The Profundity and Bifurcation of Change

The Intelligent Social Change Journey

Part I: *Laying the Groundwork*

MQIPress (2020)
Frost, West Virginia
ISBN 978-0-9985147-5-8

The Consciousness Series

*The human experience is a neuronal dance with the Universe, with each of us
in the driver's seat selecting our partners and directing our dance steps.*

Original release (as eBook): 2017
Second printing (soft cover): 2020
Copyright © 2020 MQIPress. All rights reserved.
In the spirit of collaborative advantage, with attribution,
any part of this book may be copied and distributed freely.

MQIPress
Frost, West Virginia
303 Mountain Quest Lane
Marlinton, WV 24954
United States of America
Telephone: 304-799-7267

alex@mountainquestinstitute.com
www.mountainquestinstitute.com
www.mountainquestinn.com
www.MQIPress.com
www.Myst-art.com

ISBN 978-0-9985147-5-8

Man considering the Universe of which he is a unit, sees nothing but change in matter, forces and mental states. He sees that nothing really is, but that everything is becoming and changing. Nothing stands still. Everything is being born, growing, dying. At the very instant a thing reaches its height, it begins to decline. The law of rhythm is in constant operation. There is no fixed reality, enduring quality or substantiality in anything −nothing is permanent but Change. Man sees all things evolve from other things and resolve into other things; a constant action and reaction, inflow and outflow, building up and tearing down, creation and destruction, birth, growth and death. Nothing endures but Change. And if he is a thinking man, he realizes that all of these changing things must be outward appearances or manifestations of some underlying power, some Substantial Reality.

The Kybalion (1940, p. 53

Part I*

Table of Contents

* This book is Part I of *The Profundity and Bifurcation of Change*, available from Amazon.com in hard copy and Kindle format, and in PDF format from MQIPress.

Part I
Tables, Figures, and Tools

TABLES

FIGURES

TOOLS

In Appreciation

Hundreds of people, named and unnamed, have contributed thousands of ideas to this book in the context of conversations and dialogues, articles and books, and quotes and stories. We are all indeed one, sharing ideas in groups and communities, face-to-face and virtual, appearing and connecting where we will, in an ever-looping creative embrace and continuous expansion toward intelligent activity.

Our deep appreciation to our co-authors, who each bring a unique focus and value to this work. These are Arthur Shelley, Theresa Bullard, and John Lewis. It is our sincere hope that each of them—who now are co-creators with us—will share this work largely in their day-to-day lives. Also, our appreciation to Donna Panucci, Maik Fuellmann, Jackie Urbanovic and Barbara Wheeler for their contributing and expanding thoughts, and to Mark Boyes, who co-created the thought-provoking image in Chapter 10.

Across our consilience approach, there are a handful of authors whose work has both inspired our thinking and excited our creativity. *Life's Hidden Meaning* by Niles MacFlouer provides insights from Ageless Wisdom, just coming into our realms of understanding. Serving as an example of committed knowledge sharing, MacFlouer has hosted a weekly radio show on Ageless Wisdom since 2004! This massive and incredibly insightful body of work is available on the Internet at http://www.agelesswisdom.com/archives_of_radio_shows.htm Over the past year we have listened, reflected, associated and created connections to this work, such that it is nearly impossible to follow these connections. In this regard, we try to err on the side of over-referencing, and since there is not one specific reference, but, rather, a way of thinking, we have referenced this body of work as MacFlouer (2004-16). We encourage those who resonate with this material to explore it more fully.

In 1996, Ken Wilber wrote *A Brief History of Everything*, and his brilliance continues to emerge from that point. While we applaud his continuing search for a simple and elegant theory of everything, we would be reluctant to eliminate *any* of the rich truths and theories explored in his dozens of books. *Paths of Change* by Will McWhinney served as a baseline for exploring world views and combinations of reality in the change journey. *Spontaneous Evolution: Our Positive Future* by Bruce H. Lipton and Steve Bhaerman is inspirational and informative from the viewpoint of cell biology. Jean Houston's *Jump Time* was way ahead of its time, and is a must read for any decision-maker in today's environment, and that is all of us. And where would we be as a humanity without the brilliance and wisdom of Bohm, Cozolino, Csikszentmihalyi, Damasio, Edelman, Gardner, Goleman, Goswami, Handy, Hawkins, Kant, Kolb, Kurzweil, Laszlo, McTaggart, Polanyi, Stonier, Templeton, Tiller, Wilber, and so many others! Our appreciation to all of the contributors called out in our references, and to those who may not be in our references but whose thought has seeped into our minds and hearts in the course of living.

Our continued thanks to the professionals, colleagues and thought leaders who participated in the KMTL study and follow-on Sampler Call. These include: Dorothy E. Agger-Gupta, Verna Allee, Debra Amidon, Ramon Barquin, Surinder Kumar Batra, Juanita Brown, John Seely Brown, Frada Burstein, Francisco Javier Carrillo, Robert Cross, Tom Davenport, Ross Dawson, Steve Denning, Charles Dhewa, Nancy Dixon, Leif Edvinsson, Kent Greenes, Susan Hanley, Clyde Holsapple, Esko Kilpi, Dorothy Leonard, Geoff Malafsky, Martha Manning, Carla O'Dell, Edna Pasher, W. Barnett Pearce, Larry Prusak, Madanmohan Rao, Tomasz Rudolf, Melissie Rumizen, Hubert Saint-Onge, Judi Sandrock, Charles Seashore, Dave Snowden, Milton Sousa, Michael Stankosky, Tom Stewart, Michael J.D. Sutton, Karl-Erik Sveiby, Doug Weidner, Steve Weineke, Etienne Wenger-Trayner and Karl Wiig.

There are very special people who assisted in ensuring the quality of this work. Kathy Claypatch with Ageless Wisdom Publishers served as a conduit to assure consistency with that work; Ginny Ramos, a rehabilitation counselor and Alex's daughter, served in the role of editor; and four readers played instrumental roles in assuring consistent and understandable concepts. These are Joyce Avedisian, Susan Dreiband, Denise Sumner and Deb Tobiasson, all knowledgeable explorers in the journey of life.

A special thanks to our families who ground us: from David to Steve, Melanie, John, Cindy, Jackson, Rick, Chris and the grandchildren that help to keep us young; from Alex to Ginny, Bill and Andrew and her long-lost new family; from Arthur to Joy, Cath and Helen; from Theresa to Barbara and Jay, as well as to Dennis H. and Gudni G. and her MMS friends and family; and from John to Mary, Shannon and Jonathan. Thank you to all our friends who support this work in so many ways, and who have supported Mountain Quest since its 2001 beginnings. And our continuing thankfulness to Cindy Taylor and Theresa Halterman, part of our MQI Team, and for our son Andrew Dean, who keeps Mountain Quest running while we play with thoughts and words and dive into the abyss of the unknown.

With Appreciation and Love, Alex, David, Arthur, Theresa and John.

Preface

As we move in and out of life situations, there are verbal cues, often conveyed by signs, that catch our attention and somehow miraculously remain in memory throughout our lives, popping in and out as truisms. Although we may not realize how true they were at the time, one of those sayings in an early office setting was: "Change. Your life depends on it!" Then, some 10 years later, a sign appearing on the check-in desk of the dental clinic on Yokosuka Naval Base, clearly referring to our teeth, read: "Ignore them, and they will go away."

So often we feel like victims, with some new challenge emerging from here or there, something interrupting our best laid plans, some stress or weight that sprouts discomfort or confusion. Yet we have a choice to be pulled along into the fray, dive into the flow and fully participate in the decisions and actions, or even to be the wave-setters, co-creating the reality within which we live and breathe.

Never in the history of humanity has the *need to change* so clearly manifested itself into our everyday existence. While the potential for catastrophic destruction has loomed over us since the mid-20th century, we are still *here*, admittedly a world in turmoil on all fronts—plagued with economic, political, eco-system, social, cultural and religious fragmentation—but also a humanity that is awakening to our true potential and power. Just learning how to co-evolve with an increasingly changing, uncertain and complex external environment, we are now beginning to recognize that it is the change available *within* our internal environment *and energetic connections to each other and the larger whole* that offer up an invitation to an incluessent future, that state of Being far beyond the small drop of previous possibility accepted as true, far beyond that which we have known to dream (Dunning, 2015).

In this work, we introduce the overarching concepts of **profundity** and **bifurcation** as related to change. Profundity comes from the Old French term *profundite* which emerges from the late Latin term *profunditas* or *profundus*, meaning profound (Encarta, 1999). Profundity insinuates an intellectual complexity leading to great understanding, perceptiveness and knowledge. There is a focus on greatness in terms of strength and intensity and in depth of thought. We believe that the times in which we live and the opportunity to shape the future of humanity demand that each of us look within, recognizing and utilizing the amazing gifts of our human mind and heart to shape a new world.

Bifurcation comes from the Latin root word *bifurcare*, which literally means to fork, that is, split and branch off into two separate parts (Encarta, 1999). In terms of change, this concept alludes to a pending decision for each decision-maker, each human, and perhaps humanity at large. We live in two worlds, one based on what we understand from Newtonian Physics and one based on what we don't understand but are able to speculate and feel about the Quantum Field. As change continues with every breath we take and every action we make, there is choice as to how we engage our role as co-creator of reality.

In this book, we explore very different ways to create change, each building on the former. There is no right or wrong—choice is a matter of the lessons we are learning and the growth we are seeking—yet it is clear that there is a split ahead where we will need to choose our way forward. One road continues the journey that has been punctuated by physical dominance, bureaucracy, hard competition and a variety of power scenarios. A second road, historically less-traveled, recognizes the connections among all humans, embracing the value of individuation and diversity as a contribution to the collective whole and the opportunities offered through creative imagination. This is the road that recognizes the virtues of inclusiveness and truth and the power of love and beauty, and moves us along the flow representing Quantum entanglement.

A number of themes are woven throughout this work; for example, the idea of "NOW", the use of forces as a tool for growth, the power of patterns, earned and revealed intuition, bisociation and creativity, stuck energy and flow, the search for truth, and so many more. We take a consilience approach, tapping into a deep array of research in knowledge and learning, with specific reference to recent neuroscience understanding that is emerging, pointing the reader to additional resources. And we look to psychology, physics, cell biology, systems and complexity, cognitive theory, social theory and spirituality for their contributions. Humans are holistic, that is, the physical, mental, emotional and intuitional are all at play and working together. Recognize that you are part of one entangled intelligent complex adaptive learning system (Bennet et al., 2015b), each overlapping and affecting the other, whether consciously or unconsciously, in every instant of life. As we move from science to philosophy, facts to psychology, management to poetry, and words to pictures, you will no doubt feel a tugging in the mind/brain, and perhaps some confusion. Such was the case for one of the authors when studying micro-economics and Shakespeare tragedies back to back! The good news is that this can result in a great deal of expansion and availability of a wide variety of frames of reference from which to process incoming information.

Through the past half a century, all of the authors have engaged in extensive research—much of it experiential in nature—which has led us to break through life-long perceived limits and shift and expand our beliefs about Life and the world of which we are a part. The advent of self-publishing virtual books has opened the door to share this learning globally. The concepts forwarded in the earlier works of all of the authors lay the foundation for this book.

While this book is quite large, it wrote itself. In the movie Amadeus (1984), when a complaint is lodged against his work saying there are just too many notes, Mozart responds that there are just exactly as many notes as are needed. In this book, there are exactly as many chapters as are needed, no more, no less. As you move through the information and concepts available in this text, we ask that you stay open to new ideas, ways of thinking and perceiving, and—using the discernment and discretion emerging from your unique life experiences—reflect on how these ideas might fit into your personal theory of the world. It is our hope that these ideas will serve as triggers for a greater expansion of thought and consciousness, which every individual brings to the larger understanding of who we are and how, together as One, we operate in the world.

To begin, we offer the following assumptions:

Assumption 1: Everything—at least in our physical reality—is energy and patterns of energy. We live in a vast field of energy in which we are continuously exchanging information, which is a form of energy.

Assumption 2: Creativity—nurtured by freedom, purpose and choice—is a primary urge of the human. Knowledge serves as an action lever for co-creating our experiences.

Assumption 3: Knowledge is partial and incomplete. Knowledge produces forces, whether those forces are used to push forward an idea that benefits humanity, or whether those forces are to push against another's beliefs and values (knowledge), which can escalate to warfare.

Assumption 4: The human mind is an associative patterner, that is, continuously re-creating knowledge for the situation at hand. Knowledge exists in the human brain in the form of stored or expressed neural patterns that may be selected, activated, mixed and/or reflected upon through thought. Incoming information is associated with stored information. From this mixing process, new patterns are created that may represent understanding, meaning and the capacity to anticipate (to various degrees) the results of potential actions. Thus, knowledge is context sensitive and situation dependent, with the mind continuously growing, restructuring and creating increased organization (information) and knowledge for the moment at hand.

Assumption 5: The unconscious mind has a vast store of tacit knowledge available to us. It has only been in the past few decades that cognitive psychology and neuroscience have begun to seriously explore unconscious mental life. Polanyi felt that tacit knowledge consisted of *a range* of conceptual and sensory information and images that could be used to make sense of a situation or event (Hodgkin, 1991; Smith, 2003). He was right. The unconscious mind is incredibly powerful, on the order of 700,000 times more processing speed than the conscious stream of thought. The challenge is to make better use of our tacit knowledge through creating greater connections with the unconscious, building and expanding the resources stored in the unconscious, deepening areas of resonance, connecting to the larger information field, and learning how to share our tacit resources with each other.

Assumption 6: People are multidimensional, and rarely do they hold to a single belief, a consistent logic, or a specific worldview. As identified in the recent model of experiential learning (Bennet et al, 2015b), there are five primary modes of thinking, each of us with our preferences—concrete experience, reflective observation, abstract conceptualization, active experimentation and social engagement—and each of us has a dozen or more subpersonalities offering a variety of diverse thoughts and feelings that rise to the occasion when triggered by our external and internal environments (Bennet et al., 2015a). *The human experience is a neuronal dance with the Universe, with each of us in the driver's seat selecting our partners and directing our dance steps.*

Assumption 7: We are social creatures who live in an entangled world; our brains are linked together. We are in continuous interaction with those around us, and the brain is continuously changing in response. Thus, in our expanded state we are both individuated and One, bringing all our diversity into collaborative play for the greater good of humanity.

Assumption 8: We live in times of extreme change in the human mind and body, in human-developed systems, and of the Earth, our human host. Through advances in science and technology, most of what we need to learn and thrive in these times is already available. We need only to open our minds and hearts to the amazing potential of our selfs.

There are still vast workings of the human mind and its connections to higher-order energies that we do not understand. The limitations we as humans place on our capacities and capabilities are created from past reference points that have been developed primarily through the rational and logical workings of the mechanical functioning of our mind/brain, an understanding that has come through extensive intellectual effort. Yet we now recognize that *knowledge is a living form of information*, tailored by our minds specifically for situations at hand. The totality of knowledge can no easier be codified and stored than our feelings, nor would it be highly beneficial to do so in a changing and uncertain environment. Thus, in this book, given the limitations of our own perceptions and understanding, we do not even pretend to cover the vast amount of information and knowledge available in the many fields connected to change. We *do* choose to consider and explore areas and phenomena that move beyond our paradigms and beliefs into the larger arena of knowing, and to move beyond the activity of our cognitive functions to consider the larger energy patterns within which humanity is immersed.

This extensive book is initially being published in five Parts as five separate books, which will be available in both kindle (from Amazon) and PDF (from MQIPress) formats. In support of the Intelligent Social Change Journey, these Parts are:

Part I: Laying the Groundwork

Part II: Learning from the Past

Part III: Learning in the Present

Part IV: Co-Creating the Future

Part V: Living in the Future

Each part has a separate focus, yet they work together to support your full engagement in the Intelligent Social Change Journey. A Table of Contents for all five parts is Appendix B. An overarching model of the ISCJ is Appendix A. This model can also be downloaded for A4 printing at the following location: www.mqipress.net

Workshops on all five Parts of *The Profundity and Bifurcation of Change* or, specifically, on The Intelligent Social Change Journey facilitated by the authors are available. Contact alex@mountainquestinstitute.com ... arthur.shelley@rmit.edu.au ... Theresa@quantumleapalchemy.com ... or John@ExplanationAge.com

The Drs. Alex and David Bennet live at the Mountain Quest Institute, Inn and Retreat Center situated on a 430-acre farm in the Allegheny Mountains of West Virginia. See www.mountainquestinn.com and www.mountainquestinstitute.com They may be reached at alex@mountainquestinstitute.com Dr. Arthur Shelley is the originator of *The Organizational Zoo*, Dr. Theresa Bullard is the Founder of the Quantra Leadership Academy as well as an International Instructor for the Modern Mystery School, and Dr. John Lewis is author of *The Explanation Age*. Taking a consilience approach, this eclectic group builds on corroborated resources in a diversity of fields while simultaneously pushing the edge of thought, hopefully beyond your comfort zone, for that is where our journey begins.

Introduction to
The Intelligent Social Change Journey

The Intelligent Social Change Journey (ISCJ) is a developmental journey of the body, mind and heart, moving from the heaviness of cause-and-effect linear extrapolations, to the fluidity of co-evolving with our environment, to the lightness of breathing our thought and feelings into reality. Grounded in development of our mental faculties, these are phase changes, each building on and expanding previous learning in our movement toward intelligent activity.

We are on this journey together. This is very much a *social* journey. Change does not occur in isolation. The deeper our understanding in relationship to others, the easier it is to move into the future. The quality of sympathy is needed as we navigate the linear, cause-and-effect characteristics of Phase 1. The quality of empathy is needed to navigate the co-evolving liquidity of Phase 2. The quality of compassion is needed to navigate the connected breath of the Phase 3 creative leap. See the figure below.

In the progression of learning to navigate change represented by the three phases of the ISCJ, we empower our selfs, individuating and expanding. In the process, we become immersed in the human experience, a neuronal dance with the Universe, with each of us in the driver's seat selecting our partners and directing our dance steps. Let's explore that journey a bit deeper.

In Phase 1 of the Journey, *Learning from the Past*, we act on the physical and the physical changes; we "see" the changes with our sense of form, and therefore they are real. Causes have effects. Actions have consequences, both directly and indirectly, and sometimes delayed. Phase 1 reinforces the characteristics of how we interact with the simplest aspects of our world. The elements are predictable and repeatable and make us feel comfortable because we know what to expect and how to prepare for them. While these parts of the world do exist, our brain tends to automate the thinking around them and we do them with little conscious effort. The challenge with this is that they only remain predictable if all the causing influences remain constant ... and that just doesn't happen in the world of today! The linear cause-and-effect phase of the ISCJ (Phase 1) calls for sympathy. Supporting and caring for the people involved in the change helps to mitigate the force of resistance, improving the opportunity for successful outcomes.

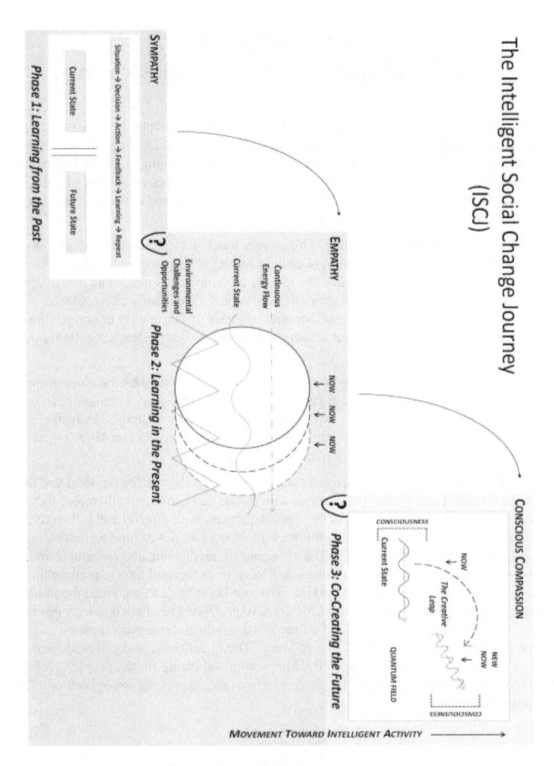

Figure ISCJ-1. *The Baseline Model.*

As we expand toward Phase 2, we begin to recognize patterns; they emerge from experiences that repeat over and over. Recognition of patterns enables us to "see" (in our mind's eye) the relationship of events in terms of time and space, moving us out of an action and reaction mode into a position of co-evolving with our environment, and enabling us to better navigate a world full of diverse challenges and opportunities. It is at this stage that we move from understanding based on past cause-and-effect reactions to how things come together, to produce new things both in the moment at hand and at a future point in time.

Phase 2, *Learning in the Present*, takes us to the next level of thinking and feeling about how we interact with our world, including the interesting area of human social interactions. Although complex, the somewhat recognizable patterns enable us to explore and progress through uncertainty and the unknown, making life more interesting and enjoyable. In Phase 2 patterns grow into concepts, higher mental thought, and we begin the search for a higher level of truth. Sustainability in the co-evolving state of Phase 2 requires empathy, which provides a direct understanding of another individual, and a heightened awareness of the context of their lives and their desires and needs in the moment at hand. While not yet achieving the creative leap of the intuitional (represented in Phase 3), we are clearly developing higher mental faculties and instinctive knowledge of the workings of the Universe, which helps cultivate intuition and develop insights in service to our self and society.

The creative leap of Phase 3, *Co-Creating the Future*, requires the ability to tap into the larger intuitional field that energetically connects all people. This can only be accomplished when energy is focused outward in service to the larger whole, requiring a deeper connection to others. Compassion deepens that connection. Thus, each phase of the Intelligent Social Change Journey calls for an increasing depth of connection to others, moving from sympathy to empathy to compassion.

<<<<<<<◇>>>>>>>

INSIGHT: **Each phase of the Intelligent Social Change Journey calls for an increasing depth of connection to others, moving from sympathy to empathy to compassion.**

<<<<<<<◇>>>>>>>

The ISCJ Baseline Model accents the phase changes as each phase builds on/expands from the previous phase. As the journeyer moves from Phase 1 to Phase 2 and prepares for the creative leap of Phase 3, the mental faculties are developing, the senses are coming into balance, and there are deepening connections to others. This will feel familiar to many travelers, for this is the place where we began. The model shows our journey is a significant change of mind, body and spirit as we operate on different cognitive and emotional planes as we progress through the developmental phases. Some people are aware of the changes they are undergoing and seek to accelerate the learning, while others resist the development, hoping (perhaps somewhat naively) to simplify the way they interact with the world.

Babies are born connected, to their mothers and families, and to the larger energies surrounding them and within them. This represents Phase 3. As one author exclaimed when exploring this reversal of the Phase 1, 2 and 3 models, "This really brings it all together for me. There is something that we admire in babies that we would like to become, and this framework makes sense of that feeling." If, and when, we return to Phase 3 in the round-trip journey of life, it will be with experience in our backpack and development of the mental faculties under our cap.

Sometime around the fourth grade, as most grade school teachers will attest, the ego pokes its head out, and, through social interactions, the process of individuation has begun, with a focus on, and experiencing in, the NOW. This represents Phase 2 of our change model, a state of co-evolving. In the pre-adolescent child, intuitional connections are subsumed by a physical focus accompanied by emotional flare-ups as the child is immersed in learning experiences, interacting and learning from and with their environment.

By the time the mid-teens come around, the world has imposed a level of order and limits, with a focus on cause-and-effect. In some families and cultures this may take the form of physical, mental or emotional manipulation and control, always related to cause-and-effect. If you do that, this will happen. For others, cultural or religious aspects of expectations and punishment may lead to the cause-and-effect focus. For the mid-teen perceived as overactive and unruly in the schoolroom, the limiting forces may be imposed through Ritalin or other drugs, which may have even started at a much earlier age. Regardless of how it is achieved, learning from the past—the Phase 1 model—becomes the starting point of our lives as we move into adulthood. From this starting point, we begin to develop our mental faculties.

The Overarching ISCJ Model

To help connect the dots, we have prepared a larger version of the Intelligent Social Change Journey, which is at Appendix A. The Overarching ISCJ Model focuses on the relationships of the phases with other aspects of the journey. For example, three critical movements during our journey, consistent with our movement through the phases, are reflected in expanded consciousness, reduction of forces and increased intelligent activity. *Consciousness* is considered a state of awareness and a private, selective and continuous change process, a sequential set of ideas, thoughts, images, feelings and perceptions and an understanding of the connections and relationships among them and our self. *Forces* occur when one type of energy affects another type of energy in a way such that they are moving in different directions, pressing against each other. Bounded (inward focused) and/or limited knowledge creates forces. *Intelligent activity* represents a state of interaction where intent, purpose, direction, values and expected outcomes are clearly understood and communicated among all parties, reflecting wisdom and achieving a higher truth. We will repeat this definition where appropriate throughout the book.

<<<<<<<◇>>>>>>>

INSIGHT: **The ISCJ is a journey toward intelligent activity, which is a state of interaction where intent, purpose, direction, values and expected outcomes are clearly understood and communicated among all parties, reflecting wisdom and achieving a higher truth.**

<<<<<<<◇>>>>>>>

Immediately below each phase of the Overarching ISCJ model are characteristics related to each phase. These are words or short phrases representing some of the ideas that will be developed in each section supporting each phase. **Phase 1,** *Learning from the Past*, characteristics are: linear and sequential, repeatability, engaging past learning, starting from current state, and cause and effect relationship. **Phase 2**, *Learning in the Present*, characteristics are: Recognition of patterns; social interaction; and co-evolving with the environment through continuous learning, quick response, robustness, flexibility, adaptability and alignment. **Phase 3**, *Co-Creating Our Future*, characteristics are: Creative imagination, recognition of global Oneness, mental in service to the intuitive; balancing senses; bringing together time (the past, present and future); knowing; beauty; and wisdom.

Still exploring the overarching model, at the lower part of the graphic we see three areas related to knowledge in terms of the nature of knowledge, areas of reflection, and cognitive shifts necessary for each phase of change. For ease of reference, we have also included the content of these three areas in Table ISCJ-1.

In Phase 1, *Learning from the Past*, the nature of knowledge is characterized as a product of the past and, as we will learn in Chapter 2, knowledge is context sensitive and situation dependent, and partial and incomplete. Reflection during this phase of change is on reviewing the interactions and feedback, and determining cause-and-effect relationships. There is an inward focus, and a questioning of decisions and actions as reflected in the questions: What did I intend? What really happened? Why were there differences? What would I do the same? What would I do differently? The cognitive shifts that are underway during this phase include: (1) recognition of the importance of feedback; (2) the ability to recognize systems and the impact of external forces; (3) recognition and location of "me" in the larger picture (building conscious awareness); and (4) pattern recognition and concept development. These reflections are critical to enabling the phase change to *co-evolving*.

In Phase 2, *Learning in the Present*, the nature of knowledge is characterized in terms of expanded cooperation and collaboration, and knowledge sharing and social learning. There is also the conscious *questioning of why*, and the *pursuit of truth*.

Reflection includes a deepening of conceptual thinking and, through cooperation and collaboration, the ability to connect the power of diversity and individuation to the larger whole. There is an increasing outward focus, with the recognition of different world views and the exploration of information from different perspectives, and expanded knowledge capacities. Cognitive shifts that are underway include: (1) the ability to recognize and apply patterns at all levels within a domain of knowledge to predict outcomes; (2) a growing understanding of complexity; (3) increased connectedness of choices, recognition of direction you are heading, and expanded meaning-making; and (4) an expanded ability to bisociate ideas resulting in increased creativity.

In Phase 3, *Co-Creating Our Future*, the nature of knowledge is characterized as a recognition that with knowledge comes responsibility. There is a conscious pursuit of larger truth, and knowledge is selectively used as a measure of effectiveness. Reflection includes the valuing of creative ideas, asking the larger questions: How does this idea serve humanity? Are there any negative consequences? There is an openness to other's ideas, a questioning with humility: What if this idea is right? Are my beliefs or other mental models limiting my thought? Are hidden assumptions or feelings interfering with intelligent activity?

Cognitive shifts that are underway include: (1) a sense and knowing of Oneness; (2) development of both the lower (logic) and upper (conceptual) mental faculties, which work in concert with the emotional guidance system; (3) recognition of self as a co-creator of reality; (4) the ability to engage in intelligent activity; and (5) a developing ability to tap into the intuitional plane at will.

Time and space play a significant role in the phase changes. Using Jung's psychological type classifications, feelings come from the past, sensations occur in the present, intuition is oriented to the future, and thinking embraces the past, present *and* future. Forecasting and visioning work is done at a point of change (McHale, 1977) when a balance is struck continuously between short-term and long-term survival. Salk (1973) describes this as a shift from Epoch A, dominated by ego and short-term considerations, to Epoch B, where both *Being and ego co-exist*. In the ISCJ, this shift occurs somewhere in Phase 2, with Beingness advancing as we journey toward Phase 3. Considerable focus to time and space occurs later in the book (Chapter 16/Part III).

....

Phase of the Intelligent Social Change Journey	ISCJ: Nature of Knowledge	ISCJ: Points of Reflection	ISCJ: Cognitive Shifts
PHASE 1: Cause and Effect (Requires Sympathy) • Linear, and Sequential • Repeatable • Engaging past learning • Starting from current state • Cause-and-effect relationships	• A product of the past • Knowledge is context-sensitive and situation-dependent • Knowledge is partial and incomplete	• Reviewing the interactions and feedback • Determining cause-and-effect relationships; logic • Inward focus • Questioning of decisions and actions: What did I intend? What really happened? why were there differences? What would I do the same? What would I do differently?	• Recognition of the importance of feedback • Ability to recognize systems and the impact of external forces • Recognition and location of "me" in the larger picture (building conscious awareness) • Beginning pattern recognition and early concept development
PHASE 2: Co-Evolving (Requires Empathy) • Recognition of patterns • Social interaction • Co-evolving with environment through continuous learning, quick response, robustness, flexibility, adaptability, alignment.	• Engaging knowledge sharing and social learning • Engaging cooperation and collaboration • Questioning of why? • Pursuit of truth	• Deeper development of conceptual thinking (higher mental thought) • Through cooperation and collaboration ability to connect the power of diversity and individuation to the larger whole • Outward focus • Recognition of different world views and exploration of information from different perspectives • Expanded knowledge capacities	• The ability to recognize and apply patterns at all levels within a domain of knowledge to predict outcomes • A growing understanding of complexity • Increased connectedness of choices • Recognition of direction you are heading • Expanded meaning-making • Expanded ability to bisociate ideas resulting in increased creativity
PHASE 3: Creative Leap (Requires Compassion) • Creative imagination • Recognition of global Oneness • Mental in service to the intuitive • Balancing senses • Bringing together past, present and future • Knowing; Beauty; Wisdom	• Recognition that with knowledge comes responsibility • Conscious pursuit of larger truth • Knowledge selectively used as a measure of effectiveness	• Valuing of creative ideas • Asking the larger questions: How does this idea serve humanity? Are there any negative consequences? • Openness to other's ides; questioning with humility: What if this idea is right Are my beliefs or other mental models limiting my thought? Are hidden assumptions or feelings interfering with intelligent activity?	• A sense and knowing of Oneness • Development of both the lower (logic) and upper (conceptual) mental faculties, which work in concert with the emotional guidance system • Applies patterns across domains of knowledge for greater good • recognition of self as a co-creator of reality • The ability to engage in intelligent activity • Developing the ability to tap into the intuitional plane at will

Table ISCJ-Table 1. *The three Phases from the viewpoints of the nature of knowledge, points of reflection and cognitive shifts.*

Cognitive-Based Ordering of Change

As a cognitive-based ordering of change, we forward the concept of logical levels of learning consistent with levels of change developed by anthropologist Gregory Bateson (1972) based on the work in logic and mathematics of Bertrand Russell. This logical typing was both a mathematical theory and a law of nature, recognizing long before neuroscience research findings confirmed the relationship of the mind/brain which show that we literally create our reality, with thought affecting the physical structure of the brain, and the physical structure of the brain affecting thought.

Bateson's levels of change range from simplistic habit formation (which he calls Learning I) to large-scale change in the evolutionary process of the human (which he calls Learning IV), with each higher-level synthesizing and organizing the levels below it, and thus creating a greater impact on people and organizations. This is a hierarchy of logical levels, ordered groupings within a system, with the implication that as the levels reach toward the source or beginning **there is a sacredness, power or importance informing this hierarchy of values** (Dilts, 2003). This structure is consistent with the phase changes of the Intelligent Social Change Journey.

<<<<<<◇>>>>>>

INSIGHT: **Similar to Bateson's levels of change, each higher phase of the Intelligent Social Change Journey synthesizes and organizes the levels below it, thus creating a greater impact in interacting with the world.**

<<<<<<◇>>>>>>

With Learning 0 representing the status quo, a particular behavioral response to a specific situation, Learning I (first-order change) is stimulus-response conditioning (cause-and-effect change), which includes learning simple skills such as walking, eating, driving, and working. These basic skills are pattern forming, becoming habits, which occur through repetitiveness without conceptualizing the content. For example, we don't have to understand concepts of motion and movement in order to learn to walk. Animals engage in Learning I. Because it is not necessary to understand the concepts, or underlying theories, no questions of reality are raised. Learning I occurs in Phase 1 of the ISCJ.

Learning II (second-order change) is deuteron learning and includes creation, or a change of context inclusive of new images or concepts, or shifts the understanding of, and connections among, existing concepts such that meaning may be interpreted. These changes are based on mental constructs that *depend on a sense of reality* (McWhinney, 1997). While these concepts may represent real things, relations or qualities, they also may be symbolic, specifically created for the situation at hand.

Either way, they provide the means for reconstructing existing concepts, using one reality to modify another, from which new ways of thinking and behaviors emerge.

Argyris and Schon's (1978) concept of double loop learning reflects Level II change. Learning II occurs in Phase 2 of the ISCJ.

Learning III (third-order change) requires thinking beyond our current logic, calling us to change our system of beliefs and values, and offering different sets of alternatives from which choices can be made. Suggesting that Learning III is learning about the concepts used in Learning II, Bateson says,

> In transcending the promises and habits of Learning II, one will gain "a freedom from its bondages," bondages we characterize, for example, as "drive," "dependency," "pride," and "fatalism." One might learn to change the premises acquired by Learning II and to readily choose among the roles through which we express concepts and thus the "self." Learning III is driven by the "contraries" generated in the contexts of Learning I and II. (Bateson, 1972, pp. 301-305)

<<<<<<<◇>>>>>>>

INSIGHT: **There is a freedom that occurs as we leave behind the thinking patterns of Phase 2 and open to the new choices and discoveries of Phase 3.**

<<<<<<<◇>>>>>>>

Similarly, Berman (1981, p. 346) defines Learning III as, "an experience in which a person suddenly realizes the arbitrary nature of his or her own paradigm." This is the breaking open of our personal mental models, our current logic, losing the differential of subject/object, blending into connection while simultaneously following pathways of diverse belief systems. Learning III occurs as we move into Phase 3 of the ISCJ.

Learning IV deals with revolutionary change, getting outside the system to look at the larger system of systems, awakening to something completely new, different, unique and transformative. This is the space of *incluessence*, a future state far beyond that which we know to dream (Dunning, 2015). As Bateson described this highest level of change:

> The individual mind is immanent but not only in the body. It is immanent in pathways and messages outside the body; and there is a larger Mind of which the individual mind is only a sub-system. This larger Mind is comparable to God and is perhaps what people mean by "God," but it is still immanent in the total interconnected social system and planetary ecology. (Bateson, 1972, p. 465)

Table ISCJ-2 below is a comparison of the Phases of the Intelligent Social Change Journey and the four Levels of Learning espoused by Bateson (1972) based on the work in logic and mathematics of Bertrand Russell, and supported by Argyris and Schon (1978), Berman (1981), and McWhinney (1997).

■■■ I

Phase of the Intelligent Social Change Journey	Level of Learning [NOTE: LEARNING 0 represents the status quo; a behavioral response to a specific situation.]
PHASE 1: Cause and Effect (Requires Sympathy) • Linear, and Sequential • Repeatable • Engaging past learning • Starting from current state • Cause and effect relationships	**LEARNING i:** **(First order change)** • Stimulus-response conditioning • Incudes learning simple skills such as walking, eating, driving and working • Basic skills are pattern forming, becoming habits occurring through repetitiveness without conceptualizing the content • No questions of reality
PHASE 2: Co-Evolving (Requires Empathy) • Recognition of patterns • Social interaction • Co-evolving with environment through continuous learning, quick response, robustness, flexibility, adaptability, alignment	**LEARNING II (Deutero Learning)** **(Second order change)** • Includes creation or change of context inclusive of new images or concepts • Shifts the understanding of, and connections among, existing concepts such that meaning may be interpreted • Based on mental constructions that depend on a sense of reality
[Moving into Phase 3] **PHASE 3: Creative Leap** (Requires Compassion) • Creative imagination • Recognition of global Oneness • Mental in service to the intuitive • Balancing senses • Bringing together past, present and future • Knowing; Beauty; Wisdom	**LEARNING III: (Third order change)** • Thinking beyond current logic • Changing our system of beliefs and values • Different sets of alternatives from which choices can be made • Freedom from bondages **LEARNINNG IV:** • Revolutionary change • Getting outside the system to look at the larger system of systems • Awakening to something completely new, different, unique and transformative • Tapping into the large Mind of which the individual mind is a sub-system

Table ISCJ-Table 2. *Comparison of Phases of the ISCJ with Levels of Learning.*

An example of Learning IV is Buddha's use of intuitional thought to understand others. He used his ability to think in greater and greater ways to help people cooperate and share together, and think better. Learning IV is descriptive of controlled intuition in support of the creative leap in Phase 3 of the ISCJ, perhaps moving beyond what we can comprehend at this point in time, perhaps deepening the connections of sympathy, empathy and compassion to unconditional love.

How to Best Use this Material

This book has, quite purposefully, been chunked into five smaller books, referred to as Parts, which are both independent and interdependent. Chunking is a methodology for learning. The way people become experts involves the chunking of ideas and concepts and creating understanding through development of significant patterns useful for identifying opportunities, solving problems and anticipating future behavior within the focused domain of knowledge. Figure ISCJ-2 shows the relationship of the Parts of this book and their content to the Intelligent Social Change Journey. *Remember*: the ISCJ is a journey of expansion, with each Phase building on—and inclusive of—the former Phase as we develop our mental faculties in service to the intuitional, and move closer to intelligent activity. As such, one needs to experience the earlier phases in order to elevate to the upper levels. Early life experiences and educational development during these earlier stages create the foundation and capacity to develop into higher levels of interactions and ways of being.

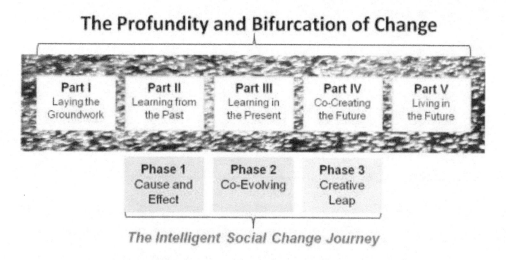

Figure ISCJ-2. *Relationship of Parts and Phases of the ISCJ.*

While many different ideas have been introduced in the paragraphs of this Introduction to the Intelligent Social Change Journey, you will discover that all of these ideas are addressed in depth during the course of this book, and each Part is inclusive of tools, references, insights and reflective questions provided in support of your personal learning journey. We also cross-reference, both within the Parts, and across all of the Parts.

This is a journey, and as such *the learning is in the journey*, the reflecting on and application of the learning, not in achieving a particular capability or entering the next Phase at a specific point in time. Similar to the deepening of relationships with others, the growth of understanding and expansion of consciousness takes its own time, twisting and curving forwards and backwards until we have learned all we can from one frame of reference, and then jump to another to continue our personal journey. That said, we suggest that those who are impatient to know the topics within this book, but reluctant to read such an extended text, jump to Chapter 11/Part III, which provides readiness assessment statements and related characteristics reflecting the high-level content of this book.

For your reference, the Overarching ISCJ model can be downloaded for printing in A3 format at www.MQIPress.net The corresponding author may be reached at alex@mountainquestinstitute.com

PART I

Laying the Groundwork

Introduction to Part I

Have you ever picked up Ken Wilber's *A Theory of Everything* with the thought in mind to read it from cover to cover? And then it just doesn't happen. While his work is extraordinary, the title and concept are mind-boggling. Even in the instant, how can there be a single theory of everything?

If you could choose one word to describe everything about our human context, what would that be? Love? Light? Energy? Consciousness? Connectedness? All good words, dependent on your worldview and belief system, nonetheless *everything* is so much more! Encarta (1999) says that everything is the entirety of all items, actions or facts *in a given situation*. When we bound our focus to a small incident, this works. But in the situation of life, there's so much to being human, to living; things like freedom, creating, learning, expanding, and service to others that they may serve others.

Could there be one theory that guides *everything*? A *theory* is a set of statements and/or principles that explain a group of facts or phenomena to guide action or assist in comprehension or judgment (American Heritage Dictionary, 2006; Bennet & Bennet, 2010a). Based on beliefs and/or mental models and built on assumptions, theories provide *a plausible or rational explanation of cause and effect relationships*. So, according to these definitions, not only is it difficult to discover a concept that covers everything, but there is the realization that "everything" is connected to a given situation, and "theory" is relative, highly dependent on the individual!

Well, you will discover a lot of *theory* and loads of *everythings* in this book. We touch on ontology, the philosophy of reality, and on epistemology, the theory of knowledge. We honor science and spirituality. No ideas are too narrow or broad to consider and reflect upon. And we understand that change is a verb and that people are verbs, continuously shifting and changing inside and out, both creating and responding to the wonderful networks of global energy of which we are all a part.

While Part I sets the stage for all that follows, it is difficult to decide what really comes first. This is the chicken or the egg problem. So, we take a guess, and try to first provide some of the thinking that helps us in understanding the changing nature of our world.

Taking a consilience approach, in this book we address change from diverse frames of reference and fields of learning. While Lao Tzu would view the human mind as two distinct minds—the worldly mind (physical) and universal mind (non-physical)—we choose to explore the workings of the human mind/brain and its interactions with reality from four distinct perspectives: the physical, emotional, mental and intuitional, with the spiritual interwoven throughout. We use the term *planes* to clarify areas of focus—physical, emotional, mental and intuitional—

although we could just as easily talk about these concepts in terms of bodies. Since these planes are all entangled and a part of who we are, each has an active voice in the other. Today's human is primarily operating in the mental, so this plane guides and drives our focus. This does not mean the plane itself has the power of focus. It is *we* who produce the energy—wherever we focus—and the plane that determines how we *engage and direct* that energy.

The first three frames of reference (physical, emotional and mental) are consistent with Lao Tzu's understanding of the physical, that is, they are very much focused on the physical reality through the physical senses of sight, sound, touch, taste and smell. To avoid confusion when it emerges, we talk in terms of seven senses occurring in all three of these planes. Lao Tzu acknowledged two additional senses in the intuitional realm, what he described as the senses of instinct and intuition, which are processed by the Universal Mind, using patterns to achieve insight (Wing, 1986). We also acknowledge two additional senses in the intuitional realm, only these we describe as connection (Oneness) and co-creation. In Chapter 4 we delve further into this.

In Part I ...

Chapter 1: Change is Natural. Everywhere we look, everywhere we go, change is at play, and play is the natural way we change. The mind is an associative patterner, engaged in a continuous learning process that is a journey of change. But that change has no significance until we discover the situation, its context, what is changing, and how that change impacts our self and those with whom we interact.

Chapter 2: Knowledge to Action. Knowledge—defined as the capacity (potential or actual) to take effective action—is a baseline for this work. We briefly explore the nature of knowledge in terms of its support to intelligent activity. Discussion topics include Knowledge (Informing) and Knowledge (Proceeding) as well as the Levels of Knowledge (surface, shallow and deep); and the knowledge-to-action loop.

Chapter 3: Forces We Act Upon. Forces are a part of our everyday world; and, while they can serve as building blocks for creativity and action, they can also hold us back from achieving our goals. We can successfully mitigate or leverage those forces to move forward with new ideas. Forces are introduced from both the viewpoint of the individual as part of a social setting, and strategic forces from the viewpoint of an organization. We also look at control as a force and ways of reducing forces.

Chapter 4: The Ever-Expanding Self. Self is an emergent quality of the human, with each self both unique and connected, both individuated and part of something larger. This idea of self is explored from the subject/object relationship, the personality, development of self, the connected self, and the power of individuation.

Chapter 5: The Window of Consciousness. What is consciousness has been a question asked for many years. We take a consilience approach to exploring this question, then delve into a deeper understanding of the threshold of consciousness, levels of consciousness, and the direct relationship between consciousness and meaning and purpose. We briefly look at the idea of consciousness as a Quantum field, and flow as the optimal experience, before exploring the idea of consciously accessing the unconscious.

Chapter 6: The Individual Change Model. This final chapter in Part I of *The Profundity and Bifurcation of Change* introduces the individual change model. We begin by looking at the human as a complex adaptive system, then take a look at the environment and the knowledge worker. In a journey towards action, the model moves through the stages of awareness, understanding, believing, feeling good, ownership, empowerment and impact.

Chapter 1
Change is Natural

If you've ever looked inside your gut during an ultrasound, you discovered entangled energy, ubiquitous movement and bouncing interactions. Our bodies have 50 trillion cells continuously changing. Nothing about us is static, and it never has been. We pulse with change: absorbing food, processing air, dividing cells, making and pushing out secretions, transmitting electrical signals. At the microscopic level, everything about us teems with change, creating patterns of activity linked with energy from our environment. Forget your early English lesson. We are, quite literally, a *verb*, not a noun!

We often think of our heartbeat as our constant rhythm of life; but even our heart must skip here and there. If it stayed in the same rut, we would wear out by the time we were 30 years old! Change is a natural part of our systems, whether we define those systems as physical, mental, emotional or spiritual, or whether our focus is the individual, family, community, nation ... or humanity as a whole. Everywhere we look, everywhere we go, change is at play, and play is the natural way we change. It is synonymous with the act of living, and life could not exist without change.

As humanity expands her horizons and our civilization has become more complex, the dimensions of change have altered in rate, speed and sequence, increasing in complexity filled with paradoxes and contradictions, and following diverse patterns with unexpected repercussions. We talk about this more in Chapter 13/Part III. Within this environment, there are hidden cause-and-effect relationships, separating time and space such that the change can no longer be identified with its creator, or with the reasons for its creation. Change has become art without an artist; sound without a melody; taste without a chef.

The 20th century multiplied human powers—military, economic, technological—have forced us to closely examine our beliefs, values, ethics and way of life. And larger changes lay ahead, challenging us—and blessing us—as individuals and as a society. As Templeton (2002, p.184) exclaims, "One of the greatest blessings to human beings is change, and the present acceleration of change in the world is an overflowing of this blessing."

Let's take a closer look at this blessing. By its own definition, *if a situation changes it is different*; it has transitioned from one state, condition or phase to another, whether environmental, physiological or perceptual/psychological in nature.

We know when something is different, and we search to discover the nuances of a situation when it changes. There is a running movie through our eyes, slices of visual time that move in 1/10 second segments as our eyes operate much like the rhythmic sound of cicadas on a clear night, both punctuated with change. We are "seeing" a living series of NOWs. While this briefly describes how we visually see our perceived external world, there are so many more systems at play with the seeing, perceiving and interpreting. The impact of actual change is significantly dependent on the *nature* of what is changing, so change is local, not general, referring to a specific phenomenon to have meaning. Change doesn't have any significance until you find out the situation and context, and what is changing.

Even our beliefs and values change! How could a rigid belief system stay the same when the reality and threshold of consciousness within which we live are continuously changing? As Cooper (2005, p. 42) so simply and eloquently says, "Growing awareness and understanding define the river of human life."

Agreeing that change is a verb, and that we live in a cycle of continuous flux, it can still be useful to consider the concept of change from both the viewpoint of a noun—as we often tend to do—and even as an adjective in terms of variation (changing and changeable). As a noun, the concept refers to a specific subject of focus, a thing or person or situation, that is, it is subjective, seen from *our* viewpoint. It also infers a specific instant in time, a state of being (shifting even as the thought is thought). Note that others may perceive the same or similar change from *their* viewpoint, in which case it could be described as a collective subjective observation; nonetheless, it is subjective. Nothing that is perceived through the human system can be considered objective. As hard as we try, we cannot eliminate our past experiences and learning, our beliefs and values, or our physical, mental and emotional feelings.

<<<<<<<◇>>>>>>>

INSIGHT: **Change has no significance until we discover the situation and context, what is changing, and how that change impacts our self and those with whom we interact.**

<<<<<<<◇>>>>>>>

To us as individuals, change is local, not general, referring to a specific phenomenon which has meaning. Change has no significance until we discover the situation and context, what is changing, and how that change impacts our self and those with whom we interact. So, within our self we explore: What is different? What is the nature of this change? What is the meaning, value and significance of this change? Why did it happen? Note that all of these questions refer to change as a noun, identifying a point in time when things are recognized as different from how they were previously perceived. In our questioning, *we lock the change concept into a slice of time that we can think about and analyze*, chunking it so that we can better understand it, although, of course, the change is continuing even as we reflect and question!

From the viewpoint of an adjective, the term "changeable" can be used in conjunction with a noun to insinuate the *possibility*, or even the expectation, of movement. The term "changing" can be used with a variety of nouns to denote a dynamic state, with the following noun representing the subject of the change. For example, the "changing nature" of humanity or society, the "changing attitudes" of a maturing adult, or the "changing landscape" of a resource-poached terrain. As we can see, when "changing" is used as an adjective it insinuates activity and movement underway, which supports the concept that change is a verb.

Change as a Verb

From a high-level context looking at *change* as a verb, the concept of change represents *the action(s) related to making something different*. The radical and startling change underway in preparation for a global consciousness shift is all-encompassing change. In that context, change is considered:

> …the shifting of any circumstance, situation, or condition, physical or nonphysical, in such a way that the original is rendered not merely different from what it was, but altered so radically as to make it utterly unrecognizable and impossible to return to anything resembling its former state. (Walsch, 2009, p. 16)

As we move from the past to the future, synonyms for change include transition, transform, transmute, alter, modify, convert, replace, vary, proceed and shift, all of which encompass movement. We as a verb *are* change. In the words of Colin Cooper,

> *It's a Funny Thing.* This growing thing—we talk about growing up but as soon as we grow up we grow old, we grow fat, or we grow thin. The common factor in growing is that we consciously or unconsciously, and whether we like it or not, are changing all the time. To be alive is to be in a process of change. That is true not only of the physical body but of ideas and convictions, character and personality. Obviously there are continuing areas of conviction and certainty but even these change in expression and in depth of assurance. (Loveridge, 1977, p. 53)

While we often consciously yearn for and search for stability, hunting for absolute truths, the concept of stability, and absolute truth, is an illusion in a changing world; nor would we want it to be otherwise! As Cooper (2005, pp. 42-43) forwards,

> The human mind does attempt to create internal stability by trying to find a foundation of absolute truths that never change. This pattern, however, is prompted by human insecurity and must be overcome. **Truth is a living, dynamic awareness that grows in its meaning and value as our consciousness**

expands [emphasis added]. Trying to rigidly define absolute truth causes separation from the world and judgment of the work. It does not allow our threshold of consciousness to grow and change.

There is stability only in the dynamic process of change, that is, the knowing that change is a dynamic process of life. There is within the human a continuous need for more and different, an underlying desire to experience, and through this experiencing the shifting and changing of desires and an ever-expanding frontier of choice. We need change. We crave change. We cannot go backwards. Change is a journey into the future, a global future requiring recognition of an entangled humanity, considering the impact of our decisions and actions on others and our environment. This is consistent with the emergence of self and the expansion of consciousness discussed in detail in Chapter 4 and Chapter 5, respectively. Knowledge and the search for truth is the focus of Chapter 24/Part IV.

<<<<<<<◇>>>>>>>

INSIGHT: **There is stability only in the dynamic process of change, that is, the knowing that change is a dynamic process of life**.

<<<<<<<◇>>>>>>>

As introduced above and as a theme running throughout this text, *change does not happen in isolation*. Much like knowledge and truth, there is a context to change. This context is required in order for change to be recognizable as change; in order to understand the movement from one perceived state to another there must be an awareness of those different states, slices in time on which the mind/brain reflects.

Within this descriptive paragraph of change we used the words knowledge, context and mind/brain. Knowledge is the subject of Chapter 2 and context is addressed in that treatment. The reference to mind inevitably pulls up a vision of the brain. For purposes of this conversation, the **brain** consists of a molecular structure and the fluids that flow within and through this structure. The **mind** is the totality of the *patterns in the brain and throughout the body*, created by neurons and their firings and connections. These patterns encompass all of our thoughts. The term **mind/brain** refers to both the structure and the patterns emerging within the structure *and* throughout the nervous system (Bennet & Bennet, 2010b).

While historically the brain has been presented as the seat of control—and it certainly plays a continuous role in the process of thought—the body-mind acts as an information network with no fixed hierarchy (Pert, 1997). As we interact with life, our neuronal circuitry rewires itself in response to stimulation. Neurons are not bound to each other physically and thereby have the flexibility to repeatedly create, break and recreate relationships with other neurons, the process of plasticity. Neurons exist throughout the body. For example, there are neurons in the spinal cord, the heart, the peripheral nervous system and the gut. While these neurons are largely focused on autonomic functions, that is, automatic activity not under voluntary control of the individual such as the heartbeat, all of these neurons provide sensory feedback to the brain, which affects emotions.

Our Changing Thoughts

Very different than a computer, the human mind is uniquely prepared to address and respond to an environment that is continuously shifting and changing, and to context-rich situations and opportunities. The mind is an associative patterner, engaged in a continuous learning process that is a journey of change. New incoming external information is mixed, or semantically complexed, with internal information (memory, feelings) creating new neuronal patterns in the mind/brain that may represent understanding, meaning, and/or anticipation of the consequences of actions; in other words, information or knowledge unconsciously tailored to the situation at hand.

Imagine a three-dimensional snapshot that lasts a tenth of a second. This picture, or pattern, is a part of the sequence of coordinated patterns and an understanding of their relationships that we call consciousness, supported by an associated set of non-conscious coordinated patterns. For example, in this picture I'm simultaneously gardening with one hand, swatting a buzzing fly away from my eye with another, and feeling the warmth of the day and the freshness of the air, while visually catching a glimpse of the blue haze of distant mountains and mentally reflecting on the potential value of a knowledge state. In the truest sense, the mind, considered to be the setting of three-dimensional neuronal patterns within the brain, as introduced above, is multidimensional, and we live every moment of our lives multi-tasking.

During that tenth of a second, visual, aural, olfactory, and kinesthetic sensory inputs combine with mental thoughts, emotional feelings and internal patterns to create an internal perception and feeling of external awareness. The firing of networks of neurons creates the internal patterns of the mind that express our awareness of the external world. As a general rule, the human brain processes at a rate of approximately 10^{15} cycles per second. (Kurzweil, 2005, pp. 123-124). While this certainly represents incredible processing power in any terms, there is an even higher number of signals continuously bombarding us, but many of these come in without being recognized. For example, light waves and sound waves outside the range of our sensors.

Aspects of these incoming patterns may cause random firings, form uninteresting patterns, or create a pattern that has historical significance. In the mind/brain, everything is relative, that is, *every individual has their own internal sets of patterns and their associations that enable them to make sense of the world*. Relationships between patterns are quasi-unique to each individual because (1) the patterns are different in each mind/brain and (2) each of us has built our personal frame of reference from different pattern relationships.

<<<<<<◇>>>>>>

INSIGHT: **Every individual has their own personal map of reality, internal sets of patterns and their associations that enable them to make sense of the world.**

<<<<<<◇>>>>>>

The patterns in the mind/brain, then, are a result of our physiology and differing representations of, and relationships with, the world. Some of these are consistent with the external world and others are only consistent and integrative within the individual. For example, my sense of the color red is consistent with the color related to red when I was a child, but it is not necessarily the same color that another individual related to red as a child. However, if I was inclined toward the study of art, I might learn to discern many variations of red, expanding my previous associations of the term and color. While still associated with red, each variation would be represented in the mind as a unique pattern. So, while over the long-term, thinking/perception may agree with physical reality much of the time, since pattern relationships are built on different sets of experiences and observations, each set is context sensitive and situation dependent. This is why the creation of knowledge is unique to each individual, such that if I try to communicate understanding of a phenomenon it doesn't necessarily mean it will make sense to someone who has a different set of patterns and pattern relationships that represent that understanding.

As we move through life and gain experience, patterns in the mind/brain are continuously expanding, connecting and shifting. As Byrnes (2001, p. 179) describes, "Experience creates new synaptic connections among neurons and also alters existing patterns of connections." For example, if you bring in a new concept, perhaps a new model such as the pattern created when you think about the organization as an Intelligent Complex Adaptive System (Bennet and Bennet, 2004), it is first associated with other related patterns you have in mind, experiences and the patterns associated with those experiences. The new pattern focused on the situation at hand is built on these associations, and it is those relationships with other patterns already in your mind that provide meaning. If the process of learning and understanding creates sets of patterns (that is, larger patterns made out of smaller patterns), they exist in the mind in relationship to patterns already there, and in relationship to new patterns coming in from the external world. See Figure 1-1.

In summary, and a foundational concept in this book, the interpretation of incoming patterns and their meaning are very much a function of preexisting patterns in the brain. As Stonier summarizes, "Meaning ... involves the integration of a message into the internal information environment of the recipient. Such a process creates a new information unit: the combination of the external information, complexed with the information provided by the internal information environment." (Stonier, 1997, p. 157) Knowledge, discussed more fully in Chapter 2, is *created by recursive interactions between, and intermixing of, external information and internal patterns of historical significance.*

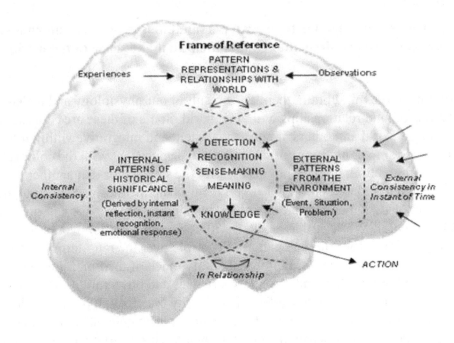

Figure 1-1: *Learning as associative patterning.*

Final Thought

When reflecting on the continuous change we are, it goes to reason that we have much experience with change. It is time to harness this experience—to learn from it, recognize its patterns and move with its continuous flow—fully embracing our role as co-creators of the future. This book is dedicated to that human journey.

Questions for Reflection:

What are the implications for me personally when I understand that my mind works as an associative patterner, linking incoming information to everything I've experienced and learned in the past?

As an associative patterner, how might I choose to prepare for the future?

Chapter 2
Knowledge to Action

SUBTOPICS: KNOWLEDGE (INFORMING) AND KNOWLEDGE (PROCEEDING) ... LEVELS OF KNOWLEDGE ... FROM KNOWLEDGE TO ACTION ... THE NATURE OF KNOWLEDGE. ... LEVELS OF COMPREHENSION ... FINAL THOUGHTS

FIGURES: 2-1. KNOWLEDGE (INFORMING) AND KNOWLEDGE (PROCEEDING) ... 2-2. THE KNOWLEDGE-ACTION LOOP ... 2-3. MOVEMENT TOWARD INTELLIGENT ACTIVITY.

Information is the connective tissue of the Universe. Knowledge is applied information to create value. Let's explore this relationship a bit further. In his three-volume study of the role of information in the structure of the Universe, theoretical biologist Tom Stonier proposed that "organization is the physical expression of a system containing information" (Stonier, 1997, p. 14). Organization means the existence of a non-random pattern of particles and energy fields, or more generally, the sub-units comprising any system. Thus, in the material world organization can be observed in space and time as a physical phenomenon and information is a basic property of the Universe—as fundamental as matter and energy. Along with Stonier, *we view information as any non-random pattern or set of patterns.*

Information has no meaning until some organism recognizes and interprets the patterns (Bennet and Bennet, 2008c). Thus, knowledge exists in the human brain in the form of stored or expressed neuronal patterns that may be activated and reflected upon through conscious thought. This is a high-level description of the creation of knowledge that is consistent with the neuronal operation of the brain and is applicable in varying degrees to all living organisms. From this process, neuronal patterns are created that may represent understanding, meaning and the capacity to anticipate (to various degrees) the results of potential actions. Thus, it is not just information that defines knowledge, but the relationships or associations (in space and time) among that information. Through this process of associating (or complexing), the mind is continuously growing, restructuring and creating increased organization (information). Taking a functional approach, our definition of knowledge then becomes: *Knowledge is the capacity (potential or actual) to take effective action in varied and uncertain situations* (Bennet & Bennet, 2004).

<<<<<<<<>>>>>>>

INSIGHT: **Knowledge is a human capacity that comes from the ability to intelligently interact with our environment.**

<<<<<<<<>>>>>>>

Knowledge is considered a human capacity that comes from the ability to intelligently interact with our environment. It may consist of understanding, insights, meaning, intuition, judgment, creativity, and the ability to anticipate the outcome of our actions. Understanding includes the description of the situation and its information content that provides the *who, what, where* and *when*. It also involves the frame of reference of the observer, including perception, assumptions and presuppositions. Much of this can be referred to as surface knowledge (Moon, 2004; Bennet & Bennet, 2008c; 2015a**).** Insight can be described as, "The capacity to discern the true nature of a situation; penetration. The act or outcome of grasping the inward or hidden nature of things or of perceiving in an intuitive manner" (*American Heritage Dictionary*, 2006, p. 906). From another perspective, insight is also the result of searching for new relationships between concepts in one domain and those in another domain (Crandall et al., 2006). It creates a recognition and understanding of a problem within the situation, including the *how* and *why* of the past and current behavior of the situation. It is often the result of intuition, competence, and the identification of patterns, themes and cue sets (Crandall et al., 2006). Insight may also provide patterns and relationships that will anticipate the future behavior of the situation.

Meaning is the significance created in the mind/brain of the knower by relating the incoming information of a perceived situation to the current cognitive structures of the learner, correlating with intelligence. Meaning can be determined only by the learner and can result from the situation, its history, and/or the implications of the situation as affecting the future (Edelman & Tononi, 2000; Sousa, 2006; Stonier, 1997). (See Chapter 5.) For example, take a bag of food. To one person, that bag may contain the food that was just purchased from the grocery store today and consists of elements that will be used for dinner tonight. To another person, that bag of food may contain the food for a friend requested to support her desire to have a picnic later that day, and to yet another person that bag of food may be excess food that will be given to a homeless shelter.

Intuition is the act or faculty of knowing or sensing without the use of rational processes; or immediate cognition (*American Heritage Dictionary*, 2006, p. 919). Creativity is the emergence of new or original patterns (ideas, concepts, or actions) that "typically have three components: originality, utility and some kind of product" (Andreasen, 2005, p. 17). Creativity is discussed in depth in Chapters 29 and 30/Part IV.

As used here, prediction is the anticipation or expectation of solutions to, and the outcomes of, proposed actions on some situation. Prediction does not imply certainty, rather it is the best estimate, expectation, or probability that an individual has for anticipating the outcome of his or her actions. For a complicated situation, it may come from identifying and understanding the causal relationships within the situation and their influence in the future. For a complex system, it may come from intuition, pattern recognition, creative exploration, or an awareness of approaches to influencing such systems. It could also include past experience with, and an understanding of, complex systems theory and practice (Bennet & Bennet, 2004; 2008a; 2013).

Predictions may happen in the instant or develop over time. For example, Canadian journalist Malcolm Gladwell (2005) wrote a book called *Blink: The Power of Thinking* without Thinking. In it, he uses the term *thin-slicing*, which is a concept representing the brain making snap decisions. He cites the case of Vic Braden, a top-class tennis coach, who can predict when a player will do a double fault before the tennis ball even touches the racket. He cites Professor John Gottman of the University of Washington as another example. Gottman can predict, up to a 90 percent accuracy level, whether a couple would still be married 15 years in the future based upon watching the two people communicate for just fifteen minutes.

While data and information both consist of patterns, they have no meaning until some organism recognizes and interprets the patterns. As introduced in Chapter 1, the human mind is an associative patterner that is continuously re-creating knowledge for the situation at hand. Knowledge exists in the human brain in the form of stored or expressed neural patterns that may be selected, activated, mixed and/or reflected upon through thought. Incoming information is associated with stored information. From this mixing process, new patterns are created that may represent understanding, meaning and the capacity to anticipate, to various degrees, the outcomes of potential actions. Thus, knowledge is context sensitive and situation dependent, with the mind continuously growing, restructuring and creating increased organization (information) and knowledge for the moment at hand.

It is only when the incoming patterns from the environment are integrated with the internal neural patterns within our brains that they take on meaning to the individual. Thus, meaning comes from the combination of non-random patterns and an observer who can interpret these patterns to create recognition or understanding (Bennet & Bennet, 2008a). These units of understanding are referred to as "semantic complexes". As Stonier explains,

> ... a semantic complex may be further information-processed as if it were a new message in its own right. By repeating this process, the original message becomes more and more meaningful as, at each recursive step, new semantic complexes are created. As these impinge on even larger areas provided by the internal information environment, whole new and elaborate knowledge structures may be built up—a process which leads to understanding (Stonier, 1997, p. 157).

Thus, knowledge exists in the human brain in the form of *stored or expressed neural patterns that may be activated and reflected upon through conscious thought*. This is a high-level description of the creation of knowledge that is consistent with the neural operation of the brain and is applicable in varying degrees to all living organisms. It took 50 years of research before this process of neuroplasticity (the capability of the external environment and learning to change the internal patterns and structure of the brain) was understood and accepted by the scientific community. From these findings we now know that *our thoughts directly impact the structure of our brain; and the structure of our brain affects our thoughts*.

Knowledge (Informing) and Knowledge (Proceeding)

For purposes of clarification and discussion, we consider knowledge as comprised of two parts: Knowledge (Informing) and Knowledge (Proceeding) (Bennet & Bennet, 2008b). This builds on the distinction made by Ryle (1949) between "knowing that" and "knowing how" (the *potential* and *actual* capacity to take effective action).

Knowledge (Informing) is the *information (or content)* part of knowledge. While this information part of knowledge is still generically information (organized patterns), it is special because of its structure and relationships with other information. Recall that knowledge is defined as the capacity (potential or actual) to take effective action. Knowledge (Informing) consists of information that may represent understanding, meaning, insights, expectations, intuition, theories and principles—all brought to bear from the past—that support or lead to effective action in the present (actual capacity) or future (potential capacity). When viewed separately this is information even though it *may* lead to effective action. It is considered knowledge when used *as part of the knowledge process*. In this context, the same thought may be information in one situation and knowledge in another situation.

Knowledge (Proceeding), represents the *process* and *action* part of knowledge. It is the process of selecting and associating or applying the relevant information, or Knowledge (Informing), from which specific actions can be identified and implemented, that is, actions that result in some level of anticipated outcome. This process occurs in the present, the NOW. There is considerable precedent for considering knowledge as a process versus an outcome of some action. For example, Kolb (1984) forwards in his theory of experiential learning that knowledge retrieval, creation and application requires engaging knowledge as a process, *not* a product. Bohm reminds us that "the actuality of knowledge is a living process that is taking place right now" and that we are taking part in this process (Bohm, 1980, p. 64). Note that the process our minds use to find, create and semantically mix the information needed to take effective action (i.e., knowledge) is often unconscious and difficult to communicate to someone else; therefore, by definition, tacit.

In Figure 2-1 below, *Justified True Belief* represents the theories, values and beliefs that are generally developed over time and often tacit. *Justified True Belief* is the philosophical definition of knowledge credited to Plato and his dialogues (Fine, 2003). The concept is based on the belief that in order to know that a given proposition is true you must not only believe it, but must also have justification for believing it.

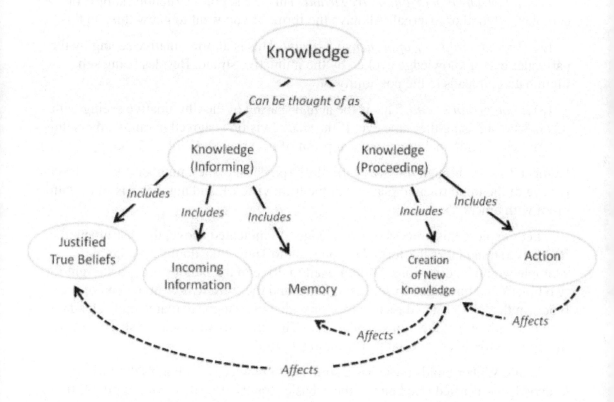

Figure 2-1*: Knowledge (Informing) and Knowledge (Proceeding)*

Note that justified true belief represents an *individual's* truth, that is, whether judging my personal experience or judging the experience of others, the beliefs and values that make up our personal theories, all developed and reinforced by personal life experiences, impact that judgment. Therefore, it is acknowledged that an individual's justified true belief may be based on a falsehood (Gettier, 1963). However, if it is used to take effective action in terms of the user's expectations of outcomes, then *it would be considered knowledge from that individual's viewpoint.* Note that this is only one part of Knowledge (Informing), and that our beliefs and theories are part of the living process described above (Bohm, 1980; Bennet & Bennet, 2008e; 2014). The term "memory" is used as a singular collective and implies all the patterns and connections accessible by the mind occurring before the instant at hand. (See Chapter 20/Part III for a discussion of memory.)

Wilber (1983) says that all valid knowledge—no matter its domain—is essentially similar in structure and has three basic components: injunction, illumination and confirmation. These basic strands of knowledge are:

(1) *An instrumental or injunctive strand.* This is a set of instructions simple or complex, internal or external. All have the form: 'If you want to know this, do this.'

(2) *An illuminative or apprehensive strand.* This is an illuminative seeing by the particular eye of knowledge evoked by the injunctive strand. Besides being self-illuminative, it leads to the possibility of:

(3) *A communal strand.* This is the actual sharing of the illuminative seeing with others who are using the same eye. If the shared vision is agreed upon by others, this constitutes a communal or consensual proof of *true seeing.* (Wilber, 1983, pp. 31-32)

Number 1 looks through the eye of the flesh (physical plane); number 2 looks through the eye of the mind (mental plane with the truth visible); and number 3 is sharing this proof with others.

Let's explore this process of knowledge. As indicated above, the instrumental or injunctive strand takes the form: "If you want to know this, do this." A simple example would be directions, "If you want to drive to the outlet store, go straight for two blocks and turn right on Jefferson Lane, and the store will be at the end of the block on the left." If the directions are provided in a language that is understandable, then the truth of the directions can be seen. The final strand would be sharing these directions with others to establish communal proof.

While Wilber builds these basic strands of knowledge on Plato's definition of knowledge—justified true belief—these basic strands also work with our definition of knowledge as the capacity (potential or actual) to take effective action. Step 1 is the expression of information in context, step 2 is the proof from the viewpoint of the individual mind in terms of effectiveness, and step 3 is the proof from the viewpoint of the communal in terms of effectiveness when shared. Note that step 3 follows the scientific approach requiring repeatability and external validation.

As a foundational concept, Knowledge (Informing) and Knowledge (Proceeding) are used as a tool for understanding ever-expanding concepts of knowledge about knowledge.

Levels of Knowledge

It is useful to think of knowledge in terms of three levels—surface, shallow and deep. It may be that we developed this way of thinking because of its close ties to navigating the high seas and our links to the naval services. Or, it may be the direct link to systems, recognizing that there are simple, complicated and complex systems. We don't consider chaos as a system, but as a condition of a system. Regardless of the reason for the original model, thinking in terms of levels of knowledge aids our understanding. These levels are not to be confused with the concepts of "tacit" and "explicit", although there is a relationship. Explicit is that which can be voiced, captured, made known. Tacit is that which cannot be pulled up from memory. See Appendix D and Bennet et al., 2015, for more detail. The terms tacit and explicit refer to the ability of the individual to express or not express what they know. The levels of knowledge refer to a quality of the knowledge itself in terms of the ease of the ability to convey it and build shared understanding.

Surface knowledge is predominantly but not exclusively simple information (used to take effective action). Answering the question of what, when, where and who, it is primarily explicit, and represents visible choices that are easily understood. Surface knowledge in the form of information can be stored in books and computers. Because it has little meaning to improve recall, and few connections to other stored memories, surface knowledge is frequently difficult to remember and easy to forget (Sousa, 2006). **Shallow knowledge** includes information that has some depth of understanding, meaning and sense-making. To make meaning requires context, which the individual creates from mixing incoming information with their own internally-stored information, a process of creating Knowledge (Proceeding). Meaning can be created via logic, analysis, observation, reflection, and even—to some extent— prediction. Shallow knowledge is the realm of social knowledge, and as such this focus of KM overlaps with social learning theory (Bennet & Bennet, 2007a). For example, organizations that embrace the use of teams and communities facilitate the mobilization of both surface and shallow knowledge (context rich) and the creation of new ideas as individuals interact, learn and create new ideas in these groups.

For **deep knowledge** the decision-maker has developed and integrated many if not all of the following seven components: understanding, meaning, intuition, insight, creativity, judgment, and the ability to anticipate the outcome of our actions. Deep knowledge within a knowledge domain represents the ability to shift our frame of reference as the context and situation shift. Since Knowledge (Proceeding) must be created in order to know when and how to take effective action, the unconscious plays a large role, with much of deep knowledge tacit. This is the realm of the expert who has learned to detect patterns and evaluate their importance in anticipating the behavior of situations that are too complex for the conscious mind to understand. During the lengthy period of practice (lived experience) needed to develop deep knowledge in the domain of focus, *experts have developed internal theories* that guide their Knowledge (Proceeding) (Bennet & Bennet, 2015a; 2008b).

The levels of knowledge will be addressed in a deeper context in Chapter 24/Part IV.

From Knowledge to Action

We've finally gotten to the most critical aspect of knowledge. *Knowledge is linked directly to action*, the way we as learners gain experience. This represents the "justified" concept introduced in Plato's definition. The only way that we can influence, and possibly change, our material world is by acting upon it. However, such action may or may not result in the desired changes, that is, may or may not be "justified" in achieving what was anticipated, may or may not be "effective" in terms of what was desired, and may or may not be "truth" in terms of the situation at hand. However, if we understand some aspect of our world—such as an undesirable situation—then we may be able to create and apply knowledge (the capacity to take effective action) and thereby improve the situation, discovering the "truth" for this situation, and possibly a conceptual truth that will carry across to other situations. Thus, the awareness, importance and application of knowledge becomes critical to our ability to survive, grow and contribute to the larger world.

There is considerable precedent for linking knowledge and action. In 2005, 34 Knowledge Management (KM) thought leaders spanning four continents participated in an extensive study exploring the field of KM and their passion for the field. When participants were asked to define knowledge, 84 percent *tied knowledge directly to action* or use. Similarly, emerging from nearly 20 years of APQC's (American Productivity & Quality Center) leading research in the field of Knowledge Management, O'Dell and Hubert define knowledge from the practical perspective as "information in action" (O'Dell & Hubert, 2011 p. 2).

Knowledge determines the quality of every single decision we make. We are continuously informed from without and within and by uniquely sifting through, focusing, and connecting the stream of information that informs our knowledge and drives our actions. Sometimes we recognize our choices, and sometimes they are beyond our conscious awareness, that is, buried in the unconscious. The knowledge we create is both triggered by external events and determined by past experiences and current learning, the process of associative patterning (see Chapter 1).

While individual experience is the primary facet for human learning (Bennet & Bennet, 2015b), learning does not occur in isolation, that is, we are social creatures who live in an entangled world. Thus, the model showing the learning-knowledge loop—focused on the learning environment—begins with experience directly impacting learning. Simultaneously, it acknowledges that social interaction (social engagement) and thinking (cognitive processes) also directly impact the learning experience, all combining to create knowledge, *the capacity to take effective action*. See Figure 2-2.

The Knowledge-Action Loop can be viewed from the framework of the individual self or from an organizational perspective. From the viewpoint of the organization, we start with the question: What completely determines the performance of an organization on any given day? We propose that the answer is: The actions taken by every employee on any given day determines the performance of the organization that day. We then ask: What determines the actions and feelings emerging from within the individual (conscious and unconscious cognitive processes) and the thoughts and feelings triggered by the external environment (social interaction and social support) (Bennet & Bennet, 2015b). It is these thoughts and feelings, Knowledge (Informing), complexed with incoming information about the environment and situations, also Knowledge (Informing), that influence the perception and effectiveness of the actions that are taken, Knowledge (Proceeding).

Think about all of the relationships and activities that occur on a given day. While these activities often seem minimal in the course of life, over time they completely determine the performance, and success or failure, of the organization. The same set of questions and comments can be applied to the individual. From this viewpoint we can see that daily actions taken become extremely important for achievement of long-term goals and sustainability. And all these actions are based on our knowledge, what we learned from past experiences (including beliefs and values), what we know about the current situation, and the anticipated outcome of our actions. The force of our knowledge is highly dependent on our capacity to learn and act.

As we consider individuals and organizational cultures the "regulators" in this capacity to learn, there are two primary orientations to consider. One orientation is a "learner" who leans towards curiosity and continuously learns and encourages the flow of knowledge and feedback. Another orientation is a "knower" who leans towards conviction, learning something new only when forced, and returning to their home base of knowing as quickly as possible. Compared to the "learner," a "knower" has more cognitive laziness and defensiveness due to confirmation seeking. This use of the label "knower" refers to subconscious knowing, that is, a limited knowing based on a set of bounded past experiences heavily tied to our personal comfort zone, which would include our beliefs and values and the limits they set. (See Chapter 36/Part V and Appendix E for a discussion of knowing as a higher order energy flow emerging from the collaboration of the subconscious *and* the superconscious). As we continue through the journey of life, truth shifts and grows with our experiences, not necessarily due to our current truths proving false, but due to our current truths *finding a higher truth*. (See the discussion of truth in Chapter 24/Part IV.)

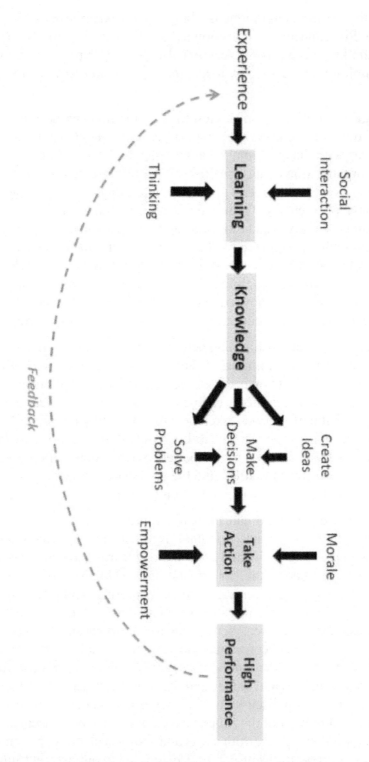

Figure 2-2. *The Knowledge-Action Loop*

The Nature of Knowledge

Let's take a quick look at the nature of knowledge. *Knowledge is dependent on context.* In fact, it represents an understanding of situations and their context, insights into the relationships within a system, and the ability to identify leverage points and weaknesses to recognize the meaning in a specific situation and to anticipate future implications of actions taken to resolve problems or meet challenges. Context is critical to *shared understanding*, the underlying purpose of communication and a primary goal of knowledge mobilization (Bennet & Bennet, 2007b). Shared understanding is taken to mean the movement of knowledge from one person to the other, recognizing that what passes in the air when two people are having a conversation is information in the form of changes in air pressure. These patterns of change may be understood by the perceiver (if they know the language and its nuances), but the changes in air pressure do *not* represent understanding, meaning or the capacity to anticipate the consequences of actions. The perceiver must be able to take these patterns (information) and—interpreting them through context—re-create the knowledge that the source intended.

This same phenomenon occurs when information is passed through writing or other communication vehicles. In other words, content and context (information) originating at the source resonate with the perceiver such that the intended knowledge can be re-created by the perceiver. If the subject of the interaction is simple and familiar to both participants, knowledge sharing (re-creation) may be relatively easy. However, if the subject is complex and the parties do not have common contexts, sharing can be very challenging. (See Bennet et al, 2015a for an in-depth treatment of context.)

Recognizing the nature of knowledge in terms of context sensitivity and situation dependence, it follows that *all knowledge is imperfect and/or incomplete*, that is, any small shift in the context or situation may require shifting or expanding knowledge, which in turn drives different decisions and actions to achieve the desired outcome(s). Since knowledge continuously shifts and changes in concert with our environment, the demands placed upon us and our response to that environment, all knowledge is imperfect and/or incomplete intelligence. A large example of this is the discovery of Quantum physics, coupled with the realization of the limitations of Newtonian physics, in representing our physical reality.

<<<<<<<◇>>>>>>

INSIGHT: **Knowledge is a human capacity that comes from the ability to intelligently interact with our environment.**

<<<<<<<◇>>>>>>

Intelligence is defined as the ability to know about, explain, define and reason; have knowledge of (Encarta, 1999). Intelligent activity represents *a state of interaction where intent, purpose, direction, values and expected outcomes are clearly understood and communicated among all parties, reflecting wisdom and achieving a higher truth.* The concept of intelligent activity, which will be discussed more fully in relationship to wisdom in Chapter 27/Part IV, will be connected throughout this book.

Let's explore the characteristic of knowledge as imperfect and/or incomplete from several frames of reference. Since each situation and its context are different, the knowledge needed to take effective action will most likely be different. The more complex the environment, the more difficult it is to take effective action. Complexity is considered as the condition of a system, situation, or organization that is integrated with some degree of order, but has too many elements and relationships to understand in simple analytic or logical ways (Bennet & Bennet, 2004). In such a situation, there are few clear cause-and-effect relationships between actions and desired outcomes. Every decision has hidden within it a guess about the future. In anticipating the results of an action, we are in fact making a guess, albeit educated or not, about what the consequences will be. This guess has many assumptions relative to the complex situation or its environment, and, as Axelrod and Cohen so succinctly summarize, "the hard reality is that the world in which we must act is beyond our understanding" (Axelrod & Cohen, 1999, p. xvii). In other words, we can never fully understand a complex situation and its context; therefore, our knowledge is imperfect and/or incomplete.

Second, people are complex adaptive systems, each having both a personal model of how we view the world and a threshold for learning (a focus) as we interact with the world (see Chapter 5). This very much has to do with our choices, previous learning experiences, and level of consciousness (see Chapter 5). Considering the external shifting and changing and the consequent internal connecting and learning, knowledge is continuously being created within the individual. Thus, at any single instant, knowledge is imperfect or incomplete.

<<<<<<<<>>>>>>>>

INSIGHT: **Knowledge represents the past, the ability to use what has already taken place in such a way that we creatively discover new directions and new ways of connecting things. It grows with use and increases when shared.**

<<<<<<<<>>>>>>>>

The activity part of knowledge manifests as energy, producing forces if the knowledge is untruthful. Activity grows us individually and collectively, enabling experiential learning and allowing life to grow, to become greater than itself. Life in part *is* activity, and the job of life is to make energy more intelligent (MacFlouer,

2004-16). When that activity is intelligent, it brings things together. When it is unintelligent, it creates negative pressure or forces that cause space to expand, putting distances between people, and leaving room for the growth of something new. The gaps opened by separation in space, what we call the environmental opportunity space, are those that human creativity can fill with new innovations (Bennet & Bennet, 2004).

Intelligent activity begins with thought as information. As energy and patterns of energy, thought produces forces. Knowledge, acting on information, produces forces. When knowledge is inward focused instead of outward focused, it produces greater forces. For example, consider a PhD professor who spent many years of life focused on developing a specific theory, and then continues to teach and push that theory year after year despite new discoveries that have negated its value, and in disservice to his students. In this example, a separation has occurred between the professor and his environment. the professor has *become* his knowledge, ceasing to learn and co-evolve with his environment. (See the discussion in Chapter 3 on the forces produced through selfishness and self-centeredness and Chapter 20/Part III on stuck energy.)

Intelligent activity involves engagement in the external reality; and the choices we make and actions we take affect the larger energy field within which we interact. Knowledge represents the past, using what has already taken place in such a way that we creatively discover new directions and ways of connecting things. It grows with use and increases when shared. Thus, through our actions we participate in expanding the field, which in turn requires new ways of thinking—new knowledge—for us to be effective. This is a continuous process of growth and expansion.

Levels of Comprehension

Another way of looking at knowledge is based on the ability of the individual to comprehend what is being shared. Knowledge encompasses *levels of comprehension* ranging from *data* (considered as a simple nonrandom pattern) to information, sense-making, understanding, meaning, intelligence, and wisdom. These levels *do* move from simple to complex, bringing out *different attributes of knowledge* and providing some measure to understand the level of comprehension an individual has relative to a particular domain of reality or situation of interest. However, unlike earlier models connecting data, information, knowledge and wisdom (Ackoff, 1989; Davenport and Prusak, 1998), while there is movement, this is *not* considered a continuum, that is, we recognize that knowledge is context-sensitive and situation dependent—what is considered data or information in one setting may be knowledge in another. Remember, information is a fundamental building block of knowledge; and knowledge is a fundamental building block of action. Different levels of comprehension may need to be engaged to act in different situations. As with all models, these levels should be considered as potentially useful guides rather than absolutes.

In the introduction to this chapter knowledge was described as a human capacity that comes from the ability to intelligently interact with our environment, helping us to move toward intelligent activity. While several of the levels of comprehension have been previously introduced, we will quickly review those definitions.

From a systems perspective, something makes *sense* when it is consistent with your own experience relative to that situation. *Understanding* means a more detailed awareness and insight into the causal relationships in addition to the elements and boundaries of the situation. Understanding applied to a complex system could include recognition of the emergent phenomena of the situation. The next comprehension level, *meaning*, considers the context of a situation in terms of its relationships to, or impact on, the environment or individuals, and other significant factors. Meaning is very personal, and heavily reliant on purpose and previous beliefs, values, mental models, etc. of the individual. *Anticipation* is the capacity to estimate the effect of a perturbation on a situation. Remember, knowledge is defined as the capacity (potential or actual) to take effective action. Effective action, then, is what is anticipated to occur, or, recognizing that in a complex situation a single decision may be part of a larger decision journey, effective action represents movement in the direction of what is anticipated. Complementing the useful and wide-spread interpretation of *intelligence* as the capacity to set and achieve goals, we add the definition introduced above: the ability to know about, explain, define and reason. *Wisdom* represents completeness and wholeness of thought. Chapter 27/Part IV is an in-depth discussion of the relationship of wisdom and knowledge.

Balancing these levels of comprehension against Lawrence Kohlberg's model of moral development can help us understand movement towards intelligent activity as part of the Intelligent Social Change Journey. According to Kohlberg, moral development is hierarchical, with each subsequent stage of six stages reorganizing and integrating the preceding one, and consequently providing a comprehensive basis for moral decisions (Kohlberg, 1981). See Figure 2-3. Although the sequence in which an individual moves through these stages of moral development is presumably fixed, the *rate* at which an individual progresses through the stages varies considerably, dependent on experience and learning capacity.

The first stage of Kohlberg's sequence is externally based with a punishment orientation, that is, concerned more with the power of authorities and avoiding punishment than with doing the right thing. In the second stage (conventional reasoning), individual acts are performed to satisfy personal needs. In the third stage (interpersonal relationships), the individual makes decisions by internalizing the rules to meet their own desires or achieve approval of significant others. All three of these stages are rooted in Phase 1 of the Intelligent Social Change Journey, connected to linear connections and cause-and-effect relationships. I do this for my personal gratification; and I do that to please my significant other.

In stage four, morality becomes more of *doing one's duty*, implying that the internalized rules are maintained for their own sake rather than the sake of others. While rules and consequences are acknowledged, patterns are recognized and conceptual thinking is emerging. Solidly moving into the co-evolving of Phase 2 of the ISCJ, stage five deals with post conventional reasoning, where individuals begin understanding abstract moral principles and considering each situation differently. Here, an individual develops their own rules and principles for good decision-making and behavior. In stage five (contractual orientation), the individual recognizes the need for flexibility and relativism in the rules of behavior, and the protection of all individuals.

As for all stages, stage 6 expands stage 5 with personal commitment rather than social consensus representing the basis for individual choices among moral possibilities (Berzonsky, 1994). At this stage an individual's conduct is driven by their own ideals and somewhat independent of the reaction of others. They vision a future and, built on a high moral ground and development of their mental faculties, they move toward that future. This final stage of moral development moves the individual into Phase 3 of the Intelligent Social Change Journey as a co-creator.

In the 2007 research study, the levels of knowledge comprehension defined above were used to help explore the relationship of knowledge and moral development in the military setting. As can be seen in Figure 2-2 from the descriptions at the point of intersection, there is a correlation between these six stages and seven of the eight levels of knowledge comprehension. The results of this study were used to develop leadership stories focused specifically at these points of intersection that demonstrated application of the organization's core values. The intent was to take advantage of the opportunity offered as an individual is developing intellectual maturity to *concurrently develop core values,* thereby producing a competent, knowledgeable and value-oriented military member. This relationship does not imply causation, rather, it indicates a deliberate conceptual correlation between the knowledge maturity of young people during military service and growth in basic values. The same learning can be extrapolated across to educational systems.

In Chapter 10/Part II, we look at Kohlberg's stages of moral development as they related to Fowler's (1995) stages of faith development.

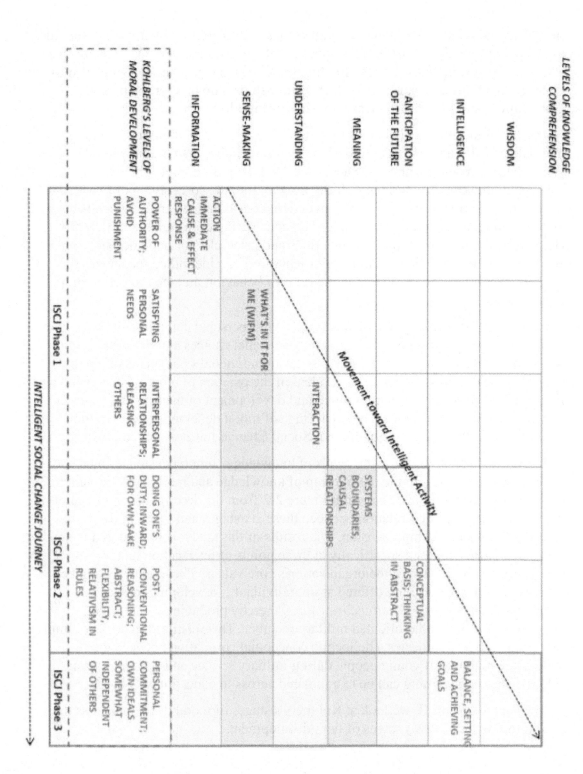

Figure 2-3. *Movement toward intelligent activity.*

Final Thoughts

As a tool for activity, knowledge has played, and continues to play, a large role in this human drama of growth and expansion. Knowledge is inextricably connected to power and energy, *giving us the ability to take intelligent action or to create forces against us*. In this drama, knowledge itself is neither true nor false, and its value in terms of good or poor is difficult to measure other than by the outcomes of actions. Knowledge includes a special form of information and all information is energy; *how that information is used and what form it takes determines its value*. Hence, good knowledge would have a high probability of producing the desired and anticipated outcome, and poor knowledge would have a low probability of producing the expected result. Note that in this context the concept of "good" or "bad" is not connected to morality but to anticipated outcome of the user. For complex situations, the quality of knowledge (from good to poor, relative to each specific situation) may be hard to estimate before the action is taken because of the situation's unpredictability. After the outcome has occurred, the quality of knowledge can be assessed by comparing the actual outcome to the anticipated outcome.

However, there is an emergent quality of "goodness" in terms of the greater good as knowledge is connected to other knowledge, shared and expanded. This is because the sharing of knowledge—that is, people collaboratively bringing knowledges together which are imperfect or incomplete—move the participants who are sharing toward intelligent activity, with the result of taking action that has a higher potential for effectiveness, spurring on creativity, and helping others serve themselves and others. This is demonstrated in the model used in the U.S. Department of the Navy included in Chapter 12/Part II. The concept of "effectiveness" is now a shared intent, with the "goodness" of the result perceived by multiple individuals, organizations, or countries. This is why *intelligent activity is described as a state of interaction where intent, purpose, direction, values and expected outcomes are clearly understood and communicated among all parties, reflecting wisdom and achieving a higher truth.*

Thus, knowledge serves as a tool for activity as we move through experiences, expanding our awareness, connectedness, growth, individuation, creativity and contribution. When all this is woven on a tapestry of inclusiveness, collaboration, knowledge sharing and wise givingness—and coupled with a striving for truth and beauty—it leads to expanded consciousness and meaning (MacFlouer, 2004-16). This is intelligent activity.

In Chapter 3 we take a closer look at the forces we act upon in our quest towards intelligent activity.

Questions for Reflection:

Am I using current knowledge resources to take appropriate actions and taking actions that will produce new knowledge and opportunities?

How often do we have conversations about what we don't know?

Chapter 3
Forces We Act Upon

SUBTOPICS: AMPLITUDE, FREQUENCY AND DURATION ... FROM THE VIEWPOINT OF THE INDIVIDUAL
... .CONTROL AS FORCE ... REDUCING FORCES ... THE SELF AND FORCES ... FROM THE SPIRITUAL
VIEWPOINT ... STRATEGIC FORCES IN ORGANIZATIONS ... CORRELATION OF FORCES ... FINAL THOUGHTS

FIGURES: 3-1. A SAMPLE FORCE FIELD ANALYSIS DIAGRAM ... 3-2. SELF-CENTEREDNESS AND
SELFISHNESS PRODUCE FORCES. SELFLESSNESS, WHEN COUPLED WITH WISE GIVING, REDUCES FORCES ...
3-3. FULLY ENGAGING THE BALANCED SENSES ON ALL OF OUR PLANES ... 3-4. DRIVEN BY INTENT,
DIRECTION IS THE JOURNEY TOWARD INTELLIGENT ACTIVITY.

TOOL: 3-1. FORCE FIELD ANALYSIS

Forces are a part of our everyday world. A force occurs when one source of energy
affects (pushes against, interferes with, influences) another source of energy, whether
with positive or negative results. Energy can never be lost; it can only be transformed.
It is through this transformation that light, heat, electricity and Life are produced.
Things in the natural setting of our planet that are not sentient are controlled by the
forces of nature. For example, consider the effects of the weather and water, and the
impacts of earthquakes and volcanos. As can be seen, forces are directly related to
change. As Walsch (2009, p. 165) describes,

> Energy acts upon itself. The transformation of energy produces energy in
> formation. Energy is life's information. Life is always in formation. It is forever
> forming itself into something it was not before it became what it is. It is through
> the becoming that life breathes life into Life itself. In simple terms, this is called
> change.

Per conventional physics, there are four fundamental forces throughout our
Universe that have been identified and are measurable by scientific instruments, and
thus scientifically accepted as "real". These four forces, found widely throughout the
cosmos and consistent with the Newtonian understanding of the molecular physical
reality, are: electromagnetic, gravity, nuclear and weak nuclear. The electromagnetic
field (which we often think of as light) is omnipresent throughout the Universe in
varying levels of intensity; although we as humans are able to see only a very small
fraction of the full spectrum of frequencies that make up light. It comes from
electrons and their interactions, and the way they are moving. Strong nuclear energy
represents the forces between nucleons in atoms (neutrons, protons) that hold together
the atomic structure. The weak nuclear force originates from the nucleus of an atom
and affects the way the atomic structure is held together. Gravity is the weakest of

these forces, although collectively it affects the Universe more than any of the other three forces. In pragmatic terms, we think of gravity as a force attracting masses; however, more recently it is considered a warping of space.

Since Einstein, science has strived to find the way these forces interact and to unify these forces. It was believed that a unified theory would explain the Universe and from whence it came. While so far this effort has been unsuccessful, Quantum theory has brought us closer to the understanding that we exist in a large probability field of energy. Further, as will become clearer as we progress through this book, we "are not mediated by forces but by exchange of energy, which is constantly redistributed in a dynamic pattern" (McTaggart, 2002, p. 23). But first, let's understand the forces we have dealt with, and currently are dealing with, in our physical, emotional and mental playground.

Amplitude, Frequency and Direction

Forces can be considered in three ways: amplitude, frequency and direction. Amplitude has to do with the amount or largeness of a force in terms of size, volume, extent or breadth. Frequency is a measure of time and space, a rate of occurrence creating a regular rhythm, the number of times something happens during a period of time. The more distance (space) between events (time), the greater the opportunity for forces to increase. Direction, or phase, is the way that energy moves, points or faces. For example, consider the destruction of a nuclear power plant where the force of an earthquake and/or tsunami directed at the plant (direction) was strong enough (amplitude) and sustained enough (frequency—length of initial quake plus smaller follow-on quakes) to cause heavy leakage of nuclear energy into the environment.

Direction is the most significant. From a Quantum field viewpoint, a force can be thought of as one type of energy moving in a different direction than another type of energy. The interaction of these energies produces force. For example, consider a boat trying to move upstream, with the force of the engine pushing against the gravity-driven force of the water, or two teams playing tug-of-war with a rope.

Forces can grow when one part of a system creates in a very different way than the other part of a system. In fact, this can produce strong conflict in terms of direction. For example, consider a start-up organization with limited resources where there is strong disagreement on whether to follow one product line or another, both requiring significant financial investments to pursue. This force is also related to amplitude (the amount of resources required) and frequency (a conflicting timeline for production), although these are variables that can be potentially negotiated through knowledge sharing, cooperation and collaboration. For example, doing some pre-work on one or both product lines to use market demand to drive the decision of which product to pursue, or agreeing on a phased production approach over time. This type of cooperation and collaboration leads toward intelligent activity.

When we deliberately create against an activity or force already in play and accomplish our objective, we produce maximum levels of force. Instead of just changing direction, we purposefully create something to destroy something already moving in a certain direction. For example, consider the take-over of a company under adverse conditions when the company desires to sustain its autonomy. This type of a power play involves all three aspects of force, which will produce strong repercussions (counter forces) for all those involved; for example, a formal or informal cessation of work.

From the Viewpoint of the Individual

This same model can be used to consider the forces in our everyday lives. Forces directly affect our physical, emotional and mental planes, whether consciously or unconsciously. For example, in the early 1900's science discovered that there is an electromagnetic field that surrounds the human body. However, since this field was not historically measurable as organic through scientific instruments—that is, it was not consistent with (it was out of phase with) our understanding of organic electromagnetic energy—it was not considered and studied as part of our physical biological system, and thus does not appear in our biology textbooks. However, that is changing. For example, researchers like Dr. Kenneth Klivington (1989) of the Salk Institute explored how unidentified forms of bioenergy interact with human electrostatic fields and published this work extensively.

There are vast amounts of non-organic electromagnetic energy bombarding our bodies in the current age. Just consider the rapid emergence of radio, television, the virtual Internet and, more recently, the cell phone, which has metaphorically become an extension of the human nervous system! There are consequences of this bombardment being paid by those whose bodies are more sensitive to these energies. For example, there are a growing number of visitors at the Mountain Quest Institute[3-1] who have electrohypersensitivity, electro-sensitivity or electrical sensitivity, more formally described as idiopathic environmental intolerance attributed to electromagnetic fields (IEI-EMF). The level of body response to electromagnetic radiation levels that are below international radiation safety standards varies, ranging from a simple tingling similar to a mild electric shock to expressing through fatigue, stress, headaches, sleep issues, multiple skin issues (prickling, burning, rashes), muscle pain and more serious long-term health decay. While this condition is not recognized in general by the medical profession, international studies have increasingly demonstrated a direct link between electromagnetic radiation exposure and symptom development.

What is increasingly clear is that our use of electric power is dramatically altering the magnetic environment in which we live, with documented negative impacts on the human body and potential connections to cancer and Altzheimers. One explanation of this negative impact is that when magnetite crystals connect to cell membranes that their rotation contributes to abnormal cell physiology. A second potential explanation is that manmade electromagnetic energies suppress the natural manufacture of melatonin in the body (Reiter, 1994). A third potential explanation is forwarded by Dr. William Tiller of Stanford University, who says that unpolarized particles exhibiting chaotic and disordered behavior damage the body's tissues as they pass through our cells (Collinge, 1998). Tiller has consulted in development of a technology that can help create a coherent polarizing field effect which would mitigate this third explanation. As can be seen, the human body is being bombarded by—and responding with internal forces to—this energy.

Our technologies have come with other forces. For example, compatibility issues emerge and capability issues abound as we try to keep up with the latest and greatest technology, regardless of its usefulness in our particular context. There are also forces created when a new platform has engaged technologies we do not understand, or lost capabilities which we have made foundational to our work processes.

Over the long term, all people are subject to forces that can lead to degradation of senses, bodies and the cessation of life. For example, aging—facilitated by gravity—reduces senses such as sight and hearing, therefore reducing the information that comes through those senses and causing faulty knowledge and a reduction of comprehension. This translates into mistakes, with more and more energy required to survive, reducing the time to deal with other necessities of life, a diminished ability to be free and creative, and a steady increase in forces. Concurrently, our consciousness level and ability to gain meaning from life can diminish.

While humans have evolved, and have achieved some level of balance among the physical, emotional and mental planes that form our interactions, the balance that the spiritual brings to all planes of existence has lagged behind. This is largely due to the emphasis on mental development, which has escalated almost exponentially during the last decade. A considerable loss of physical capability has also accompanied this advancement of our mental faculties. Survival is no longer based primarily on the physical. Today, as a race, it would be difficult if not impossible to survive physically in the wild without technology. While survival is still a very real issue, the survival forces of today are headed a very different direction than those of the past, largely based on economic worth. Further, since living at a survival level involves strong forces in terms of amplitude, frequency and direction, there is little energy left for being creative. For example, when you are working two jobs to put food on the table it is difficult to break out of that pattern in order to pursue your dreams.

Further, as we have increasingly discovered (too many times) as we moved into the new century, extremists, or outliers, can significantly create large forces and have a strong effect on the overall average in terms of potential disruption and force. This is the principle of terrorism, where the whole can be adversely affected by a small number of people.

Control as a Force

You cannot force people to change, at least not for the long-term. History has proven that you cannot choose to take something else over and control it. Yet humans have a propensity for wanting to control. For example, consider the way we use the three lower kingdoms—animal, plant and mineral—and our abuse of all three in the name of progress, creating forces that eventually have, and will continue to, come back and harm us. MacFlouer (2004-16) calls the need to control a human foible, a paradox of individual understanding. However, he notes that as people grow in consciousness they also grow in understanding, which offers the opportunity for better choices.

Many people think that in order to create you must control that which you create. This is an illusion. The greatest benefit (and joy) to a creator is the self-sustainability of a creation. A simple and simultaneously complex example is the raising of a child. While initially a parent may desire to control a child's behavior, an intelligent parent realizes that this is not possible, and that the desired outcome is not control, but the ability of the child to create their own future—a future moving beyond what is possible for the parent. This occurs as the child learns through experience and interactions with others the relationship of cause and effect, and begins to understand larger concepts that move closer to intelligent activity.

We can, however, if we choose, *control ourselves* in a way that is intelligent, conscious and creative in its own right. Things create themselves and are cooperative within themselves to sustain life. Humans also have the capability of bringing people together and, while acknowledging and supporting their right to self-control, cooperatively working together to reduce forces and achieve common goals. For example, consider a not-for-profit organization with a diversity of partners and individuals, each with a personal agenda yet striving in the same direction. By discovering the common ground and focusing together on what *can be achieved* in that area, forces are reduced and progress is made.

<<<<<<<◇>>>>>>>

INSIGHT: **History has proven that you cannot choose to control others, at least for the long term. However, we *can* choose to *control ourselves* in a way that is intelligent, conscious and creative.**

<<<<<<<◇>>>>>>>

The founders of the U.S. Constitution believed that people have the right to control themselves. It is based on a "Naturalism" viewpoint of the world, not the relative conditions of the times. This, of course, is what civilization is all about, learning to control ourselves and bringing people together to head in a common direction, choosing those things that are best controlled by the common collective and pursuing those as a society.

Looking from the larger viewpoint of society, the more developed a civilization the fewer the forces, that is, increased or higher civilization reduces forces. Forces are reduced as people learn to live and work together. Civilization is considered an advanced level of development in society marked by complex social and political, organization and material, scientific and artistic progress (Encarta, 1999). It is not surprising that the social aspect of society is important to our definition of civilization. *Most activities have more forces pushing against them than the ability to join together and head in the same direction.* The more people are heading in the same direction, that is, wanting the same rights such as freedom and choice, and working together to ensure these rights, the fewer forces are created. This can only occur through social interaction based on intelligent activity. In general, the higher the consciousness level of the citizens on average, the fewer the forces. (See Chapter 5 for a deeper understanding of consciousness.)

As we have developed civilizations, we have simultaneously developed governments, and specific organizations within those government structures, as controls to ensure that laws and rule sets are obeyed. In a country where freedom is recognized as necessary for people to develop, expand and contribute their unique views and abilities to the larger whole, the laws and rule sets are collectively agreed-upon. The forces engaged in the latter situation are considerably less than the forces necessary to control a dictatorship, absolute monarchy, sultanate, theocracy or other form of totalitarian or authoritarian government where state authority is imposed on all or many aspects of citizens' lives.

MacFlouer (2004-16) provides an excellent example of the forces used in policing collectively-agreed upon laws and rule sets, what he refers to as the spiritual use of force, that is, the balancing out of surrounding forces that are destructive to freedom, purpose and creation, which leads to the destruction of love, inclusiveness and consciousness. The freedom to act, and the ability to choose to act wisely, are paramount to the spiritual use of forces. A police officer is repeatedly involved in actions where he must employ force (physical force such as restraints, use of weapons, ignoring some laws, etc.). Since there is not a single answer in every circumstance of its use, such policing demands both intelligence—development of the mental faculties and emotional intelligence—and wisdom (see Chapter 27/Part IV).

Using MacFlouer's example, imagine a home invasion where the perpetrator seeks to steal valuables and has the desire and means to eliminate any forces (you) that stand in his way. In terms of our earlier discussion, our police officer will consider amplitude (the amount of power employed), frequency (time and space, when and where) and direction (toward whom and what) both in terms of the forces being used by the perpetrator and in terms of the police officer's response to those forces. A response in terms of amplitude would perhaps be the surprise entry of a cadre of police officers to "forcefully" subdue the perpetrator. Power alone has a short life expectancy; failing to be as effective and with diminishing returns as time passes. In our example, the "surprise" only works if the perpetrator is in the right location and is not holding a hostage, both having to do with frequency and direction. If the perpetrator *is* in the right location and confronted by this amplitude of force, the element of fear (as a force that is a physical force avoidance response) may shift his direction, that is, moving the perpetrator away from his original plan and causing him to run for his life, out of the house and away from doing harm to the inhabitants of the house. Now force is moving with the perpetrator away from the police officer. This shift is closer to the police officer's direction, and with sufficient police and/or firepower (amount) and wise planning, the perpetrator will be apprehended. As can be seen, the time-space issue (frequency) can be effective for a longer period of time than amplitude (amount).

Based on the need to wisely use all three aspects of force, the spiritual use of force to overcome the non-spiritual use of force requires three times or more the power of the non-spiritual force (MacFlouer, 2004-16). It also requires a good deal of planning, creativity and intelligent use of time and space issues. Finally, there needs to be an understanding of direction to ensure that the perpetrator doesn't have a better perspective on the police officer's direction and therefore the ability to change the direction of that force, countering and negating the forces that are being used. For example, perhaps the perpetrator is carrying a trigger to a bomb planted on a hostage. Regardless of the amplitude of the police offer's effort, greater forces are now engaged.

When forces are created, it becomes more difficult to move through those forces to achieve intelligent activity. For example, let's look at a country with a two-party political system, where one half of the country supports the incumbent and the other half of the country is very unhappy about his election. Now, the incumbent is killed in an accident, which, because of the forces already in play, is perceived by his supporters as an assassination by non-supporters. In an emotional state, some supporters immediately retaliate and, with no one in power to rein them back or present a voice of reason, mayhem results. While in this hypothetical example it may be easy to see the larger pattern underway, when these events are occurring in the complex, uncertain and changing environment of today, deep emotions are triggered and it would be difficult to keep a clear mind. Thus, when more forces are created, all participants suffer. We have long understood the disempowerment and continuous suffering of retaliation and revenge, a continuous loop which never gets done whether played out between different families, different colors, different cultures or different countries.

<<<<<<<◇>>>>>>>

INSIGHT: **When you create forces, it becomes more difficult to move through those forces to achieve intelligent activity.**

<<<<<<<◇>>>>>>>

Working through another scenario, let's say the incumbent survives the accident and begins to enact wrongful legislation against these non-supporters. When this occurs, it is the right, and responsibility, of the non-supporters to use force—within the framework of the political and legal system—to fight such legislation.

As a result of the diversity in our world, a moral issue that repeatedly emerges is that of non-conflict. The question becomes: Is it more violent to be a receiver of greater violence than engaging the amount of force needed to succumb and reduce those that are being destructive to us? The choice is either to allow others to be violent to you and others without preventing it, or using force on others. MacFlouer (2004-16) believes that in some circumstances it is not appropriate to be nonviolent; that you actually invite violence from others in some situations. Rather, his response is to respond in such a way that you try and reduce violence to the minimal level necessary to prevent violence, using the principles of force to create a Spiritual circumstance when others are seeking to do violence. An example is the use of nuclear force. You want to use the least amount of force necessary to prevent the forces that your adversary is seeking to use. In this case, you would focus on what was required to completely negate the negative forces, and, after using all other alternatives, applying force with the least amount of loss of life and only the destruction necessary to dismantle the infrastructure.

When used, force must be used intelligently and wisely, not randomly (MacFlouer, 2004-16). There needs to be a "clear and present danger" so the force being used is for goodness rather than a random act of violence. Thus, any pre-emptive strike requires the necessity of understanding and conscious awareness on the part of those using it, and a continuous testing with wisdom when exercising it. This, of course, can be difficult when a sudden dilemma presents itself requiring an instant response.

Reducing Forces

The likelihood of reducing forces to zero while living in our world is minimal; it would be difficult to have any kind of life without force, and indeed forces can accelerate learning and incentivize creativity. On the other hand, persistent forces can destabilize a system, causing change and inducing conflict. As Kurt Lewin (1997; 1946) demonstrates in his force field model, a situation will stay stuck as long as there is a balance of opposing forces. Changes can only come by upsetting the balance.

Balancing can also serve as a tool to reduce forces. (See Chapter 32/Part V on Balancing and Sensing.) One of the ways to balance opposing forces and reduce conflict is through counter-invention, that is, a *communion of opposites* (Wagner, 1975), which occurs naturally in change. When we invent something, we are simultaneously counter-inventing its opposite. For example, in trying to differentiate when applying for a job, an individual's education and training, which may be similar to other applicant's since it was a requirement for the job, may prevent recognition of difference. Conversely, when trying to conventionalize, the act of attaching a conventional name to something that is different may help an individual who recognizes the misfit to better perceive that difference (McWhinney, 1997, p. 70). The bottom line is that the more successful we are at change *the greater the chance that we will end up where we began*. It is critical to understand the total process of change from a system's viewpoint in order to manage this paradoxical backlash of counter-invention and unexpected outcomes (forces).

****

TOOL 3-1: Force Field Analysis

A Force Field Analysis can be used to help identify forces in place that support or work against a solution, issue or problem. It helps illustrate the driving forces that can be reinforced or the restraining forces that could be eliminated or reduced. It also helps identify positive forces that can be strengthened to propel a project forward.

The process begins with a "T" diagram. Write the current problem and the ideal situation or solution to the problem at the top of the diagram. Evaluate the forces driving the ideal state and list those on the left-hand side of the diagram. List the restraining forces, or forces that are holding the team or organization from attaining the ideal situation, on the right-hand side. When all the forces have been identified and listed, evaluate the list. Ask which restraining forces might be reduced, or which driving forces may be enhanced, to bring you closer to the ideal situation. Prioritize the driving forces that can be strengthened, and restraining forces that would allow the most movement toward the ideal state if they were removed. Decide how to strengthen the positive elements and decrease the occurrence and ramifications of the negative elements, and *take actions to do so*. Here is a simple Force Field Analysis dealing with forces related to an individual's fear of public speaking.

****

The fundamental cause of conflict is separation. Forces grow from this one element more than any other. We are social creatures. Our brains are linked together. As Cozolino and Sprokay (2006, p. 3) say, "We are just beginning to understand that we have evolved as social creatures and that all of our biologies are interwoven."

Figure 3-1. *A sample Force Field Analysis diagram (DON, 1999) (used with permission).*

How we interact with each other plays an important role in the amount of force we experience. For example, if you are a member of a team or focus group and closed to other people's ideas while promoting your own, you are producing forces that will need to be dealt with. When you are engaged in dialogue, listening to other's ideas with openness, humility and appreciation, you are not producing forces, and the thoughts of the group are coming closer to heading the same direction. Cooperation and knowledge sharing can facilitate the reduction of forces through an increase in shared understanding. Such a group can survive impact forces from outside sources as well as reduce the forces in their lives, providing they are doing so for themselves *and* for others with whom they interact. Note that shared understanding provides a safe environment from which to act, and the freedom to act based on a connectedness of choices, that is, heading you in the same direction.

Actions that connect people without producing forces, and helping to reduce forces already in play, are based on inclusiveness, wise givingness and love. Consider these three aspects in terms of amplitude, frequency and direction, and it is clear how powerful they are in reducing forces both inside and outside ourselves. One outcome is the goodwill of others and, working together, the opportunity to bring about positive changes that keep on growing outwards.

A number of years ago a movie came out which included the idea of "pay it forward". In terms of behavior modeling and learning, this is similar to the effective "train-the-trainer" and "educate-the-educator" approaches emerging near the end of the last century. As we were just beginning to recognize our interconnectedness and morph into a global world—and the necessity of moving forward together while simultaneously tapping into the amazing diversity of thought and individuation—we discovered a secret. *Our thoughts and feelings coupled with collaboration and knowledge sharing were actually creating our future* (see Chapter 23/Part IV). If what we project outward is force with the power of that force dependent on amplitude, frequency and direction, then we are going to bang up against other forces, weaker or stronger and with similar characteristics. *If we create together with others in service to the greater whole, then fewer forces accompany that creation process.* For example, consider development of an innovation that will help other people live more creative lives, that is, creating something that saves others time and effort so that they have a larger opportunity to create.

The ability to collectively engage diversity and individuation in intelligent activity not only reduces forces but causes expansion of all those involved, as well as positively affecting those they touch and those that are touched by the resulting products and processes. In other words, similar to the butterfly effect in complexity theory, there *is* the potential to change the world. We *are* creators and innovation *is* an outcome of our creativity.

<<<<<<<◇>>>>>>>

INSIGHT: **Similar to the butterfly effect in complexity theory, there *is* the potential to change the world. We *are* creators and innovation *is* an outcome of our creativity.**

<<<<<<<◇>>>>>>>

When conscious of a situation and recognizing the forces related to that situation, erratic forces can be eliminated. In every circumstance, there is a way to improve a situation where strong forces are in play by working with others, engaging in planning and having the freedom to act intelligently and wisely. Who are these others with whom we engage? They come from all walks of life, from all of the social groups of which we are a part at the family, community, organizational, country and global levels. *The value of inclusiveness is additive.* It builds on openness and the recognition of the creative power of diversity and variety, while simultaneously seeking close relationships built on personal resonance, an event significant beyond surface meaning, connecting values, beliefs and dreams. For example, in the journey of developing friendships you might ask: Is this person virtuous? Do they seek consciousness-expanding experiences? How do they treat others? Or, you might look for places where you can be with people less selfish than yourself.

The Self and Forces

Selfishness (looking after your own interests, needs and desires while ignoring those of others) and self-centeredness (tending to focus on your own needs and affairs and showing little or no interest in those of others) are traits that produce strong forces in our lives (Encarta, 1999). Conversely, selflessness (putting other people's needs first) decreases forces (see Figure 3-2). For example, consider a marriage or business partnering relationship where self-centeredness and/or selfishness occurs on a regular basis. From our personal experiences in life we know that, depending on the strength of the forces created, these relationships are certainly going to be troubled and short-term ones. Further, selfishness produces emotive forces—both within ourselves and from others—with many of these forces becoming "stuck" energy and heavily impacting the health of our physical bodies (see Chapter 20/Part III).

DECREASED	[FORCES]	INCREASED
Selflessness	**Self-Centered**	**Selfishness**
•Puting other people's needs first	•Tending to focus on your own needs and affairs and to show little or no interest in those of others	•Looking after your own interests, needs and desires while ignoring those of others

Figure 3-2. *Self-Centeredness and Selfishness produce forces. When coupled with wise giving, Selflessness reduces forces.*

Wise giving is an important element of a relationship that can help reduce forces. Wise giving is helping others to help themselves and others. The object of wise giving is to reduce forces over the long term by cooperating and sharing with others the amount of energy they need in the short term. For example, lending a hand with a difficult task that requires more than one person, or providing a short-term loan to get through a rough spot, which is then repaid in some way as promised, or sharing knowledge and objects in an equitable relationship. On the other hand, unwise giving can produce selfishness in others, thereby *producing* forces. Unwise giving can be characterized as taking care of other's issues and problems without their participation. For example, paying someone's debt without them learning from the experience, thereby repeating it again and again, or building a dependency on you such that they cease their own creativity and growth, and give away their freedom and personal power.

Relationships—and the forces created through relationships—are ultimately about people and the way they interact with each other over long periods of time. From the business perspective, Relationship Network Management (RNM) recognizes the need for and power of connecting and collaborating with others, and the impact of those relationships on our future decisions and actions (Bennet et al., 2015c). Critical concepts tied to successful RNM include interdependency, trust, openness, flow and equitability. RNM attempts to raise awareness of these relationships to enable individuals at all levels of life to consciously choose and manage their relationships in terms of amplitude, frequency and direction. RNM is presented as a tool in Chapter 10/Part II.

Another way that individuals increase internal forces is by being irresponsible with their abilities. For example, when a worker claims to have a capability they do not have, or perhaps responding to what others *think* they can do while knowing they do not have that capability. While this can be balanced by a continuous cycle of learning, expanding and working with others, wisdom must be engaged to ensure that insurmountable forces are not put in play.

At a personal level, we have a tendency to choose to reduce forces as we age. The sheer weight of navigating traffic, waiting in lines, repeatedly accomplishing mundane tasks, and generally navigating the ins and outs of life in terms of paperwork and deadlines begs us to change our life style. Humans have a propensity for increasing the complexity of their lives when they stay in a specific situation, year after year expanding their baseline of activity and taking on new responsibilities and obligations, and thereby increasing the forces in their lives. The secret, of course, is to know ourselves and our capabilities, choose our environment carefully, set limits and ensure that our thoughts and activities are outward focused, creatively and wisely serving others so that they may serve others, collectively engaging in intelligent activity.

From the Spiritual Viewpoint

The greater the spiritual thought and direction to any movement, the fewer forces are present. Since this term will appear throughout this text, we take pause to develop a common understanding of its meaning. Spiritual is taken to mean pertaining to the soul, or "standing in relationship to another based on matters of the soul" (Oxford, 2002, p. 2963). Soul represents the *animating principle of human life in terms of thought and action*, specifically focused on its moral aspects, the emotional part of human nature, and higher development of the mental faculties. From the philosophical aspect, it is the vital, sensitive or rational principle in human beings (Oxford, 2002, p., 2928).

Csikszentmihalyi (2003, p. 19) says that "an enduring vision in both work and life derives its power from soul—the energy a person or organization devotes to purposes beyond itself." It is also noted that an alternative definition of spiritual is *of or pertaining to the intellect* (intellectual, the capacity for knowledge and understanding, the ability to think abstractly or profoundly) (*American Heritage Dictionary*, 2006) and of the mind (in terms of highly refined, sensitive and not concerned with material things) (*Oxford English Dictionary*, 2002, p. 2963). In this book, then, spirituality is **the elevation of the mind as related to intellect and matters of the soul—the animating principle of human life reflected in thought and action**. This includes moral aspects, the emotional part of human nature, and higher development of the mental faculties.

The concepts of inclusiveness, wise givingness and love, as well as knowledge sharing and collaboration, truth and beauty, combined with a focus on helping others help themselves and others (the pass-it-on or pay-it-forward approach), provide the foundation for understanding spiritual thought and direction. While in this paragraph we are referencing these attributes as spiritual in nature, we are increasingly learning as a humanity that these are virtues applicable on the physical, mental and emotional planes. For example, cooperation and collaboration indeed trump the heretofore perceived value of survival of the fittest (Kropotkin, 1902; Darwin, 1998; Swomley, 2000). Further, as we will explore in Chapter 33/Part V, beauty—which is very much context sensitive and situation dependent, that is, in the eye of the beholder—has the capability of balancing the senses across all three of our planes of existence! Thus *beauty, when shared, has the potential to reduce forces*. With this in mind, think of the impact on our children when funding is cut for educational programs in the arts.

As we become more spiritual in the way we live, we reduce the amount of force in our lives. By opening our minds and hearts and working together in co-service to a global world, co-evolving and expanding *with* that world and in service to others who in turn can serve others, we move closer to that state. As MacFlouer (1999) contends, forces *can* go to zero when you become a master and your senses are all unified, enlightened and working together as a unit. As shown in Figure 3-3, this is when we are able to fully engage in cooperation and sharing on the physical plane, in love and compassion on the emotional plane, in truth on the mental plane, and in beauty generated from the intuitional plane, using all these together to create an incluessent future, a state that is far beyond that which we know to dream (Dunning, 2015).[3-2]

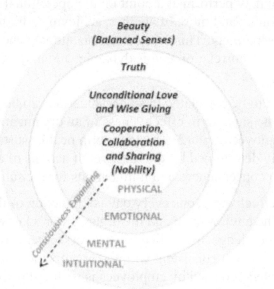

Figure 3-3. *Fully engaging the balanced senses on all of our planes.*

Strategic Forces in Organizations

[An example of the use of force in the Intelligent Complex Adaptive System model of organizations (Bennet and Bennet, 2004).]

While we have focused above on ways to reduce forces, we also need to recognize that *forces serve as sources of growth.* A system or field, including our organizations, can simply not stay in stasis for very long: sustainability requires growth. As discussed in Chapter 15/Part III, organizations are complex adaptive systems. A good organizational strategy identifies the major strengths, or forces, within the organization, and those that help mitigate—and take advantage of—changing day-to-day external threats and opportunities. Thus, an important aspect of strategy development is recognizing and monitoring the fundamental forces within the organization to ensure that these forces are aligned to maximize their effectiveness in creating sustainable collaborative advantage. Alignment means that these forces are moving the organization in the same direction, and they are coordinated such that they reinforce each other rather than push against each other.

In the complex adaptive system that is an organization, there are many forces at work. This makes sense considering the multitude of people involved and activities underway that affect the sustainability of the organization. By harnessing, directing, and/or nurturing the major forces, the organization can work with its partners and stakeholders to correlate its major resources to achieve maximum effectiveness. The correlated organization may perform at a point on the operational spectrum that utilizes less of one resource and more of another, achieving a higher gain than if these resources were added separately. This creates organizational synergy through the correlation of resources, a correlation that is dynamic, and may be highly responsive to external pressures.

The forces that need to be correlated in an organization can be considered in light of the following: (1) The short-term effectiveness of an organization depends on the actions of all of its employees, and (2) The long-term health (sustainability) of an organization is partially determined by the same set of actions of all employees seen from their downstream consequences and implications for the future.

Being able to take effective actions every day is a function of the knowledge and intent of employees. The environment and the organization's knowledge are correlated when that knowledge, as applied by the workforce, is directly related to those areas in the environment consistent with the organization's direction and needs, that is, knowledge created and used by employees is within the knowledge space of the organization as influenced by the environment.

Thus, at a high level we have identified three of the four forces used in an intelligent complex adaptive system to directly influence an organization's success. The four forces are the force of direction, the force of intent, the force of knowledge, and the force of knowing (Bennet and Bennet, 2004).

Direction serves as the compass for the organization as it moves into an uncharted future. It both limits organizational activities within some action space surrounding the chosen direction, and conserves energy by defining what areas in which the organization is *not* interested. To determine direction there must first be a vision and understanding of what is required to make the journey. Direction is the journey toward that vision, acting on the organizational reason for being and providing spirit and purpose to all employees. It is also used to explain why the organization must be as it is—providing sound reasons for collaboration, empowerment, etc.

The strength of the force of direction is measured by organizational cohesion, the line of sight, and the connectedness of choices. A *connectedness of choices* in this context means that decisions made at all levels of the organization, while different, are based on a clear direction for the future. Simultaneous, they are made in a cohesive fashion based on an understanding of both (1) *why* that direction is desirable and (2) the role that individual decisions play with respect to immediate objectives in support of the larger shared vision. While approaches and methods may shift and change in the journey, planning serves as a powerful mental tool. The level of communication, the alignment of work activities, and the effectiveness of operations all impact the force of direction. This is the journey toward intelligent activity.

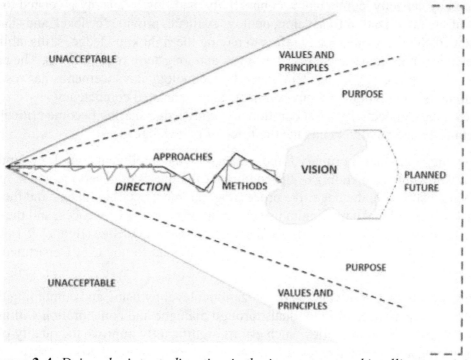

Figure 3-4. *Driven by intent, direction is the journey toward intelligent activity.*

Intention is an act or instance of determining mentally upon some action or result. Change occurs from the perceived current state of reality and, by choice, in the direction determined by the reality of *intention* and with the intended result taking control, leading from the problem to the solution. There can be no second-order change without intention to sustain the direction of change, with blindness to inconsistencies and courage of conviction serving intentionality. (See Chapter 25/Part IV on Attention and Intention.) Intention includes the purpose and attitude toward the effect of one's action, the outcome, with purpose implying having a goal or the determination to achieve something and attitude encompassing loyalty and dedication. Intent focuses the energy and knowledge of the organization, and is the power and consistency that gains the admiration of the marketplace. Knowledge is the "know how"—at least to the best of our current understanding—and intent is the power to focus the knowledge and sustain the direction. The strength (amplitude) of the force of intent is measured by the desire, willingness, and energy of every member of the organization. (Intention is discussed in-depth in Chapter 25/Part IV.)

Knowledge is the fundamental force of the organization, tied directly to action, and, as introduced in Chapter 2, consists of the creation, sharing, dissemination, leveraging, and application of knowledge. The strength of the force of knowledge is measured by capacity, competency, connectivity, and flow. Capacity is related to the ability of the organization to develop, deploy, evaluate, provide feedback and sustain the planned change. Competency refers to having the right knowledge, skills, abilities and behaviors needed to meet both short-term and long-term requirements. The pace of change (frequency), which is stimulated by technology advancements, has resulted in continuously evolving work environments and associated competency requirements. Connectivity, collaboration and knowledge sharing become critical assets to fully and positively engage the force of knowledge.

Knowing is the fourth primary force engaged by the intelligent complex adaptive system. Knowing is a blending of the cognitive capabilities of observing and perceiving a situation, the cognitive processing that must occur to understand the external world and make maximum use of our intuition and experiences, and the faculty for creating deep knowledge and acting on that knowledge (Bennet & Bennet, 2013). (Appendix E is a treatment of knowing developed for the U.S. Department of the Navy.)

Knowing can be elevated to the organizational level by using and combining the insights and experiences of individuals through dialogue and collaboration within teams, groups, and communities. Such efforts significantly improve the quality of understanding and responsiveness of action of the organization. It also greatly expands the scope of complex situations that can be handled through knowing because of the great resources brought to bear. Knowing is the tip of the intelligent complex adaptive system spear, penetrating the haze of complexity by allowing workers to think beyond normal perception and dig into the meaning and hidden patterns in a complex world. As an analogy, knowing represents fog lights into the future. The strength of the force of knowing is measured by the organization's ability to collectively perceive, interpret, and make sense of the environment and take effective actions.

The Correlation of Forces

The objective of a correlation of forces strategy is to create a specific organization with its unique environment in which the right set of critical success factors are managed, such that each of the four forces (knowledge, intent, direction and knowing) are maximized to support the organizational goals and objectives through the actions of individual knowledge workers. This can only be successful, of course, when the goals of the organization are those of service to others, empowering or facilitating others to be of greater service to themselves and to others, that is, making a contribution to the larger whole. To understand this, consider the organization as an individual and apply the earlier conversation regarding the concepts of selfishness and self-centeredness. The same patterns emerging within an individual can emerge within an organization, and, because larger forces are at play, have consequences potentially fatal to the organization.

These four forces must work together in a synergistic manner so they can mutually support each other through the critical success factors and the day-to-day operation of collaborative leaders and knowledge workers. When this occurs, the organization achieves its maximum probability of co-evolving with the environment, and creating sustainable collaborative advantage. Bennet et al. (2015c) is an extensive resource on collaborative leadership and thought leadership.

Consider the four forces: direction, intent, knowledge and knowing. Direction sets the compass, gives meaning to the trip and offers a vision of what to strive towards. Intent provides the energy and consistency of movement, the power of creativity. Knowledge provides the competency to take the right actions. Knowing provides a deeper understanding of the environment and how to deal with it over the long term. These forces are aligned when:

* Direction is set and understood.

* Intent moves the organization in the desired direction.

* Knowledge ensures actions follow intent and direction.

* Knowing improves knowledge, bolsters intent, and signals the organization whether the actions and directions are on track.

The correlation of forces, which is the movement of these forces in the same direction, is consistent with the pursuit of intelligent activity. As introduced in our earlier discussion, when intelligent activity becomes unintelligent activity, there are additional forces produced that are out of phase with the initial forces being employed for growth. This out-of-phase energy produces a series of incidents that can clog or stop the system. See Chapter 20/Part III, Stuck Energy: Limiting and Accelerating.

Final Thoughts

We think of ourselves as separate, which introduces limits to our ability to cooperate and share. When we can't or don't share, forces are created, and we struggle and/or compete against others. Indeed, competition, whether in business, academics or sports, has been a hallmark of the 20th century, producing negative life experiences. It doesn't matter if you "win" the game of force or "lose" it, there are negative results in terms of ego, separation, arrogance, loneliness, anger, frustration, desperation, etc., which all lead to a reduction of consciousness. As we intuitively know, it's time for a model based on collaboration.

Questions for Reflection:

What forces are acting upon me?

What forces am I creating and what impact are they having?

Chapter 4
The Ever-Expanding Self

SUBTOPICS: THE SUBJECT/OBJECT RELATIONSHIP ... THE PERSONALITY ... CHARACTERISTICS OF PERSONALITY ... DEVELOPMENT OF SELF ... THE HEALTHY SELF ... THE CONNECTED SELF ... INDIVIDUATION ... THE POWER OF HUMILITY ... FINAL THOUGHTS

FIGURES: 4-1. WE REFER TO THE PHYSICAL, EMOTIONAL, MENTAL AND INTUITIONAL FOCUS AREAS AS PLANES ... 4-2. THE INTERRELATED GROWTH OF THE ONE AND THE WHOLE ... 4-3. INDIVIDUATION AND CONNECTEDNESS ARE PART OF THE SAME CONTINUUM ... 4-4. THE SEASHORE SELF-AS-AN-AGENT-OF-CHANGE MODEL ... 4-5. RELATIONSHIP OF HUMILITY, EGO AND ARROGANCE ... 4-6. INTEGRATING FOUNDATIONAL PIECES.

TOOL: 4-1. SELF BELIEF ASSESSMENT ... 4-2. HUMILITY

Each and every human being is unique, whether considered from the frame of reference of DNA, experience, culture, family, thought patterns, beliefs, values, or emotions and feelings. At the core of all this difference is the *self*, with a subjective mind, exploring the world from the inside out, a protagonist ready for action. Yet in the magical environment of the womb, self does not exist. The thinker of the future that we become (the self) is a blank slate, even as energies entangle to create the unique web of associations and responses that will help ensure survival of the budding human, what we describe as the "personality".

Self is an emergent quality of the human which moves beyond biological drives and cultural habits. For purposes of this discussion, self is defined as the totality of the conscious and unconscious mind, the brain and the body. Note that while there is a close relationship of self to our understanding of consciousness (see Chapter 5), we take an expanded view with self inclusive of the personality, and—as our consciousness expands and becomes co-creator of our reality—inclusive of every aspect of what it is to be human. As Csikszentmihalyi (1993, p. 22) says, "Inside each person there is a wonderful capacity to reflect on the information that the various sense organs register, and to direct and control these experiences." This is rather like a figment of our imagination, "something we create to account for the multiplicity of impressions, emotions, thoughts, and feelings that the brain records in consciousness." (Csikszentmihalyi, 1993, p. 216)

Every self has a mind. According to Csikszentmihalyi (1993, p. 28), "Nowadays learning to control the mind may have become a greater priority for survival than seeking any further advantages the hard sciences could bring." We agree. As defined in Chapter 1, the mind is the totality of the *patterns* in the brain and throughout the body created by neurons and their firings and connections.

From a Quantum field perspective, the mind can be described as:

... a field of possibilities in which at least one-half of the field has chosen the same direction for its choices, with these choices having the potential to further limit a smaller field that the larger could be a creator of and is therefore potentially connected to. (MacFlouer, 1999, p. 162)

When thoughts are heading the same direction, what can be referred to as a *connectedness of choices*, force is not created and there is a higher probability of that thought becoming a reality. The Quantum field is a probability field, which is quite different than ordinary uncertainty. When something is uncertain, that uncertainty is due to lack of information. A Quantum state includes all possibilities at the same time prior to when it is revealed. Evolution in a Quantum state comes in two varieties, one when it is not observed and another when it is observed. When not observed, evolution is deterministic, much like that of classical mechanics. However, when it is observed, the wave function suddenly collapses and the outcome cannot be determined, rather, it includes all possibilities (Schrödinger, 1983).

This field can also be thought of in terms of focused consciousness, or will. The mind is the seat of consciousness, enabling awareness of our self as a knower, an observer and a learner, and as one who takes action. Knowing, observing, learning and taking action are not static, nor is the self. Self emerges from lived experience and reflection; thus, the perception of self is a *learned pattern*, beginning early in the journey of individuation and shored up by the subject/object relationship. In short, as introduced in Chapter 1, **we are a verb, not a noun**, continuously associating incoming information through the senses with stored patterns, creating and recreating a continuous series of Nows that become our source of thoughts and actions. From this perspective, self can be thought of as a self-organizing complex adaptive system. As such, it cannot remain static for long, but must either learn and expand, or fall into entropy, which is confusion, disorder, the waste of energy and the inability to work and achieve goals.

Self—including self-referential memory, self-description, self-awareness and the personality—coevolves with, and is the creator of, its environment (see Chapter 23/Part IV). As forwarded in *Urantia* (1955, p. 1227), "Physical life is a process taking place not so much within the organism as *between* the organism and the environment." This is a theme that emerges from many different frameworks cited throughout this text. Our self-awareness—which represents the unique ability to reflect on the past and potential future of ourselves, our world and the Universe—is possible *because* of the relationship between ourselves and our environment.

<<<<<<<◇>>>>>>>

INSIGHT: **Self awareness is possible because of the relationship between ourselves and our environment.**

<<<<<<<◇>>>>>>>

Self has many facets. We often perceive ourselves as the roles we play, the identities we take on, but those are just the *way we choose* to manifest self. Self is so much more. As American psychologist William James argues, "Although the self might feel like a unitary thing, it has many facets—from awareness of one's own body to memories of one's self to the sense of where one fits into society" (Zimmer, 2005). Thus, there is no single point within the mind/brain/body complex where we could situate self. It is the interactions among *all* of these neuronal patterns, firings and connections that create the self.

Similarly, contemporary neuroscience does not identify a separate neurological function or structure where self—or consciousness, which enables the recognition of self—exists. Self is the Quantum leap that occurred after the emergence of self-reflective consciousness, a distinct self that could take charge of the domain of consciousness, and determine which feelings or ideas take precedence. "Having had this experience of something inside us directing consciousness we gave it a name—the self—and took its reality for granted. And the self became an increasingly important part of human beings." (Csikszentmihalyi, 1993, p. 23)

The Subject/Object Relationship

At the material level of self in our perceived physical reality is the *perception of separation*, with boundaries of self encompassing a set of physical, mental, emotional and spiritual characteristics and beliefs (Bennet et al, 2015b). A learned pattern, this perception of separation expanded as humankind focused first primarily on the physical strength of the body, then primarily on mental strength, with physical strength still retaining a place of honor. Today, in our educational and work systems, we have reached a point of recognition of—and focus on—*the holistic and individuated human,* each with unique physical, mental, emotional and spiritual characteristics.

****

TOOL 4-1: Self-Belief Assessment

Beliefs can separate us from others. From the viewpoint of openness to change, take an inventory of your current beliefs. This is an awareness-raising exercise in which you explore your beliefs. Remember, change begins with awareness, and only you can change yourself (see Chapter 6).

STEP (1) Find a place where you can be comfortable and uninterrupted. Have a pad of paper and pen in front of you. Draw three columns on the paper, with the one on the left the thinnest and the other two equals.

STEP (2): One-by-one, bring each of the following concepts into your mind, putting the concept in the left-hand column, and quickly jotting down your feelings about each of them in the middle column, the first thoughts and feelings that come to mind. Here are the concepts: Voice Accent, Spirit, Egotism, Judgment, Gratitude, Skin Color, Education, Diversity, Life, Arrogance, Experience, Connection.

STEP (3): Consider other concepts that will trigger beliefs that you have, and repeat Step 2, bringing each of those concepts to mind. Push your edges, your comfort zone, bringing to mind concepts based on old beliefs.

STEP (4): Review your thoughts/feelings.

STEP (5): Think about a person that you respect and admire, someone who has high moral standards. Imagine you are that person. Now, go back and review your thoughts/feelings from that individual's perspective. This will require a longer period of time as you reflect on how (as that individual) you feel about these items. Write your responses in the third column.

STEP (6): Now compare the responses in column 2 and column 3. Where the two responses are different ask: Are there any beliefs that caused me to respond in this way? Is there a belief I have that is not helping me to be the best person I can be? Can I improve my response? How would I go about doing that?

STEP (7): As appropriate, act on your thoughts.

****

While the understanding of self in the "self-world" distinction has shifted, nonetheless there has been development through the years of the "I-as-subject" concept, with considerable debate around immunity to error as an essential ingredient of being self-conscious in terms of thought and experience (Eilan et al., 1995). For example, the substantive self-consciousness thesis considers the self as a persisting object with self-consciousness, the recognition of self as an object. Gibson (1979) forwarded that the self and the environment are co-perceived, that is, our perception of self coevolves with the perception of the environment as we move from infancy into adulthood. We are leaning toward agreement.

This awareness of self as a persisting object (the substantive self-consciousness thesis) supports connecting the self to the physical body and the perceived boundaries of the body as separate from our environment and other "selfs" within that environment. (Note that the substantive-consciousness thesis does *not* explain whether the self as an object is a mental or physical self.) For the next two paragraphs we will adopt this stance, looking from the viewpoint of the physical self as an object, which has—and projects—characteristics of mind, emotion and spirit.

As one object in a world of perceived objects, we can now consider the relationship between subject and object, bringing in the "I-as-Subject" Thesis, with "I" as the self-conscious subject of thought (me), which includes experiences producing knowledge that help build the idea of self. From the viewpoint of associative patterning, interactions in the environment have provided incoming information that, when complexed with internal information, produce *new patterns of thoughts and feelings*. These patterns—part of a continuous information stream— produce our ever-changing internal map of self and the world within which we live. In the brain, a network of neurons mimics the structure of the body parts to which they belong and *literally map the body*, creating a virtual surrogate of it, what Damasio (2010) refers to as a neural double.

In brief, neurons are *about the body*, and this "aboutness," this relentless pointing to the body, is the defining trait of neurons, neuronal circuits, and brains. When the body interacts with its environment, changes occur in the body's sensory organs such as the eyes, ears, and skin; the brain maps those changes, and thus the world outside the body indirectly acquires some form of representation within the brain.

There is considerable precedence for considering the *information processing system* of self as subject. The subject of experiences is linked to the point of view of the self, that is, a specific way of looking at a field of consciousness. Taking a reductionist approach, this would mean that "perceptual states are conscious just when they are representations from the subject's point of view" (Eilan, 1995).

In literature, as in life, the awareness of events from a specific point of view is in their associations through comparison or contrast. This question of association is a basic and indispensable principle in the description of any system. The process of selection depends on comparison and contrast, similarities and differences. When the "I" as subject perceives the "things" around the "I" as objects, it is through the unconscious lens of association, and through comparison to other objects in the environment. The illusion of self as separate, with boundaries, is what enables this process, with the self being the observer and the objects outside the self being what is observed. Note that the observer cannot be the thing observed; the process of evaluation demands some degree of transcendence of the thing which is evaluated.

Damasio forwards that *conscious minds begin when self comes to mind*. He describes three distinct steps to achieving self, starting with the *protoself*, that is, the generation of primordial feelings. The *core self*, all about action, is the next step, which "unfolds in a sequence of images that describe an object engaging the protoself and modifying that protoself, including its primordial feelings" (Damasio, 2010, p. 24.). The protoself (and its primordial feelings) and the core self are what constitute the *material me*, the physical me.

The *autobiographical self* is the final step and includes biographical knowledge that pertains to the past, as well as anticipation of the future. The higher reaches of the autobiographical self embrace "all aspects of one's social persona ... a 'social me' and a 'spiritual me'" (Damasio, 2010, p. 24). Note the emphasis on the holistic self. The combination of the core and autobiographical selfs construct a *knower*, another variety of subjectivity. As Mulvihill (2003) forwards, during the initial processing and linking of information from the different senses "it becomes clear that there is no thought, memory, or knowledge which is 'objective,' or 'detached' from the personal experience of knowing" (p. 322). While we agree, conscious awareness of the autobiographical self moves the self into the position of both the observed and the observer, an expansion of self-conscious awareness, enabling the living of life more fully and increasing our engagement with choice.

In Quantum physics there is an Observer Effect, recognition that the act of observing or measuring some parameter *changes that parameter*, that is, the observer affects the observed reality. This description emerged out of research by the Weizmann Institute of Science noting that, when observed, particles can also behave as waves (Buks et al., 1998). The import of this phenomenon shifts the focal point of the subject/object relationship back to the observer (as subject). This leads us to explore the power of intent. (See Chapter 25/Part IV).

While this quick treatment is far too thin to do justice to these concepts—and the many related concepts—the intent [pun intended] is to set the stage for looking at the experiential learning process in terms of self and the social interactions occurring in, and social support coming from, the environment.

The Personality

According to Merriam-Webster (2016), personality is a set of emotional qualities and/or ways of behaving that make a person different from other people. Working together, personality and self are part of what it is to be human.

Human beings are not blank slates at birth, and our slates become increasingly rich and multidimensional as we grow and learn. We are bubbling cauldrons of preferences, wants, sentiments, aspirations, likes, feelings, attitudes, predilections, values, and devotions. We aren't slaves to our desires; we have the capacity to reflect on them and strive to change them. But they make us who we are. It is from these inclinations within ourselves that we are able to construct purpose and meaning for our lives. (Carroll, 2016, p. 393)

In the following paragraphs, our exploration of personality will follow a flow of thought in terms of nature and nurture, and similarities and differences. Human nature and nurture include that which is innate, "common characteristics of humans—the shared motives, goals and psychological mechanisms that are either universal or nearly universal" (Buss, 1999). A part of this is the human decision-making process—the progression from knowledge to action—including response to, and influence and manipulation of, the environment within which we exist.

While much of the research into personality leans towards emergence of the personality, we contend that *we come with personality*, that our primary personality traits are already imprinted at the time of our birth, although, of course, these traits are thereafter affected by the environment and experiences of life. On the other hand, we believe that the self *does* emerge, and evolve, in concert with the environment, and, when/if it grows strong enough in terms of mental and emotional development, the self is quite capable of choosing to change its personality patterns. Thus, in our discussion below, we forward that the personality is very much a product of both nature (initially) and nurture (when and if it matures as a partner to self).

As early as 2500 B.C. in Babylon, and most likely earlier coming from ancient mathematicians, the Enneagram was emerging (taken from the Greek word *ennea*, or "nine") to represent different types of personalities. The Enneagram maps out nine basic personality types with traits and an inner change dynamic related to each type. The nine general types are: reformer, helper, motivator, artist, thinker, loyalist, generalist, leader and peacemaker. Each type is related to two others, one representing a change that is positive and the other a change that is negative. But the Enneagram goes beyond labeling a personality. Moving through self-observation, self-understanding and self-transformation, the Enneagram helps us focus on our fears and desires, strengths and weaknesses, defenses and anxieties, frustrations and disappointments, and our truest capacities and greatest strengths. As Rohr and Ebert (2000, p. 4) describe: "It confronts us with compulsions and laws under which we live—usually without being aware of it—and it aims to invite us to go beyond them, to take steps into the domain of freedom."

Another type indicator developed in the 1950's and 1960's is the Myers-Briggs (MBTI), which demonstrates the fundamental differences between people in terms of preferences (choice, whether unconscious or conscious). There are eight preferences based on four dichotomies. A preference for the way we perceive the world is either through our senses or intuition. A preference for making judgments is through thinking or feeling. These perceptions and judgments, then, are influenced by our interests in the inner world of ideas and concepts (introversion) or the outer world of objects and people (extraversion). Finally, we are asked whether we have a preference to rely on perception or judgment (Myers & Myers, 1995). Note that this is not a matter of one or the other, but rather the strength of one preference over the other. A forced scale is used such that here is no neutral point, although there can be a very weak preference of one over the other.

Other methods of assessing the personality place more emphasis on specific traits. For example, the Neuroticism-Extraversion Openness Personality Inventory rates individuals in terms of consciousness, agreeableness, openness, extraversion and neuroticism (Time-Life Books, undated). A specific personality trait explored by German researcher Elisabeth Noelle-Neumann (2008) was "personality strength." Personality strength is related to extroversion and self-esteem, and people with high scores on this trait tend to be leaders and influencers. Regardless of class, people with strong personalities are willing to try many new things and they enjoy influencing others. The really good news is that, as Csikszentmihalyi (1993, p. 99) says,

> … people with strong personalities seem to be less selfish and more concerned with helping others than those whose personalities are less strong. Apparently whatever trait makes for success and influence also includes a feeling of responsibility for the community.

This is consistent with the understanding that with knowledge comes responsibility.

Characteristics of Personality

We could take to the bookshelf of the Mountain Quest Institute Library and quote one "expert" after another, with varying viewpoints, on the characteristics of personality. However, all of that material is accessible to each of you, and, as interesting as those views are, the authors of this text do not have a unique contribution to add to that material. So, shifting our frame of reference, we dig into *Ageless Wisdom* (MacFlouer, 2004-2016) to explore the personality from that distinctive frame of reference, searching for and finding thoughts that resonate with our life-times of experiential and education-based learning to bring about a new understanding of a well-investigated topic. Building on that resource, and bringing in other learning in support of this line of thought (appropriately referenced), we forward the following:

The initial personality, simple and by nature over-controlling, is designed for the first ten years of life to help ensure survival of the budding human and its developing self. The personality is limited, existing without a sense of itself or an understanding of its own attributes. Charged with self-maintenance, self-perpetuation and self-gratification, the personality is aware of the self that it assists, yet does not have enough consciousness to understand who and what it is in relationship to that self, or anything else. Yet, it serves as the unifier of all the factors of reality as well as the coordinator and integrator of relationships, uniquely suited to its interactive role as the process of physical life takes place *between* the organism and the environment (*Urantia*, 1955).

The personality is pre-programmed with pre-existing properties, and focused on achieving our wants and desires, formed before mental clarity is developed and consciousness of choice is achieved. For example, the hypothalamus has a functional characteristic suggesting "a vague mixture of anxiety and desire—best described perhaps by the phrase 'I want', spoken with or without an object for the verb" (Konner, 1990). The *I want* mechanism makes sure that we are alert and watching out for new opportunities to control more energy, which is useful for our survival. As Csikszentmihalyi (1993, p. 31) describes, "The mind seems to operate under the general instruction to be constantly alert to improving one's chances, because if it is not someone else will surely take the advantage." Rough and tough and focused on acting in the physical world, the personality is energy-based and able to manipulate energies because it *is* energy focused on keeping us alive, experiencing pleasure, protecting us, avoiding pain, and eliminating fear.

Is this kind of control necessary? Evidently it is. Created before birth and operating from the subconscious realms, the personality is autonomous and mechanical, and has the role of helping us survive in what can be perceived as a threatening world. As the young child with limited consciousness and an undeveloped self attempts to navigate the physical body, with increasing input from the emotional body in terms of desires and wants, it is difficult to stay aware of, much less understand, the dangers in the largely unknown physical world. We will never know just how many accidents our unconscious prevented during these early years!

Since a child's senses are not very well developed, in the beginning the child has a narrow existence in terms of awareness and consciousness. Nor can the young mind connect one event to the next, so there is little memory. However, the self does not suffer from this lack as long as the senses are not very well developed. The self is virtually asleep, slowly becoming, and doesn't know it is losing out. However, *enriched environments facilitate the growth of self*, and once such exposure occurs it is important to continue that enriched environment. For example, take two infants 8 months old, one with continuous exposure to an enriched environment and with developing self, and the other one who is given things that are then removed from its environment. The child who receives more and more input grows all of its senses in the physical, emotional and mental bodies faster than the second child. This child is joyful and has a sense of self emerging. The second child, who no longer lives in an enriched environment, suffers. The giving, then taking away, has a greater impact and, over time in an impoverished environment, causes suffering without growth, producing a disorder which is similar to an animal level of development (MacFlouer, 2004-16).

Made up of thought forms and connected to what can be described as part of the lower mental mind, the personality, operating in the unconscious, is superior to self in its ability to process information. All information coming from the senses of all of our bodies goes through the personality. If we were fully conscious of all that the personality does, no doubt we wouldn't be able to do anything well, so it is necessary to have this part of us on auto pilot. It is the personality that initially drives the memory selection process, with its limited judgment collecting stuff most relevant to its perceived needs and throwing out a bunch of stuff that we do not yet have the capacity to use.

The development and connection of information resources in the mind/brain is a slow and tedious process, becoming more and more complex as more and more information is processed through the senses. Fortunately, we are designed to handle this increasing complexity. As Csikszentmihalyi (1993, p. 172) describes:

> What makes the evolution of complexity possible is the fact that we also have a built-in predilection for learning new skills, for doing difficult things that stretch our abilities, for creating order in our consciousness and in our environment … [and] this propensity can be used to create the kind of self that might contribute to a harmonious future.

Although initially focused on the physical body, the more information that is processed from all the senses (including focus points from the physical, emotional and mental planes), the greater the ability of the mind to act, the more interactions the mind can choose to have, and the larger opportunity to move toward intelligent activity. Concurrently, since self is co-evolving with its environment, problems can occur when the self is separated from information. Let's explore this further.

In the early years, acting from the subconscious, the personality is making all the choices, and it does this rapidly. The self does not yet have a high enough level of consciousness to take over this role and become who it chooses to be. Over 99 percent of the information coming in through the multiple senses and bodies is discarded, with the personality choosing what it allows to move into the consciousness of self (MacFlouer, 2004-16). Focusing on the mundane and pragmatic, the personality is the part of us that thinks about concrete things, material concepts, in short, survival and pleasure.

While the personality is structured to put together incoming information, sometimes the personality is inadequate in development or is too over controlling to do this well. This results in a lack of organization in the way the personality inputs and connects vital information into the lower mental brain. Remember, the personality does not understand who and what it is, or where and what it wants to be in the future. Interestingly, and in deference to the emotional body, the subconscious would rather be "right" in a fake way than accurate. This can rear its ugly head in the business environment. "Right" does not refer to truth or accuracy; it means convincing others that it is right, a social acceptance of right. This is done by filling in and making up things to explain to others *why* it is right! Most humans have participated in this type of response at some point in their lives.

While the maturing self is destined to become a co-creator through conscious choice and change, the personality *does not like* change. Thus, the personality is *not* supportive of creativity, because that means something new, change, which is prone to unknown threats that may cause pain. Imagine your personality saying, "I believe in [am comfortable with] these old ideas and don't want to change them" or "These things have kept you alive up to now. Why change?" Deeply embedded in our subconscious, we can get caught up in this fear of change.

Unaware that the personality exists, the developing self can actually be pushed by its unconscious to victimize itself, holding back from experiences and growth and reducing its level of consciousness in order to feel safer (from the personality's viewpoint). This, of course, has vast ramifications for how we interact in the world, and how meaningful our life is. When consciousness is reduced, it directly impacts our experience in life, suppressing our creativity and reducing meaning (see Chapter 5). Interestingly, this cycle also impacts the personality, the culprit, when lack of meaning may push an individual to seek stimulation through substance abuse and other physical excesses.

Even when unaware of the influence and power of the personality, the self can have a strong impact on the personality. For example, since one of the personality's reasons for being is to pursue pleasure and avoid pain, suffering is intolerable. When the personality picks up suffering from the self, the subconscious reacts, generating fear, limiting the flow of information, causing the mind to become disoriented, perhaps even affecting development. When the personality becomes disordered, it may make the wrong choices on what to keep and what to throw away, and make misconnections among incoming information. This can manifest as a psychological disorder, affecting behaviors and mental health. As more and more mistakes are made, it becomes more difficult to make choices. There is a reduction in consciousness, the self shrinks, and permanent damage can occur to the physical brain.

As the individual moves toward maturity, the personality is less and less capable of making its existence meaningful alone. Since the personality's initial development ceases around the age of 10 (MacFlouer, 2004-16), in order for the personality to become more it must give way to the self. Slowly, the self has been experiencing and learning, expanding its consciousness and, eventually, becoming aware of itself, and perhaps even the attitudes, feelings and actions driven by its personality, choosing to keep some of those traits and to shift others. Self now has the opportunity to move into the leadership role, albeit bringing personality biases along with it. That said, do not yet dismiss the significance of the personality. It continues the unconscious processing of incredible amounts of information through all 21 senses (7 senses on each of three planes: physical, mental and emotional). And, as we shall see in Chapter 37/Part V, as the self grows and consciousness expands, the personality has the opportunity to move into a new role.

We now take a closer look at the development of self.

Development of Self

During the years that personality has been in control, the child primarily operates on automatic, with actions very much driven at the subconscious level. From the viewpoint of the self, unaware of the personality's protective control, it has the freedom to develop who it chooses to be.

Initially, the child is focused on immediate physical needs such as safety and food and comfort. *Living* is the first step. As forwarded in *Urantia* (1955, p. 1228):

> In all concepts of selfhood it should be recognized that the fact of life comes first, its evaluation or interpretation later. The human child first *lives* and subsequently *thinks* about his living. In the cosmic economy insight precedes foresight.

While these physical needs certainly remain essential, for most people relationships rapidly become more important. Most humans are family-centric. Development and differentiation start with the nuclear family, parents and parental figures, and expands through the extended family of male and female relatives, friends and teachers. The self has the desire to be accepted, loved and respected by these people. Csikszentmihalyi (1993) warns that there is a danger if the self remains in this mode that life might be reduced to thoughtless conformity. This is consistent with our discussion of the personality above.

<<<<<<<>>>>>>

INSIGHT: **In the cosmic economy, insight precedes foresight**.

<<<<<<<>>>>>>

Education often takes a lead role as the self continues expansion, and with adulthood, there is a focus on the new family structure, with the rearing of children becoming a dominant factor. As the child connects with larger groups, social values become important, although the focus is still on the self.

The emergence of the individual self begins with our senses. If there is no information coming into the mind then the mind is mindless, that is, it doesn't have the resources—or the truth—to construct itself. Similar to how we view millions of water molecules as a single thing (the ocean), "we experience the coming together of information in consciousness as the self" (Csikszentmihalyi, 1993, p. 217).

As introduced at the beginning of the book, we as humans have seven senses, the five senses of form (seeing, hearing, tasting, smelling and feeling) and two inner senses, connecting us to each other and informing our role as co-creator. These two inner senses increasingly come into awareness with maturity, as the self grows and consciousness expands. The two inner senses are located in the heart and crown. The heart has long been associated with love and the recognition of Oneness, the connectedness of all things. This sixth sense develops as we move through the Intelligent Social Change Journey, expanding from sympathy to empathy to compassion and deepening our connections to others. The seventh sense is located in the crown energy center, connecting us to the larger Universal whole and our role as co-creators.

All of these seven senses can be perceived from a physical, emotional or mental focus. While these areas of focus are often referred to as bodies, for purposes of this book, and as referenced in the Introduction to Part I of this book, we choose to refer to each of these focus areas as *planes*. From this viewpoint, as humans we have a physical plane focus, an emotional plane focus, and a mental plane focus. Information is continuously coming in through all of our senses on each of our planes. For example, *seeing* from the physical plane refers to the physical qualities of what my eyes are viewing, *seeing* from the emotional plane refers to the emotions or feelings emerging from what I am viewing, and *seeing* from the mental plane refers to the connections of what I am viewing as representations to other activities and larger concepts, which is a determinate of truth. Thus, there is an abundance of information coming through the various senses. Factorially speaking, the 21 senses viewed from the three planes provide 51,070,942,170,709,440,000 different potential combinations of incoming information!

In the middle of all this incoming information, every once in a great while, there is a "woosh" of *intuitional thought*, a wonderful download brimming with possibilities. And then it is gone. In Figure 4-1 we show four planes, the lower three of which can be fully engaged by the individual as we progress through life. The fourth plane, the intuitional plane, will be discussed in Chapter 28/Part IV. While spiritual tacit knowledge moves throughout all the planes, the closer we expand toward the intuitional plane the fewer forces there are pushing against us and the greater our ability to tap into spiritual energy.

Please note that "intuitive tacit knowledge" is related to the mental plane. In this treatment and because the word "intuitive" has been used in so many ways in our everyday reality, we refer to intuitive tacit knowledge as the result of continuous learning through experience. In contrast, we use the word "intuitional" to refer to a higher order of thinking, a higher plane, that is informed by spiritual tacit knowledge, knowledge based on the soul, which represents the animating principles of human life in terms of thought and action. In Chapter 5 we introduce the concept of tacit knowledge more fully, and in Appendix D we discuss ways to engage tacit knowledge.

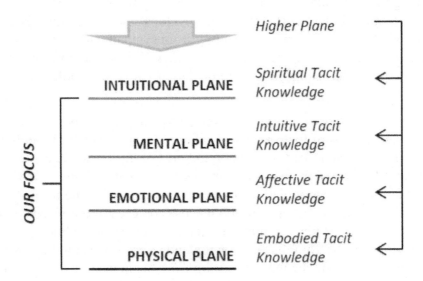

Figure 4-1. *We refer to the physical, emotional, mental and intuitional focus areas as planes.*

As information continues to flood through the senses and life becomes more complex, eventually the mind begins to weave this information together in new ways to develop a greater level of understanding. The creation of knowledge requires connecting information from a number of senses. Discernment and discretion (D^2) are necessary to plan for the future. D^2 is first the process of differentiation, and then the process of choosing to utilize our personal guidance system including values, purpose and goals, feelings, and mental faculties. For example, given alignment with values and goals, mental senses may aid recognition of a pattern that has been seen before, and therefore suggest a proven solution, while the emotional senses may feel something unsettling about a specific individual providing information. It is necessary to integrate *all* the incoming information in order to discover the best way ahead.

Learning from the past and living in the NOW, the self begins to plan for the future, "seeing" future events and making predictions with some degree of accuracy based on interactions with its environment. As the mental faculties grow, knowledge increases and the outcomes of actions take on a higher truth (see Chapter 24/Part IV).

Pliable and adaptable, self develops better with a variety different experiences and interactions. For example, we have long recognized the value of travel and living in different cultures. These experiences and interactions expand our knowledge of self, develop an appreciation for differences, and help us determine who and what we are in relationship to the world around us. This is happening more today than ever before. As cross-cultural interactions accelerate with the advent of global connectivity and ease of travel, the potential for expanded consciousness increases. The more exposure and interaction with people and other cultures, the greater the diversity of thought, the greater opportunity for recognition of patterns and development of elevated conceptual thinking and truth, and the greater the opportunity to engage our creativity with and for others.

With the individuation of self and the illusion of separation comes development of the ego, often associated with power and control. Ego, a sense of self-esteem or self-importance, emerged through the negative emotions of desire and fear. As Cooper (2005, p. 125) described,

> Because physical reality was so unpredictable, it was continuous fear that drove the animal mind to develop the capacity to reason. Reason came about through the animal desire to attain a higher level of gratification and physical security. It is here that we witness the birth of the conscious ego ….

With a direct line to the personality residing in the subconscious, yet visible in interactions with others, we can see the relationship of fear to ego. When a child is free to think and make mistakes without punishment, the mind continues free thinking and trial and error throughout life. If a child is fearful of making mistakes, then it quickly develops ego as part of its defense. This can lead to a position of narrow-mindedness, with answers regurgitated from limited, controlling minds and intolerance of others' thoughts. Often, ownership of possessions is used to provide concrete evidence of power and control, although certainly artificially so, and human relationships are used for building the image of self. For example, consider the practice of name dropping. (See Grounding Change in Chapter 10/Part II.)

Note that self does NOT denote ego. As can be seen, the ego was an important and necessary part of the early development of the human. However, in today's world this is reversed. As the individuated self evolves, it moves away from separation dominated by ego towards reconnecting, which is the road to greater growth and contribution.

The Healthy Self

The healthy self is continuously asking questions. *What is reality?* The Hindu say that what we think, see and believe are illusions, what they call the *veils of Maya*. By lifting these veils, we get a closer look at what life is all about. Similarly, more than 24 centuries ago, the pre-Socratic philosopher Democritus (460-357 B.C.) is credited with saying: *Nothing is real, or if it is, we don't know it. We have no way of knowing the truth. Truth is at the bottom of an abyss*.

What is truth? Truth changes. Truth is relative to the amount of information that has been garnered and is, like knowledge, at some level context sensitive and situation dependent. Since we are continuously learning and the situation is continuously changing, new information, different knowledge, expanded knowledge, and new concepts are always emerging. Even concepts, which can provide a higher level of truth than single events, are shifting and changing. When a new situation occurs where a concept that was considered truth does not fit, then a larger concept is discoverable that has a greater level of truth. Our job is to continue this search for truth, the highest virtue on the mental plane. (See Chapter 24/Part IV.)

As awareness of self emerges through interactive experiences and reflection, and as consciousness expands, creativity is unleashed. This creative urge is our birthright. While the personality is still locked in its mode focused on survival, seeking pleasure, following its desires and wants and avoiding fear and pain, the self has developed an understanding of who and what it is. Much like the behavioral model of the child coming of age—and often concurrent with full development of the executive brain which occurs around 28 years of age—the self chooses to overrule the personality, making conscious decisions through its mental faculties and in anticipation of the outcomes of decisions and actions. Not only is the self creating its life through a conscious understanding of *who and what it is* in relationship with others, but it also understands *who and what it wants to be*, with the aspiration to be anything and the inspiration to be something great (MacFlouer, 2004-16).

<<<<<<<◇>>>>>>>

INSIGHT: (MacFlouer) **As the self matures, not only does it create its life through a conscious understanding of *who and what it is* in relationship with others, but it also understands *who and what it wants to be*, with the aspiration to be anything and the inspiration to be something great.**

<<<<<<<◇>>>>>>>

Unable to fathom any of these things, the personality continues to take care of the mundane processing of information, only now doing so more in alignment with the choices of what is important to the self. This processing in alignment with self continues as self sleeps, a critical need for the healthy functioning of self. And while the personality still initially receives most information from the senses, information that deals with the higher focus levels, that is, the virtues of each of the planes, goes directly to the self. From the viewpoint of the physical plane this would include cooperation, collaboration and sharing; from the viewpoint of the emotional plane this would include compassion and love; and from the viewpoint of the mental plane this would include truth and wisdom. It would also include intelligent activity and beauty, which is the balancing of all senses (MacFlouer, 2004-16).

The focus of self has now gone beyond the illusions of personality, culture and ego to a contribution to others and concern for all life, *moving from an inward focus to an outward focus*.

By choice, the self and personality become partners, using their uniqueness and individuation to partner with others to co-create their rules and their reality. This is a state of transcendence, moving beyond personal limitations and adopting larger goals that encompass community, humanity and the planet. Csikszentmihalyi (1993, p. 235) sees this growth of self as an ascending spiral, "where concern for the self becomes steadily qualified by less selfish goals, and concern for others becomes more individualistic and personally meaningful." The self is choosing the manner of its life, contributing to the larger humanity, and happy with its choices. When we look at the world in which we live—a world that has the capability of destroying itself and its environment—this state of transcendence is not surprising, for "Selfishness, conformity, and even the development of unique individuality are no longer sufficient to give life a meaningful purpose …" (Csikszentmihalyi, 1993, p. 236-7).

The Connected Self

To be conscious, one must be able to connect to that which is perceived as outside of one's self. While we often have instinctive reactions to perceived external events and people, we also have responses which are thought out. *Connecting through responses requires a level of giving*, even if only of the intellect and in terms of the time needed to understand those with whom you connect.

When Darwin first published his book in 1859, *On the Origin of Species,* he voiced conclusions regarding the superior strength of individuals. His conclusion, *survival of the fittest*, became an accepted business mantra leading to and supporting hard competition. What is lesser known is that in his later book, *The Descent of Man*, Darwin had realized his mistake. As he summarized, "Those communities which included the greatest number of the most *sympathetic* [emphasis added] members would flourish best and rear the greatest number of offspring" (Darwin, 1998, p. 110). This will be discussed further in Chapter 14/Part III.

When we explore the workings of the mind/brain, this is not surprising. The human mind/brain is designed to think socially, forming and reforming social groups and relationships every day of our lives. Neither a single neuron nor an individual human brain exists in nature; rather, as introduced earlier and is rapidly becoming an interweaving theme, "all of our biologies are interwoven" (Cozolino & Spokay, 2006, p. 3). Mahoney and Restak look at the neuron as a model for corporate success, a design based on networking. "Our identity as social creatures is hardwired into the very structure of our brain ... this pattern of interconnectedness and sociability exists at every level of brain function." (Mahoney & Restak, 1998, p. 42) Gazzaniga (2008) feels that, metaphorically, humans are much more of a sociological entity than a single self. We agree, and from what we are learning through neuroscience and from our early understanding of Quantum, perhaps this is not so metaphorical. People are in continuous two-way interaction with those around them, with the brain continuously changing in response (Bennet et al., 2015b). And today, we recognize cooperation and collaboration as virtues of the physical plane.

<<<<<<<◇>>>>>>>

INSIGHT: **The human mind/brain is designed to think socially, forming and reforming social groups and relationships every day of our lives.**

<<<<<<<◇>>>>>>>

While there are many ways to learn—self-reflection, observing others, our own instincts, etc.—in our networked world the art of communication and social networking has become an essential part of our organizations and communities. Global connectivity has assured the availability of massive amounts of information and a wide diversity of thought and opinion on every subject imaginable, and the ability to share this information with others. This shift has prompted an exponential growth in learning from each other, with a plethora of new ideas emerging from the bisociation of ideas and the creative imaginings of people. Little wonder that the field of Knowledge Management—with a focus on connectivity, cooperation, collaboration, creativity and knowledge sharing—has continued to expand its influence since before the turn of the century. As an early graphic used in the U.S. Department of the Navy—a starter for Conversations that Matter—reads: *As one grows, all grow ... as all grow, the one grows ...*

Individuation

This is a long chapter, yet a necessary focus of the journey of self is individuating, which has been referenced a number of times but not explained. In his *Two Essays on Analytical Psychology*, Jung (1972) says you will not be able to face social

Figure 4-2. *The interrelated growth of the one and the whole.*

problems until you have gone through the process of individuation, which is Jung's equivalent to understanding the self. This sets the stage for us to face that which is often conceived as a contradiction, or *what could be called a paradox*: individuation and group consciousness, or separateness and Oneness. As we have learned from failed world experiences with socialism and communism, and through the expansion of globalism, individuation in terms of learning, passion and freedom of thought bring the energy and diversity into cooperation and collaboration that is necessary for innovation and a sustainable global economy.

<<<<<<<>>>>>>>

INSIGHT: **Individuation in terms of learning, passion and freedom of thought bring the energy and diversity into cooperation and collaboration that is necessary for innovation and a sustainable global economy.**

<<<<<<<>>>>>>>

A parallel example is our growing understanding of the importance of interdependence, which has a higher value than independence or dependence. Consider a marriage, where two people with different characteristics choose to intertwine their lives and potentially bring new lives into existence. If an individual in relationship is fully independent, then there is no relationship, limited mutual growth and no synergy created. If an individual in the relationship is fully dependent, then it falls to a single individual to make choices and provide in a changing, uncertain and complex environment. This limits the choices, setting forces in play and curtailing growth for both parties, with the result of reducing consciousness. In interdependence, there is a common ground supported by responsibility and commitment, some independence and some dependence balanced out, a give and take, with each having a voice and each listening, resulting in a growing synergy far beyond the win/win relationship that it already is. In an interdependent relationship, there is a mutual reliance on each, a balance not denoting sameness but taking full advantage of the strengths of the diversity of each individual.

Jung's process of individuation involves "letting go of all the false images of ourselves that we have allowed to be built up by our environment and by the projected visions of parents, teachers, friends, and lovers" (Crowley, 1999, p. 136). In other words, *there is an authenticity and integrity of self that comes with individuation.*

Individual differences, or individuation, has been a primary focus in personality psychology research (McCrae & John, 1992). Whether crediting this individuation to evolution by selection, divine creation, or seeding by extraterrestrial organisms, or perhaps all three, what is clear is that, while acknowledging that no two people are or ever have been identical *and* the possibility of randomness, the foundation of these differences is largely a specification of human nature developed through adaptation (Buss, 1999). It is the personality that lays the groundwork for the individuation of self, with development of personality and self heavily affected by social contexts, role experiences and changing historical and cultural norms (Caspi & Roberts, 1999). In turn, *all that is observed in the external world is affected by the observer.* (See the discussion above on subject/object relationship.)

<<<<<<<◇>>>>>>>

INSIGHT: **There is an authenticity and integrity of self that comes with individuation.**

<<<<<<<◇>>>>>>>

There is no conflict between individuation, built through expansion of the individual consciousness, and development of, participation in, and contribution to the collective consciousness. Quite the contrary. For those evolved integrators who connect to the collective consciousness, the contribution of individual consciousness—when acting with humility, that is, as a learner and recognizing that all knowledge is partial and imperfect—releases ownership of thought, which opens one fully to the contribution of, and connections to, others' thoughts. The individuated self doesn't go away or diminish. While still acting as an individual, we are dynamically connected to the collective, providing growth and expansion, enabling increased opportunity for the creative bisociation of ideas, and offering the discovery of higher truths. Thus, in Figure 4-3, individuation and connectedness are shown as part of the same continuum. See the discussion of Oneness in Chapter 36/Part V.

INDIVIDUATION	CONNECTEDNESS
SELF	ONENESS
•Creativity	•Inclusiveness
•Expansion	•Understanding
•Contribution	•Loving
	•Sharing
	•Giving

Figure 4-3. *Individuation and Connectedness are part of the same continuum.*

From the perspective of art rather than science, we offer the *Myst* phenomenon that began at Mountain Quest Institute in the Fall of 2010 and continues today, as a demonstration of the energetic possibilities offered through the simultaneity of individuation and Oneness. The *Myst*—which is formed by electromagnetic energies called orbs and appears as a collective in the instant in a dark night sky—represents a deeper look into the natural energies surrounding us each and every day, energies that are often invisible and rarely capture our awareness and attention. In the prose and picture analogy of *An Infinite Story*, individuated orbs (electromagnetic energy dots which we perceive as points of consciousness) attract the moisture in the air to come together (amplitude), forming a tapestry of *Myst* that represents a larger concept (direction), perhaps conveying a message, then falling back to their individuated state. This analogy serves as an example of the potential offered through cooperation and collaboration. See Appendix C.

Individual uniqueness and differentiation are related to the state of "self-actualization" credited to the psychologist Abraham Maslow (1968), although the term was originally introduced by Goldstein (1939). Self-actualization is one of the six levels of human needs, which include basic physiological needs, safety needs, belongingness needs, esteem needs, self-actualization needs (Maslow, 1971) and transcendence (Roberts, 1978). Maslow emphasized that self-actualizing people are involved in a larger cause beyond themselves, working with joy at something they love, all the while searching for what Maslow calls the being values, *B-Values* for short. As he describes, B-Values are,

> ... the ultimate values which are intrinsic, which cannot be reduced to anything more ultimate ... including the truth and beauty and goodness of the ancients and perfection, simplicity, comprehensiveness, and several more ... (Maslow, 1971, p. 42)

We will return to the virtues of truth, beauty and goodness throughout this book. Self-actualizing people are not content with normalcy, rather striving toward becoming exceptional. They have a naive creativity, looking at the world with fresh perceptions (Maslow, 1968).

Maslow (1971) describes eight ways for individuals to engage self-actualizing: (1) experiencing life fully and selflessly; (2) making growth choices consistently; (3) listening to the voice within; (4) being honest and taking responsibility; (5) courageously daring to be different; (6) using one's intelligence; (7) recognizing peak experiences; and (8) opening oneself up to oneself. This is a good set. Note that self-actualizing is a dynamic experience, much like learning and very much related to learning, occurring when individuals are performing at their optimal level and consistent with the understanding that we are verbs, not nouns.

From a leadership viewpoint, Seashore et al. (2004) propose a framework that relates key factors that are important in maintaining and increasing our individual capacity as change agents, leaders, task facilitators, etc. The model (Figure 4-4) considers the world as we perceive it and act on it, and the simultaneous or consequent, intentional or unintentional, change that occurs within ourselves. (An in-depth treatment of this model is included in Bennet et al., 2015b.) In the Seashore model, the self is an integration of, at the unconscious level, the defensive self, the shadow self, the lost self, and the robotic self; and, at the conscious level, the performing self, the creative self, the beautiful self and the evolving self. Intentions, styles, patterns, habits, defenses and needs all contribute to the differentiation or individuation of self.

In this model, the individual's competence and effectiveness are functions of many elements, including self-efficacy, agency, skills and the use of support systems to optimize those. Self-efficacy refers to an individual's belief that they can achieve desired ends. Agency refers to the ability and capacity to act on those beliefs (knowledge). Support systems are the pool of resources (individuals, groups, organizations) that an individual can draw on selectively "to help one be at their best in moving in directions of their choice and to grow strong in the process" (Seashore et al., 2004, p. 58). Examples of potential barriers to conscious awareness are transference, anxiety, and external threats. Transference refers to the ability to

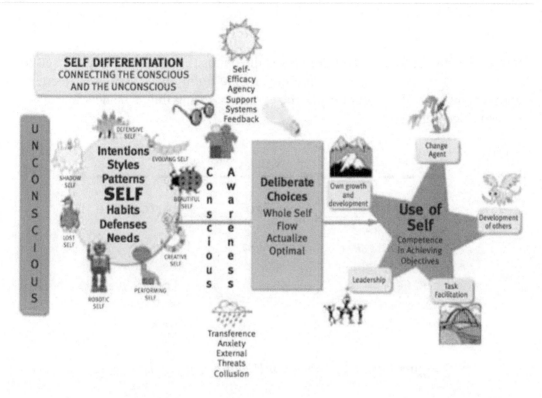

Figure 4-4. *The Seashore Self-as-an-Agent of Change model* (used with permission).

perceive situations through the projection of oneself onto others, a process that can both potentially aid or interfere with understanding. Note that conscious awareness lays the groundwork for choice. Deliberate choices and the use of self as a change agent—for leadership and development of others, and for task facilitation and personal development—requires an understanding of the connections and relationships among others and the self. The deepening of connections is the movement from sympathy to empathy to compassion that is part of the Phase changes in the Intelligent Social Change Journey. (See Chapter 35/Part V on Conscious Compassion.)

The Power of Humility

Simple, yet profound, the conscious choice of humility is a powerful tool for change. The greatest barriers to learning and change are egotism and arrogance, which are fundamental difficulties in a rapidly-developing, mentally-focused business environment. Egotism says, "I am right." When egotism advances to arrogance, it says, "I am right. You are wrong. And I don't care what you think or say."

As can be seen, egotism shuts the door to learning, and arrogance ceases to listen to or consider others at all, which is necessary for growth and expansion of an individual and an organization. Since others are non-existent, an arrogant individual does not care what harm is inflicted on others. Both egotism and arrogance increase the forces being produced. Humility takes the opposite stance, opening the self to others' thoughts and ideas, and providing an opportunity for listening, reflecting, learning and expanding. Humility is the choice of letting things be new in each moment. See Figure 4-5.

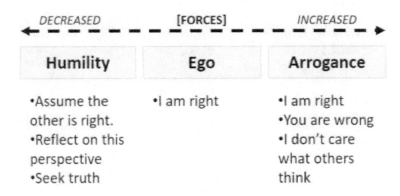

Figure 4-5. *Relationship of Humility, Ego and Arrogance.*

When you remedy egotism, the self grows. Since the self is now listening to and considering others' ideas, there is larger opportunity for the bisociation of ideas, and creativity expands. Even a small amount of change can have a large impact on an individual or humanity at large! For example, consider the creation of floss for cleaning teeth.

****

TOOL 4-2: HUMILITY

This tool was developed from the teachings of Niles MacFlouer (2004-2016).

STEP (1): To develop humility, first *open your mind* to accept that, by nature, at this point of development human beings have egos and desires, both of which can have strong emotional tags connected to them. It can be quite difficult for an individual to recognize egotism and arrogance in themselves. Remember, the personality, not the self, is often in control, so the individual may or may not be aware of their projection or position. This is potentially true of the individual with whom you are interacting, as well as yourself.

STEP (2): Second, *assume the other is right*. Set aside personal opinions and beliefs for the moment, accept what is being said, this idea or concept, and reflect on this new perspective in the search for truth. While this may prove quite difficult for an individual who is highly dependent on ego and arrogance to survive in what can be a challenging world, almost every individual has someone or something they love more than themselves. Try imagining that this new idea is coming from that someone or emerging from that something that you love. This simple trick will help increase your ability to engage humility.

STEP (3): Adopting this new idea or concept, *try to prove it is right*, pulling up as many examples as you can and testing the logic of it. If all the examples you can pull up fit this new perspective, then you have discovered some level of truth. If the examples contradict the concept, then bring in your ideas and test the logic of those. Again, if the examples do not all fit, continue your search for a bigger concept that conveys a higher level of truth. The critical element in this learning approach is giving up your way of thinking so that you can understand thoughts different than your own. You can compare the various concepts, asking which is more complete.

One issue that may emerge is the inclination for people to think how they feel first, then think about the logical part to determine truth. The "feeling" has already colored their higher conceptual thinking, which may result in it being untrue. It is necessary for us to develop a new sense of self that does not require us to be right in order to feel good about our thinking.

STEP (4) Once we come to a conclusion, we need to take action. It is time to affirm our incorrectness to those with whom we have potentially lacked humility, and to show gratitude for them sharing their thoughts with us. Note that the expression of appreciation and gratitude reduces forces. It is not enough to say that you were wrong, nor is that an important issue. What *is* important is to acknowledge that someone else is right, and that you are appreciative of learning from them.

STEP (5) Finally, *ensure that your motive for adopting humility is your search for truth*. Motive eventually comes out, and the wrong motive will defeat the purpose in hand. In this search for truth, you are using mental discipline to develop greater wisdom. It is difficult to overcome the urge to "look good" and to be righter than others. When we are "full" there is no room for new thought. When choosing humility as part of our learning journey, we discover that it is not about being right, rather it is about the continuous search for a higher truth.

****

Final Thoughts

We are now in a position to conceptually integrate a few thoughts. Figure 4-6 shows the balancing of passion and desire (driven by personality and subconscious) and will of self, all tittering on, emerging from, the preferred world view of self.

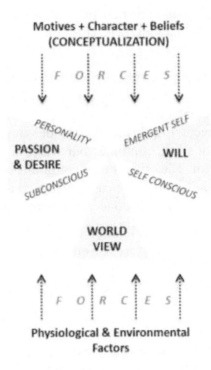

Figure 4-6. *Integrating foundational pieces.*

As we enter a world full of forces, the personality (upper left), operating in the subconscious and focused on survival, pleasure and avoidance of pain, serves as a protector to the growth of self (upper right). As we experience life, we become increasingly conscious of our self and begin to develop preferences and make choices, simultaneously developing an internal model of how the world around us works (world view) of which we may or may not be aware. Nonetheless, this personal world view affects our thoughts, feelings and actions. In the next chapter, we deep dive into the concept of consciousness.

Questions for Reflection:

Am I able to engage humility when listening to other's ideas?

How well connected am I to myself and to others? And what synergies does this create for intended and actual Oneness?

Chapter 5
The Window of Consciousness

SUBTOPICS: PROPERTIES OF CONSCIOUSNESS ... THE THRESHOLD OF CONSCIOUSNESS ... LEVELS OF CONSCIOUSNESS ... MEANING AND PURPOSE ... CONSCIOUSNESS AS A QUANTUM FIELD ... FLOW AS THE OPTIMAL EXPERIENCE ... CONSCIOUSLY ACCESSING THE UNCONSCIOUS .. FINAL THOUGHTS

TABLE: 5-1. RELATIONSHIP OF PHASES OF THE INTELLIGENT SOCIAL CHANGE JOURNEY WITH LEVELS OF CONSCIOUSNESS

FIGURES: 5-1. RELATIONSHIP OF PHASES OF THE INTELLIGENT SOCIAL CHANGE JOURNEY WITH LEVELS OF CONSCIOUSNESS.

TOOLS: 5-1. ENGAGING TACIT KNOWLEDGE (SEE APPENDIX D.)

We all know what consciousness is, but find it very difficult to talk about in an objective way, or even to find the words to describe it. We give up consciousness every time we go to sleep. Yet in the morning, we pick it up as if nothing happened in between. We see consciousness as a march of sequential events, inter-playing on multiple levels, that arise either from the environment getting our attention, or from our own internal ruminations. "It involves wakefulness, receiving and responding to sensory inputs, imagination, inner experience, and volition." (Carroll, 2016, p. 319) You *exist* and you are *aware* that you exist.

The difficulty of defining consciousness, which has historically caused great confusion among thinkers trying to sort out the phenomenon, still remains today, although recent work over the past several decades has narrowed the limits of reasonable interpretation. As Chalmers (1999, p. 287) describes,

> Conscious experience is at once the most familiar thing in the world and the most mysterious. There is nothing we know about more directly than consciousness, but it is extraordinarily hard to reconcile it with everything else we know.

A private, selective and continuously changing process, consciousness includes a sequential set of ideas, thoughts, images, feelings and perceptions. In a way, consciousness is sense-making, that is, integrating incoming information from the senses as we move through experiences and interactions in order to build awareness and understanding. It is difficult to understand something that we have not directly sensed.

Perhaps the most lucid description of consciousness comes from John Searle in a paper entitled "Consciousness, Free Action and the Brain." He says,

> Consciousness is a real biological phenomenon. It consists of inner, qualitative, subjective, unified states of sentience, awareness, thoughts and feelings. These states begin when we awake in the morning from a dreamless sleep, and they continue throughout the day until we become unconscious again. Dreams are a form of consciousness on this account, though they are in many respects different from normal waking consciousness. Some of the defining features of consciousness, on this conception, are that it is qualitative, subjective and unified. (Searle, 2000, p. 4)

Qualitative, subjective and unified.

Noting that consciousness and the self are terms that are often used interchangeably, in Chapter 4 we introduced self as the totality of the conscious and unconscious, the brain and the body. In *The Courage to Create*, Rollo May (1975) sees consciousness as the awareness emerging out of what he describes as the dialectical tensions between possibilities and limitations. Consciousness requires awareness, knowing that we exist and others exist, which is the result of information coming in through our senses, but is *more* than awareness. It is when this information is engaged in thought that consciousness occurs. Consciousness *requires* thought, the ability to link together internal and external Knowledge (Informing) such that it leads to a better understanding of our self and our environment, and the *relationships* among our self and others. In short, it is the sum total of who we are, what we believe, what we say, how we act and the things we do (Dunning, 2014). As a working definition, we consider consciousness as a state of awareness and an understanding of the connections and relationships among that of which we are aware and our self (Bennet, 2001).

Although we often refer to states of mind, in fact, the neurons in the brain are always firing at different rates and changing their activity and interconnection strengths. This can easily be seen from measurements such as electroencephalography (EEG), magneto-encephalography (MEG), Positron emission tomography (PET), and functional magnetic resonance imaging (fMRI). From a Quantum Field perspective— with the term field representing patterns of relationships—consciousness is the *directionality* of thought itself, a way to connect one thought to another, allowing us to connect choices and affect future choices. William James (1890/1980) was amazed at the continuity of human consciousness. Similarly, Dewey noted that, "the principle of continuity of experience means that every experience both takes up something from those which have gone before and modifies in some way the quality of those which come after" (Dewey, 1938/1979, pp. 35-44 in Kolb, 1984, p. 27). This concept of directionality of thought is consistent with the emerging understanding of the Quantum field and the increased probability for change as more and more thought is heading the same direction.

Properties of Consciousness

Edelman and Tononi (2000) postulate that consciousness is a subset of coherently connected neuron patterns. Thus, similar to William James and Dewey, they believe that consciousness must be a process. They forward two other empirical properties of consciousness: **unity** and **informativeness.** To these we add **optimum complexity**. Let's explore these properties.

Unity means that each conscious state is experienced as a whole. The mind is continually integrating the incoming signals from the environment as well as connecting many different processing areas within the brain and combining them into a coherent flow of conscious thinking or feeling. When we see a snapshot of the visible world, it appears as a coherent, unified whole. This is the same concept of the "unified" element of consciousness voiced by Searle in our introduction. The mind/brain insists on this result. For example, the need for conscious states to be coherent is seen in a number of visual pictures where two interpretations are possible, yet it is impossible for anyone to see them both at the same time. Even though alternating perceptions are easy, the incongruent superposition of two objects or pictures cannot happen. Without this property survival would not be possible because the mind's perception of external reality would be confusing and incomprehensible. As Edelman and Tononi (2000, p. 18) note, "Many neuropsychological disorders demonstrate that consciousness can bend or shrink and, at times, even split, but it does not tolerate breaks of coherence." This unity and coherence requirement also explains the so-called capacity limitations of the human brain. Examples include Miller's rule of seven to nine numbers and the fact that we generally cannot keep in mind more than four to seven objects at one time. Albert Einstein once stated, "The hardest thing to understand is why we can understand anything at all" (Kaku, 1997, p. 338). Separate from the Universe's objective order, man's brain also assists in its comprehensibility.

Optimum complexity allows the processing of divergent signals from within the individual and from the external environment. A life of harmony is one that is ordered, and when this occurs consciousness becomes more complex. This complexity involves far more than cognitive functions. As Csikszentmihalyi (1993, p. 207) describes:

Complexity of consciousness is not a function of only intelligence or knowledge, and is not just a cognitive trait—it includes a person's feelings and actions as well. It involves becoming aware of and in control of one's unique potentials, and being able to create harmony between goals and desires, sensations and experience, both for oneself and for others.

Informativeness covers several concepts. The mind is continually filtering and selecting from an extremely wide range of external signals entering through the body's sensory systems. This ability to discriminate among billions of continuously incoming patterns or states of affairs in the environment is one of the mind's dominant characteristics and is known as informativeness. As Edelman and Tononi (2000, p. 18) describe: "Within a fraction of a second each conscious state is selected from a repertoire of billions and billions of possible conscious states, each with different consequences." The richness of the mind is not in how many states it can store or work with, but in its ability to discriminate among a large number of possible states, created in part by external impinging sensory information and in part from the multitude of possible internal states. The ability to tell the difference among these states is the reduction of uncertainty. This creates information. Because artificial intelligence has been unable to replicate this discriminatory capability of the mind, computers cannot understand context nor derive meaning. What they can do (that brains cannot) is process large chunks of data and information. (Edelman & Tononi, 2000, p. 126)

Thus, consciousness is very much related to the action journey of life, creating order and continuity as we move through the phases of the Intelligent Social Change Journey toward intelligent activity in a search for higher truth. Recall from Chapter 2 that intelligence is the ability to know about, explain, define and reason, and intelligent activity represents *a state of interaction where intent, purpose, direction, values and expected outcomes are clearly understood and communicated among all parties, reflecting wisdom and achieving a higher truth.* As we move toward this goal, consciousness expands.

<<<<<<◇>>>>>>

INSIGHT: **Ultimately, consciousness is that which provides us our life experience, times of joy and times of despair.**

<<<<<<◇>>>>>>

In relationship to information and knowledge, consciousness is the ability to understand information such that it can be turned into knowledge to act upon and interact with the world around us. This includes the ability to connect a diversity of knowledges, enabling us to expand our self beyond what it is, that is, to apply knowledge in greater and greater ways. Thus, consciousness is extremely relevant to the amount of information coming through the senses and how it is organized and categorized, which, as we learned in Chapter 4, is a primary focus of the personality. We agree with MacFlouer (1999) that consciousness is a measure of self. It is, ultimately, that which provides us our life experience, times of joy and times of despair. For example, conscious reflection helps us determine what is good for us and what is not good for us; helping us determine the actions that will head us toward our purpose in life. As Csikszenmihalyi (1993, p. 29) says, "If we don't gain control over the contents of consciousness we can't live a fulfilling life, let alone contribute to a positive outcome of history." We focus specifically on conscious compassion—a critical growth element of the Intelligent Social Change Journey as we move toward Phase 1II—in Chapter 35/Part V.

The Threshold of Consciousness

The mind is the seat of consciousness, enabling awareness of our self as a knower, as an observer and learner, and as one who takes action. But knowing, observing, learning and taking action are not static. The perception of self is a *learned pattern*, beginning early in the journey of individuation and shored up by the subject and object relationship. **Remember, we are a verb, not a noun**, continuously associating incoming information with stored patterns, creating and recreating a continuous series of *Nows* that become our source of thoughts and actions. Since all consciousness is a process of change, the permanency of form, or reality, is an illusion. Thus, consciousness is a process in which thoughts, images and feelings are constantly evolving, and reality is created and recreated as the mind is focused and refocused (see Chapter 23/Part IV).

At any given moment, each individual and each organization functions from a very definable band or region of thinking, talking and acting, an attention space with upper and lower thresholds. Even if reality is hitting us in the face, we still must translate that through our personal lens. Within these thresholds, knowledge and events make sense. If a proposed new idea or strategy or initiative is above the upper threshold, it cannot be comprehended and has no perceived value. If a proposed new idea or strategy or initiative is below the lower threshold, it is so well-understood, so common, that it may be dismissed as unimportant. See Figure 5-1. Pushing the edges of this threshold produces discomfort, and we seek to bring the environment and our values and beliefs back into balance. As we are able to integrate new experiences and knowledge into this space, understanding increases and, by definition, the thresholds adjust to accommodate this learning.

Within each individual's (or organization's or country's) thresholds are deep pockets of focus, that is, areas that are of particular interest (or passion) to the individual (or organization, or country). For example, a concert pianist may have a deep focus on a specific kind of music with a developed set of preferences and beliefs around the value of other music. A farm growing organic crops will have a bounded focus on specific methodologies, with a strong prejudice against insecticides, etc. An IT organization may have deep knowledge that is bounded by a focus on non-Apple products (or vice versa), supporting their belief in the value of one over the other. A state or country with high elevation would have a focus on winter sports and would, most likely, value winter sports over other sports in terms of fitness, etc. Conversely, the focus and beliefs of those living on a Caribbean island would be quite different.

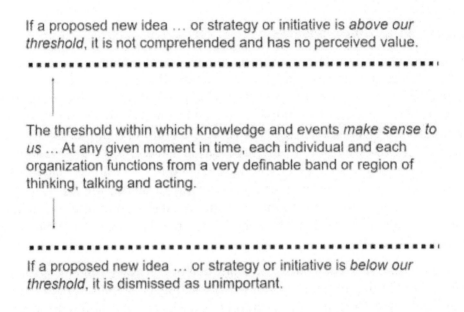

If a proposed new idea ... or strategy or initiative is *above our threshold*, it is not comprehended and has no perceived value.

The threshold within which knowledge and events *make sense to us* ... At any given moment in time, each individual and each organization functions from a very definable band or region of thinking, talking and acting.

If a proposed new idea ... or strategy or initiative is *below our threshold*, it is dismissed as unimportant.

Figure 5-1. *The threshold of focus and consciousness.*

With the advent of the Internet came global connectivity such that people had greater access to an exponentially expanding amount of information. Thought that has been vibrating around the world collides with the expanding minds of thought leaders at all levels of the organization and society. This incoming thought (information) is now associated with all that is already known and brought into the situation and context of the moment, that is, creating a cohesive world view from the learner's point of view. Out of this melee patterns appear and new thought emerges, and both individual and organizational thresholds for learning move higher and higher, with expanding knowledge bringing them ever closer to intelligent activity.

Levels of Consciousness

Levels of consciousness span the spectrum from subconscious to self-conscious to superconscious (Murphy, 1992; Wade, 1996; Wilber et al., 1986; Wilber 2000). This *Great Chain of Being* is said to range from matter to body to mind to soul to spirit (Smith, 1986). Another viewpoint sees the spectrum of consciousness as ranging from prepersonal to personal to transpersonal (Murphy, 1992; Walsh, 1999). Wilber (2000) presents over 100 models of the levels of consciousness, but credits each as a different human construct to help understand consciousness. He points out that each individual possesses different capacities, intelligences and functions, thus moving through the various developmental levels at a different rate (Wilber, 2001).

Hawkins (2002) uses the concept of *levels of consciousness* to represent calibrated levels correlated with a specific process of consciousness—emotions, perceptions, attitudes, worldviews and spiritual beliefs. As the culmination of research over a 20-year period involving thousands of people of all ages and personality types, Hawkins (2002, p. 67) *mapped the energy field of consciousness*, with the levels ranging from 0 to 1,000. The progression is as follows: 20 (Shame); 30 (Guilt); 50 (Apathy); 75 (Grief); 100 (Fear); 125 (Desire); 150 (Anger); 175 (Pride); 200 (Courage); 250 (Neutrality); 310 (Willingness); 350 (Acceptance); 400 (Reason); 500 (Love); 540 (Joy); 600 (Peace); 700-1,000 (Enlightenment). The 200 level, that associated with integrity and courage, serves as a critical response point, "the balance point between weak and strong attractors, between negative and positive influence" (Hawkins, 2002, p. 70). This generally occurs during Phase 1 of the Intelligent Social Change Journey. Attitudes, thoughts, feelings and associations with levels below 200 make people weaker and are associated with force; those above make people stronger and are associated with power. As people move from the lower negative emotions into Courage, increasingly the well-being of others becomes more important. By the 500 level,

> The happiness of others emerges as the essential motivating force. The high 500s are characterized by interest in spiritual awareness for both oneself and others, and by the 600, the good of mankind and the search for enlightenment are the primary goals. From 700 to 1,000, life is dedicated to the salvation of all of humanity. (Hawkins, 2002, p. 70)

According to Hawkins, there are several important points to note regarding this progression. First, it is a logarithmic progress, that is, the level 200 is not a doubling of 100, but rather 10^{200}, representing an enormous increase in power as you move up the scale. Second, these are not considered pure states, that is, an individual may operate at a specific level of consciousness in one area of life, and a different level of consciousness in another area of life. This is still a development model, with the sum total of these mixed levels of consciousness representing an individual's overall level of consciousness.

Table 5-1 shows the relationship of the levels of consciousness to the Phases of the Intelligent Social Change Journey. Note that full range of negative emotions can occur during Phase 1, and, since this is a development model and because an individual operates at different levels of consciousness in different focus areas, indeed can continue into Phase 2. However, as referenced in the previous paragraph, the sum total would be higher as individuals move into Phase 2.

Phase of the Intelligent Social Change Journey	Levels of Consciousness (Hawkins, 2002)
PHASE 1: *Cause and Effect* (Requires Sympathy) •Linear, and Sequential •Repeatable •Engaging past learning •Starting from current state •Cause and effect relationships	20-150: Moves through Shame, Guilt, Apathy, Grief, Fear, Desire and Anger
	175: Pride
	200: Courage
	[Moving out of negativity]
PHASE 2: *Co-Evolving* (Requires Empathy) •Recognition of patterns •Social interaction •Co-evolving with environment through continuous learning, quick response, robustness, flexibility, adaptability, alignment.	250: Neutrality
	310: Willingness
	350: Acceptance
	400: Reason
	500: Love [Interest in spiritual awareness]
PHASE 3: *Creative Leap* (Requires Compassion) •Creative imagination •Recognition of global Oneness •Mental in service to the intuitive •Balancing senses •Bringing together past, present and future •Knowing; Beauty; Wisdom.	540: Joy
	600: Peace [Good of mankind becomes primary goal]
	700-1,000: Enlightenment

On the Cusp (bracketing 175: Pride, 200: Courage, [Moving out of negativity], 250: Neutrality, 310: Willingness)

Table 5-1. *Relationship of Phases of the ISCJ with Levels of Consciousness.*

Hawkins' model can also be used to measure the energy of human thought. For example, Hawkins contends that only 15 percent of the populations of the world achieve the consciousness level of 200 (the critical level to move out of negativity). However, because power advances logarithmically, a single individual at the highest consciousness level (1,000, an Avatar) can "counterbalance the negativity of all mankind" (Hawkins, 2002, p. 282). As Hawkins explains,

> Were it not for these counterbalances, mankind would self-destruct out of the sheer mass of its unopposed negativity. The difference in power between a loving thought ($10^{-35 \text{ million}}$ microwatts) and a fearful thought ($10^{-750 \text{ million}}$ microwatts) is so enormous as to be beyond the capacity of the human imagination to easily comprehend. ... even a few loving thoughts during the course of the day more than counterbalance all of our negative thoughts. (Hawkins, 2002, p. 283)

Note that Hawkins made these comments in 2002. A great deal of global activity, and there learning, or opportunity for learning, has occurred since that date. Since more people have greater access to more information, it has become more difficult to manipulate and control others through the promulgation of negative emotions, primarily fear. People are becoming smarter, and recognizing their ability to co-create their reality as they move into Phase 2 of the Intelligent Social Change Journey. While this is certainly not the case for everyone—and indeed the journey is a very individual one offering the opportunity for learning and expanding skill sets during each Phase—we would contend that percentage of the world population to achieve the consciousness level of 200 is much higher today. We challenge you, from your unique point of view, to consider just what that level might be in today's world. The levels of consciousness were introduced in Chapter 5.

Meaning and Purpose

When contemplating values, it is important to distinguish between that which *is* value and that which *has* value (situational). As the appreciative consciousness of values, meaning is something which experience adds to value. Thus, values are experiential while, through mental association, realities are meaningful when the relationships of those realities are recognized and appreciated by the mind. While values are real, they always depend on the fact of relationships, and these relationships are not arbitrary. As LeShan (1976, p. 90) explains:

> Nothing is arbitrary; nothing occurs by chance. Everything has meaning and is charged with implications and power. Things, however, may look arbitrary because it can be hard to trace the connections between the various parts of a unity as these connections, from the sensory viewpoint, range over objective and subjective, past and future, things and symbols, until they come to that one arbitrary act of will underlying the whole thing that neither needs explaining nor is explainable.

Like knowledge, values are both actual and potential, what is and is to be. Actuals and potentials equal growth, the *experiential realization* of knowledge and values. (This is why knowledge is defined as the actual and potential capacity to take effective action.) As knowledge, the construction of meaning is relative, highly individualized and subjective, using our creative juices to move us toward the reality we desire (see Chapter 23/Part IV). It is also an intimidating responsibility (Carroll, 2016). As Carl Sagan says, "We are star stuff, which has taken its destiny into its own hands." (Sagan, 1973, p.189-190).

We are the determinants of meaning. As Walsch (2009, p. 79) describes,

> Events are events, and meanings are thoughts. *Nothing* has any meaning *save the meaning you give it*. And the meaning you give to things does not derive from any event, circumstance, condition, or situations exterior to yourself. The Giving of Meaning is entirely an internal process. *Entirely.*

Positive psychology couples meaning with positive emotions, engagement, relationships and accomplishment (PERMA) as the permanent building blocks for a life of profound fulfillment (Seligman, 2011). These are considered the pillars for individuals, organizations, communities and nations to get the most out of life. We would add "thoughts" to this equation, as a reminder that our internal environment creates our external environment.

<<<<<<<<>>>>>>>

INSIGHT: **Our internal environment creates our external environment.**

<<<<<<<<>>>>>>>

Similar to knowledge, meaning expands as we experience growth. *Urantia* (1954, p. 1097) points out that meaning can never be static. "Reality signifies change, growth. Change without growth, expansion of meaning and exaltation of value, is *valueless*." The greater the quality of change and adaptation, the more meaning an experience possesses. This is no clearer than in the co-evolving phase of the Intelligent Social Change Journey. Note that while man can affect his growth by his choices, he cannot *cause* growth. Whether physical, intellectual or spiritual, growth is unconscious.

However, there *is* a limit to the growth of self. For example, a world renown pianist will eventually reach a point where that individual has gone as far as she can go. Once this point is reached, playing the same piece over and over again does not add any additional value, and may even diminish value in terms of the frustration resulting from the replaying with no additional progress. The more you attempt to play, the less meaning there is in the playing. As Conner (1998, p. 25) describes,

One of the great myths about humans is that repetition results in expertise. Iteration may lead to heightened proficiency, but only if new learning is associated with each interaction. **Recurring episodes of change that lack the benefit of new learning produce little more than redundant experiences** [emphasis added]; no cumulative value is realized.

Now, add the factor of a new audience, someone the pianist can connect to and share with, someone new to this piece but clearly filled with joy and love in the listening. As the pianist connects with this person, moving beyond self, there is an expansion of the music far beyond the skill set producing the music, and a larger meaning flows with this expansion. This is consistent with the need to share energy in order to expand individual growth, and consciousness.

The amount of meaning in life is directly related to an individual's level of consciousness. Primary consciousness is the ability to construct a mental scene, but with limited semantic or symbolic capability and no true language. An incoming scene, say an image, is immediately (within fractions of a second) evaluated by the brain's value systems and, through the interaction of the memory system with its previous experiences and the incoming signal, *a meaning is associated with the perception*. This new perception may be put into memory, depending on its importance to the individual. Edelman calls this perception the remembered present because it is a combination of past memories, individual values and incoming signals (Edelman & Tononi, 2000, p. 78). We never just see some "thing". The mind automatically mixes the external scenes with our own history, feelings and goals (the associative patterning process introduced in Chapter 1) to give it context and meaning. In other words, meaning is created out of external events and signals complexed with internal resources.

> The ability of an animal to connect events and signals in the world, whether they are causally related or merely contemporaneous, and, then, through reentry with its value-category memory system, to construct a scene that is related to its own learned history is the basis for the emergence of primary consciousness. (Edelman & Tononi, 2000, p. 109).

Higher-order consciousness, as seen in humans, includes primary consciousness together with a sense of self and an ability to *build past and future scenarios*. In its highest form it includes a language capability. It emerges from the creation of new communication networks that connect and coordinate the multiple neuronal groups that gave rise to primary consciousness. With the emergence of language and social interaction comes the emergence of higher-order consciousness found in humans.

These communication circuits provide for functional integration between perception and memory, resulting in a stable sense of unity and personal identity (Edelman & Tononi, 2000, p. 110)

<<<<<<<◇>>>>>>>

INSIGHT: **The amount of meaning is directly related to an individual's level of consciousness.**

<<<<<<<◇>>>>>>>

In early development when the personality (subconscious) is in control and there is minimal awareness of self, the ability to create more consciousness is limited. Recall that in Hawkins' model detailed above, levels of consciousness falling below 200 are weak attractors and represent negative energy. They are focused inward, centered around self. For example, consider level 150 (Anger). We always say "I'm angry at …." Or "I'm angry because …" and give credit to an external source. However, the anger is within you; our emotions are *our* emotions. Two examples of this are provided in Chapter 19/Part III.

As you move up the levels of consciousness, the increased awareness that comes with expanded consciousness offers greater choice as life unfolds. We are no longer victims to our environment in terms of our emotional responses, but can use those very human emotions as the guidance system they were intended to be, thanking them, then engaging our mental faculties to consider our next actions and interactions. Feelings—the inward response to emotions—can also serve as indicators of your consciousness level. As MacFlouer (2004-16) says, if you are trying to gain consciousness, there are a lot of crutches that can help you figure out when you are less loving or less wise in your giving. Love is level 500 on Hawkins' model and wise giving is an attribute accompanying higher levels of consciousness (see Chapter 19/Part III and Chapter 22/Part IV, respectively). MacFlouer examples feelings of boredom and loneliness as indicating lack of consciousness. By being more inclusive, connecting more with others and becoming more giving, consciousness expands and meaning increases.

Carroll (2016) points out that ideas like meaning and purpose are not part of the core theory of Quantum fields, the physics of our everyday life. This is not surprising, since, as discussed above, meaning and purpose are not a science, but rather an emergent quality of self. As Carroll (2016, p. 389) describes:

The source of these values isn't the outside world; it's inside us. We're part of the world, but we've seen that the best way to talk about ourselves is as thinking, purposeful agents who can make choices. One of those choices, unavoidably, is what kind of life we want to live.

Consciousness as a Quantum Field

The Quantum field—which has many names such as Noosphere, Akashic field, the Zero Point or God field—refers to an unlimited field of possibilities. When things within this field are heading in the same direction, they group together and create a subfield; uniquely different from the infinite field, pursuing a probability, yet pulling along related elements outside that probability. So, it is with consciousness; and in this subfield, uniquely different, we become the co-creators of our self and our life. In short, consciousness as a Quantum field is a creative field that is self-defining, self-creating, self-conscious, self-controlled, self-sustaining and self-limiting. It can grow and change, connect itself with the larger field, and affect other fields. As with all Quantum fields, ultimately, it is controlled by thought (MacFlouer, 2004-16).

<<<<<<<◇>>>>>>>

INSIGHT: **Consciousness, as a Quantum field, is a creative field that is self-defining, self-creating, self-conscious, self-controlled, self-sustaining and self-limiting**.

<<<<<<<◇>>>>>>>

A fascinating characteristic of the Quantum field is its ability to suddenly change or jump. This Quantum leap is defined as an abrupt change, sudden increase, or dramatic advance (Merriam-Webster, 2016). This exciting concept intrigued television audiences in the U.S. through a TV series of that name showing from 1989 through 1993, even inspiring a cult of followers. As Donald P. Bellisario, the show's creator who got the idea from a physics book, says,

> I was reading a book called *Coming of Age in the Milky Way* and it took man from when he looked up at stars and all the way to Quantum physics, and it gave the history of everything. And the Quantum leap is a physical thing that happens that you can't explain. That was it. (Mental Floss, 2016)

While we still can't explain it, glimpses of the truth of this concept are emerging through various scientific disciplines. An example is punctuated equilibrium, a rapid change resulting in a new species occur in a species that has been stable for millions of years (Eldredge & Gould, 1972). From the Quantum perspective, this leap occurs when enough thought is consistent with consciousness (the direction of creation and choices in the field) that the smaller field connects with a larger field while maintaining the integrity within its own field, that is, the ability to be conscious of itself while connecting to the larger field consciousness (MacFlouer, 2004-16).

Flow as the Optimal Experience

Psychic negentropy—the state described by Csikszentmihalyi as the optimal experience, or flow state—occurs when "**all of the contents of consciousness are in harmony with each other**, and with the goals that define the person's self … the subjective conditions we call pleasure, happiness, satisfaction, enjoyment" (Csikszentmihaly & Csikszentmihalyi, 1988, p. 24). Having the contents of consciousness in harmony with the goals of self is consistent with the Quantum field perspective, a connectedness of choices moving energy in the same direction.

Individuals involved in the flow state feel a sense of exhilaration and joy. As these optimal experiences are repeated, they develop a sense of experiencing their real reason for being, coupled with a strong feeling of being in control. Csikszentmihalyi says that the flow experience is a central goal of the self. This is consistent with the primary goal of the personality to seek pleasure. Indeed, the tendency of humans to set goals is itself as embedded as genetics or culture.

<<<<<<<◇>>>>>>

INSIGHT: **The tendency of humans to set goals is as embedded in the human as genes and culture.**

<<<<<<<◇>>>>>>

An individual or team in a state of flow is so involved in the goal at hand that nothing else seems to matter. The activity in which they are engaged becomes so intense that the normal sense of time and space disappears, and all energy is invested in the task, what Csikszentmihalyi (1988) describes as a *merging of activity and awareness*. In a team setting, individuals lose the sense of identity or separateness during this experience, then afterwards emerge from the experience with a stronger sense of self. "In flow, the self is fully functioning, but not aware of itself doing it, so it can use all the attention for the task at hand" (Csikszentmihalyi & Czikszentmihalyi, 1988, p. 33). This facilitates accomplishment of the task at hand. For example, the writing and publishing process involved with this book was achieved through the authors connecting with this state of flow. We're not sure it would have become a reality in any other way!

In a later work, Csikszentmihalyi (1993) identified eight characteristics involved in the flow experience: (1) Goals are clear and there is immediate feedback; (2) the actions involved are relatively high and the capabilities of the actors are well matched for the challenge; (3) the merging of activity and awareness; (4) attention and concentration on the challenge at hand; (5) the feeling of being in control; (6) a sense of being a part of something larger accompanied by loss of self-consciousness; (7) an altered sense of time; and (8) the autotelic experience, that is, doing something that is worthwhile in its own right.

The flow state is, ultimately, part of the human experience, a very important part that facilitates growth and the expansion of consciousness. As Csikszentmihalyi (1993, p. 367) sums up, "It is through the flow experience that evolution tricks us to evolve further." He contends that after every flow experience we are a little different, better than we were before.

Consciously Accessing the Unconscious

The term unconscious refers to *not* conscious, or occurring in the absence of conscious awareness or thought, without conscious control; involuntary or unintended (*American Heritage Dictionary*, 2006, p. 1873). People do all sorts of things for reasons of which they are not consciously aware. As described by Uleman (2005, p. 3), the unconscious includes "internal qualities of mind that affect conscious thought and behavior, without being conscious themselves."

In our treatment, we consider the unconscious as an integrated unit comprised of unconscious functions that include the *subconscious* (where the personality resides) and the *superconscious*. The subconscious directly supports the embodied mind/brain and the superconscious focuses on tacit resources spiritual in nature involving larger moral aspects, the emotional part of human nature and the higher development of our mental faculties. It also connects to the larger energy field, what we have called the Noosphere in deference to Pierre Teilhard de Chardin, a French geologist/paleontologist. The Noosphere is defined as "a human sphere of reflection, of conscious invention, of conscious souls" (deChardin, 1966, p. 63).[5-1] In Figure 5-2 the superconscious is described with the terms spiritual learning, higher guidance, values and morality, and love. It is also characterized as "pre-personality" to emphasize that there are no personal translators such as beliefs and mental models attached to this form of knowing.

The flow of information from the superconscious is very much focused on the moment at hand. In contrast, the memories stored in the subconscious are part of the personality, and the self as it takes over, and dependent on the individual's perceptions and feelings at the time the memories were formed. *The human subconscious is in service to the conscious mind*. Knowing is the sense gained from experience that resides in the subconscious part of the mind *and* the energetic connection our mind enjoys with the superconscious. (An extensive treatment of Knowing developed for the U.S. Department of the Navy is Appendix E.)

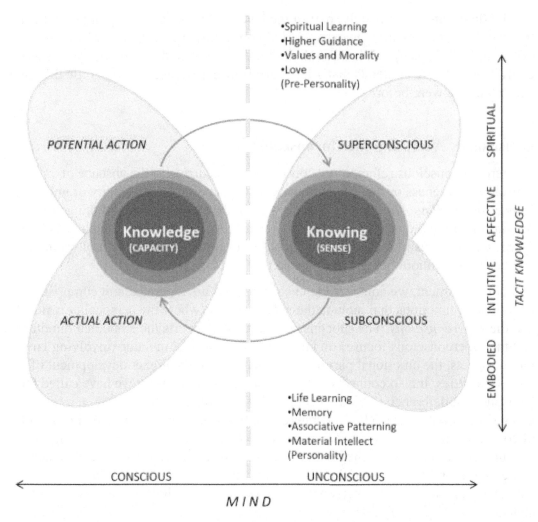

Figure 5-2. *The eternal loop of Knowledge and Knowing.*

<<<<<<<◇>>>>>>>

INSIGHT: **Knowing is the sense gained from experience that resides in the subconscious part of the mind *and* the energetic connection our mind enjoys with the superconscious.**

<<<<<<<◇>>>>>>>

The unconscious mind is multidimensional and has a vast store of tacit knowledge available to the self. It has only been in the past few decades that cognitive psychology and neuroscience have begun to seriously explore unconscious mental life. Polanyi felt that tacit knowledge consists of *a range* of conceptual and sensory information and images that could be used to make sense of a situation or event (Hodgkin, 1991; Smith, 2003). We agree. The unconscious mind is incredibly powerful, on the order of 700,000 times more processing speed than the conscious stream of thought. The challenge is to make better use of our tacit knowledge through creating greater connections with the unconscious, building and expanding the resources stored in the unconscious, deepening areas of resonance, and sharing tacit resources.

Tacit knowledge can be thought of in terms of embodied, intuitive, affective and spiritual. Embodied tacit knowledge, both kinesthetic and sensory, is represented in neuronal patterns stored within the body. Examples are riding a bicycle, dancing, or the smell of something burning. Intuitive tacit knowledge, the result of continuous learning through experience, is that "mysterious mechanism by which we arrive at the solution of a problem *without* reasoning toward it" (Damasio, 1994, p. 188). Affective tacit knowledge is connected to emotions and feelings, with emotions representing the external expression of some feelings. Spiritual tacit knowledge can be described in terms of knowledge based on matters of the soul, with the soul representing the animating principles of human life in terms of thought and action, specifically focused on its moral aspects, the emotional part of human nature, and higher development of the mental faculties (Bennet & Bennet, 2007c). See Appendix D for a deeper treatment of tacit knowledge.

****

TOOL 5-1: ENGAGING TACIT KNOWLEDGE

Four ways to engage tacit knowledge, that is, to have conscious access to or use of knowledge that is stored in your unconscious, are thorough surfacing, embedding, sharing and creating resonance.

External triggering and self-collaboration can SURFACE tacit knowledge. Triggering occurs by putting yourself in situations that will excite your thoughts. For example, engaging in conversations with experts in your field, or attending a seminar with thought leaders, or visiting a facility engaged in an area about which you have passion. To collaborate with yourself, take the time to quiet the monkey chatter in your mind and, in that quietness, open to a conversation with yourself. For example, sit with nature and listen to yourself. (See the tool *Quieting the Mind* in Chapter 29/Part IV.)

EMBEDDING can also involve attending special events around your passion and engaging in conversations and dialogue with experts. Even if thoughts are not immediately triggered, you are planting those ideas into your unconscious for future use. Embedding can also occur through mimicry, copying someone else's actions, and practice, repeating an action over and over again. The act of reflection aids in embedding, that is, contemplating an event or thinking about a concept you are trying to understand.

While SHARING tacit knowledge can happen at the conscious and unconscious levels, there can also be a conscious choice to share unconscious knowledge. For example, working closely with someone on an assembly line, or through mentoring or shadowing acquiring a deeper understanding of their work.

INDUCING RESONANCE can occur by planning a debate around two sides of an issue, thus causing an internal response from listeners who, before this debate, didn't have an opinion. (See Appendix D for more detail.)

****

Final Thoughts

Recent findings in cell biology beg us to ask the question: From where does consciousness originate? Lipton (2005) says that, similar to a computer, a cell has no behavior if it is disconnected from the environment. In his research, Lipton discovered that cells are not controlled by the nucleus as previously thought, but rather through receptor and effector proteins, a set of antennas, that appear on the outer membrane of the cell. Thus, Lipton sees consciousness as a simulation information field, still evolving, with identity and ownership, being picked up in the environment. What are the implications of these findings? As was advanced at the beginning of this chapter, considerable confusion remains among thinkers trying to sort out the phenomenon of consciousness. We will explore this concept further later in the book.

Questions for Reflection:

How consciously aware are you of the things that have meaning for you and why?

Reflecting on the levels of consciousness in relationship to a specific part of your life where do you think you are operating? How might you expand your consciousness in that area?

What are some things you do routinely during the day that if you thought about you may do differently? What are the implications of consciously making a change to your routine?

Chapter 6
The Individual Change Model

SUBTOPICS: The Human as a Complex Adaptive System ... The Environment and the Knowledge Worker ... The Model ... Applying the Model ... Final Thoughts

TABLES: 6-1. Workplace progression expanding through IQ, EQ and SQ ... 6-2. Frame of reference for change program activities to assess whether personal action learning will take place at every level of the model.

FIGURES: 6-1. Mobilizing personal action ... 6-2. The individual change model from the individual learning perspective.

Not too many years ago in the world of business, assembly line workers were asked to just do certain tasks, repeatedly and well. They were paid for the physical actions of their bodies and hands, often without knowledge of what happened next or how the work they did related to the whole. This "management" knowledge was held closely by the supervisor or the manager or the owner, and served as a source of power.

Then, businesses began to realize that good ideas could emerge from people throughout the workplace, and as these ideas added to the bottom line, the power of mental thought in terms of new products and processes came to the fore. The focus of work began to shift from the product of the physical body to the product of the mental plane, with physical strength still retaining a place of honor. This mental focus flourished in the bedrock of bureaucracy, where knowledge continued to be held close since position and remuneration were highly dependent on that knowledge, i.e., knowledge as power. The self that was valued, then, was determined in a dualistic fashion, that is, the capabilities of this physical body versus the capabilities of others; the knowledge of this manager versus the illiteracy of others. Intelligence was determined by an IQ test, and competition moved to the front line, determining success in sports, education and business, and creating winners and losers.

It wasn't until the latter part of the 20th century that it was generally recognized that emotional intelligence had a great deal to do with success. As previously believed, emotions could *not* be left at the door when entering the workplace. Discernment and discretion (D^2)—decisions and judgment—engage emotions, whether occurring with conscious awareness or being processed in the unconscious. Thus, the emergence of emotional intelligence along with the physical and mental, but for goodness sakes leave your spirituality and religious beliefs at the door! They don't belong in the workplace! Only, as we moved toward the 21st century, we began to realize that basic spiritual and religious grounding play a very large role in values, beliefs, and ethics that are core to an employee's, and an organization's, success! Table 6-1 details this journey.

In addition to physical activity, recognition of power in, need for, and potential value to the organization of worker's:

Thinking Capabilities (Mental body)	Emotions and Feelings (Emotional body)	Values and Meaning (Spiritual body)
1970 Beginning of post-bureaucratic era. (More benign and malleable structure.)	**1980-2010→** Rise of Information and Knowledge Organization (Full employee involvement)	**1998→** Emotional Intelligence (Can effectively manage ourselves and relationships.)	**2012→** Spiritual Intelligence (Ability to behave with wisdom and compassion.)
Building on new theories such as Theories X, Y and Z, Charismatic and Transformational Leadership, General Systems Theory and Organizational Linking Pins, Tayloristic time and motion mgmt and participative mgmt bring in worker responsibility and empowerment. Language of innovation in and out of the spotlight.	Technological advancements and virtual connectivity on a global scale enabled increased communication, collaboration and networking, both virtual and real. Wide knowledge creation, sharing and application. Increased economic affluence of the worker in developed countries coupled with increased education level.	Focused on learning more about ourselves and others: self-awareness; self-management; social awareness and social skill. EI recognized as a basic requirement for effective use of the intellect. Recognition that emotions/feelings are a necessary part of judging and decision-making.	Spiritual is standing in relationship to another based on matters of the soul, the animating principle of human life in terms of thought and action focused on its moral aspects, the emotional part of human nature, and higher development of the mental faculties. Pertains to the intellect and the ability to think abstractly or profoundly and to the sensitivity of the mind beyond material things.

Table 6-1. *Workplace progression expanding through IQ, EQ and SQ.*

<<<<<<<<>>>>>>>

INSIGHT: **Since 1970, there has been progression in the workplace toward valuing the full capacity and capability of what it is to be human.**

<<<<<<<<>>>>>>>

We had finally recognized that people are complex adaptive systems, and that the entangled physical, mental, emotional and spiritual systems *cannot be separated from each other.* Reality System Theory says just that, taking a holistic approach to management and leadership in organizations, comingling the dynamically interacting influences of the intellectual, emotional and spiritual. Reality System Theory specifically focuses on how this comingling *energizes* organizational culture, thereby improving individual, team and organizational performance. As Stebbins (2010, p. 2) describes, "The human reality is a dynamic holistic system subject to the continuous ebb and flow of intellectual, emotional, and spiritual influences."

Reality System Theory looks through the lens of Quantum physics, building on Heisenberg's uncertainty principle (Marshall & Zohar, 1997; Prigogine, 1996) and the contextualism of the Quantum field (Zohar & Marshall, 1994). The now-classic uncertainty principle refers to the particle/wave fluctuation and contextualism refers to context sensitivity, that is, change as a function of surroundings. Of contextualism, Wilber (2000, p. 89) reminds us that, "Meaning is context-dependent, and contexts are boundless."

Humans are integral parts of a larger whole, part of a holistic human potentially capable of intelligent decisions and actions. As Zohar and Marshall (2012, Intro) quote, "Neither IQ nor EQ [nor SQ], separately or in combination, is enough to explain the full complexity of human intelligence nor the vast richness of the human soul and imagination." It is with this understanding that we explore the various elements of individual change, which directly correlate to group and organizational change, and must be considered in any change effort, whether choosing to change yourself or to influence others.

The Human as a Complex Adaptive System

Human beings and the organizations we create are complex adaptive systems. A **system** is a group of elements or objects, the relationships among them, their attributes, and some boundary that allows one to distinguish whether an element is inside or outside the system.

In 1984 the Santa Fe Institute was created to better understand complex systems (and complexity) and, specifically, complex adaptive systems (CAS). Taking a consilience approach, the Santa Fe Institute pulled together a consortium of leading researchers in such diverse fields as biology, physics, economics, and management. This group defined complexity as,

... the condition of the Universe which is integrated and yet too rich and varied for us to understand in simple, common mechanistic or linear ways. We can understand many parts of the Universe in these ways but the larger and more intricately related phenomena can only be understood by principles and patterns—not in detail. Complexity deals with emergence, innovation, learning and adaptation. (Santa Fe Institute in Battram, 1996, p. 12)

Building on this definition, we consider complexity as *the condition of a system, situation, or organization that is integrated with some degree of order, but has too many elements and relationships to understand in simple analytic or logical ways.* Complex adaptive systems, that is, partially ordered systems that unfold and evolve through time, contain many agents (people) that interact with each other. They are mostly self-organizing, learning, and adaptive (Bennet & Bennet, 2004).

Stacy (1996) considers complex adaptive systems as having a large number of people with multiple, non-linear relations that allow the system to learn and adapt. Morowitz and Singer (1995) see complex adaptive systems as involving numerous interesting agents, "where aggregate behaviors are to be understood. Such aggregate behavior is non-linear; hence it cannot simply be derived from summation of individual components behavior" (Morowitz & Singer, 1995, p. 2). As used in this book, *a complex adaptive system is a system composed of a large number of self-organizing components that seek to maximize their own goals, but operate according to rules and in the context of relationships with other components and with the deterministic and inherently unpredictable external world.*

As complex adaptive systems continuously interact with their environment and adapt, they operate at some level of perpetual disequilibrium, which contributes to their unpredictable behavior (Bennet & Bennet, 2004). Having nonlinear relationships, complex adaptive systems create global properties that are called emergent because they emerge from the multitude of elements and their relationships and actions. Axelrod and Cohen (1999) define emergence as a property of a system that its separate parts do not have. The example they point out has to do with consciousness, "No single neuron has consciousness, but the human brain does have consciousness as an emergent property" (Axelrod & Cohen, 1999, p.15). Emergent properties cannot typically be understood through analysis and logic because of the large number of elements and relationships. As Johnson points out, "It wouldn't truly be considered *emergent* until those local interactions resulted in some kind of discernible macro-behavior" (Johnson, 2001, p. 19). Examples are life, ecosystems, economies, organizations, and cultures (Axelrod & Cohen, 1999).

Other potential properties of a complex adaptive system include: nonlinearities, feedback loops, time delays, tipping points, power laws, correlations, unpredictability, and butterfly effects (Battram, 1996; Buchanan, 2004; Gell-Mann, 1994; Gladwell, 2000). Simultaneously, a system has multiple connections, relationships, and is often surprise prone. Variety is one measure of complexity, representing the number of possible states a complex system can have. Variety also represents the number of options or possible actions that a person or organization has when interacting with its environment. Ashby's law of requisite variety says that for a complex system to survive in a complex environment, it must have greater variety than its environment in areas relevant to the system's health. "Optimum complexity is that level of variety needed to manage the complexity of the present and deal with the anticipated future level" (Bennet & Bennet, 2004, p. 303). See Bennet and Bennet (2013) for an in-depth treatment of systems and complexity.

As complex adaptive systems, people and organizations both contain many components that interact with each other. They are both partially ordered systems that unfold and evolve through time, and are mostly self-organizing, learning, and adaptive. To survive they are always creating new ideas, scanning the environment, anticipating the future, trying new approaches, observing the results, and changing the way they operate. From this brief description of complex adaptive system behaviors, it is easy to see how important it is to have learned the lessons of cause and effect (Phase 1 of the Intelligent Social Change Journey) to build on as you move into co-evolving (Phase 2 of the ISCJ). To continuously adapt, complex adaptive systems must operate in perpetual disequilibrium, which results in some unpredictable behavior.

An organization has a large number of options and choices of actions it can take to adjust itself internally or when responding to, or influencing, its environment. The people in organizations are semi-autonomous and have varying levels of self-organization. They operate and direct their own behavior based on rules and (hopefully) a common vision of the organization's direction, working in small groups to take advantage of the local knowledge and experience of coworkers. It is the aggregate behavior (actions) of all these workers that can be observed as organizational performance. The interactions that create this performance are numerous, complex, and often nonlinear, making it impossible to derive global behavior from local interactions. The variety and diversity of individuals also contributes to the creation and characteristics of the aggregate behavior.

If one person leaves an organization, the others immediately reorganize to fill the vacuum and the firm internally adapts to its new structure, often with some stress (and presumably some learning). As people move in and out of the organization, its global behavior may shift and change, adapting to its new internal structure as well as its external environment. This continuous flexing of complex adaptive systems keeps them alive and gives them the capacity to quickly change pace and redirect focus.

In the midst of all this change—and despite the need for the disequilibrium to adapt—most individuals and organizations have a tendency to seek stability. For example, emergent characteristics of an organization represent stable patterns that are qualitative and exert a strong influence back on the individuals and their relationships (Bennet and Bennet, 2004). Examples are culture, team spirit, attitudes toward customers, trust, consciousness, laughter, and individual emotions.

A typical organizational intervention is to require a specified series of actions done in a specific fashion to ensure a desired outcome. These directives may or may not be cohesive with the culture, or the way work is done. If the new procedures *are* consistent, they may well be fully adopted. Even when the new procedures are *not* consistent with the culture, when oversight is strong, employees may follow the steps of the process to the letter, at least for awhile. When management focus changes, or a management personnel change occurs, employees will slip back to earlier behaviors consistent with the culture. This phenomenon has been well-documented in the literature on management and culture (Forrester, 1994; Munck et al., 2002, Schein, 2004).

Complex adaptive systems seek organization, which is often achieved through increased complexity. They can only stay in stasis for a short period of time; they either need to change and expand and grow, or they fall into chaos or dissipate.

The Environment and the Knowledge Worker

From the viewpoint of our knowledge and learning research, we talk about the natural cycle of change introduced in Chapter 1 and Chapter 2 in this way: *With learning comes knowledge, with knowledge comes action, and with action comes change.* As our understanding of the mind/brain unfolds in concert with neuroscience research findings, new ways to think about learning, knowledge and change are emerging. Exploring these new frames of reference can provide insights that suggest new behaviors. This chapter offers one such frame of reference.

With the recognition of knowledge as an organizational asset came the awareness that knowledge could not be "managed" but rather had to be nurtured (Bennet and Bennet, 2004), and that an individual could not be ordered to learn, but could learn best only if they *wanted* to learn. Being pressured or forced to learn minimizes the learning rate because it creates a level of stress and fear that will most likely significantly detract and reduce learning capacity (Jensen, 1998). This concept is important enough to be repeated several times in this book. Similarly, Choice Theory (Glasser, 1998) is based on the belief that we are internally motivated. Outside events cannot make us think and act. The only person who can change us is ourselves.

<<<<<<<<◇>>>>>>>

INSIGHT: **The only person who can change us is ourselves.**

<<<<<<<<◇>>>>>>>

This is not to say that the environment does not have an impact on our choices. Research in neuroscience has validated that the human mind/brain co-evolves with its environment,

> ... endowing it with the flexibility to adapt to the environment it encounters, the experiences it has, the damage it suffers, the demands its owner makes of it. The brain is neither immutable nor static but is instead continuously remodeled by the lives we lead (Begley, 2007, p. 130).

What has been discovered is that the genes cannot be expressed (released to influence the cells) without some external influence outside the cell body. The implication is that humans can no longer assume their destiny is in their genes. This new field is called Epigenetics, the study of the mechanisms by which the cell environment influences gene activity. When describing this new area of research, Bruce Lipton, a cell biologist, asserts, "The belief that we are frail bio-chemical machines controlled by genes is giving way to an understanding that we are powerful creators of our lives and the world in which we live" (Lipton, 2005, p.17). This is a theme that will emerge again and again from different frames of reference as we move through the three phases of change toward the ultimate choices that faces us as a humanity.

Similarly, James Byrnes, an educator, suggests that the "neural organization of an adult brain is not set in stone at birth" (Byrnes, 2001, p. 171). Eric Jensen, also an educator, takes the strong stand that, "... it is now established that contrasting, persistent, or traumatic environments can and do change the actions of genes" (Jensen, 2006, p. 10). Colin Ross, a psychologist, describes the causality in brain development as a "dance between two partners, DNA and the environment" (Ross, 2006, p. 32). As Lipton explains,

> Genes are simply molecular blueprints used in the construction of cells, tissues and organs. The environment serves as a "contractor" who reads and engages those genetic blueprints and is ultimately responsible for the character of a cell's life. It is a single cell's "awareness" of the environment, not its genes, that sets into motion the mechanisms of life (Lipton, 2005, p. 15).

In short, research suggests that what we believe leads to what we think, and what we think leads to knowledge—the effective actions we take. Thus, what we believe and how we think determine what we do. It is our actions that primarily determine our success, not our genes (Bownds, 1999; Lipton, 2005; Rose, 2005; Begley, 2007).

<<<<<<<◇>>>>>>>

INSIGHT: **What we believe and how we think determine what we do. It is our actions that primarily determine our success, not our genes.**

<<<<<<<◇>>>>>>>

This idea of cell awareness and learning as a dance between two partners lays the groundwork for exploring the personal action learning change model presented here. This model describes a set of factors through which an individual can initiate and *implement personal change from the inside out,* that is, from our own volition. The job of the individual is to be open to—and choose to—change. The job of the manager is to create an environment where these factors can occur. See Figure 6-1.

The Model

Although change and adaptation is a natural characteristic of the brain, so, too, is the search for safety, security and comfort. As people grow and live, they develop and become comfortable with their way of working and will usually resist any external influence to change. This is what makes change management so challenging in organizations.

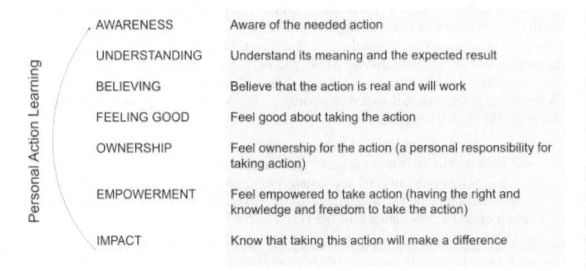

Figure 6-1. *Mobilizing personal action.*

Change is particularly difficult if it impacts who we are, that is, our self-image. For example, you cannot successfully tell a knowledge worker to share their knowledge, trust others, be creative, or collaborate with their peers. They will only do these things if, and when, they decide to do them. So how can we get workers to change, or better, to *want* to change? We offer that the following seven factors are instrumental in determining whether or not an individual will change: awareness, understanding, believing, feeling good, ownership, empowerment (AUBFOE), and impact. For ease of exploring these factors, we will use the term "actor" to describe the individual we wish to embrace change.

First, our actor must be **aware**. Awareness means that something has come into your attention; it is perceived; it has been mentally engaged. Attention is a cerebral phenomenon which the scientist Michael Posner hypothesized as caused by three separable-but-integrated systems in the brain (Medina, 2008). The first system is the Alerting or *Arousal Network*, a surveillance and monitoring system paying attention to the environment in the condition of Intrinsic Alertness (what would be the amygdala). When something unusual is detected, this Intrinsic Alertness transforms into specific attention, or Phasic Alertness. The second system is the *Orienting Network* (what would be an increase in neuronal firings and connections with incoming information patterns engaged with an emotional tag), which uses the senses to gain more information about the subject of the alert. The third system is the *Executive Network* (engagement of the executive function in the frontal cortex), which is the stage where a response is, or is not, determined (Medina, 2008). A deeper treatment of attention is included in Chapter 25/Part IV.

Once aware, our actor must **understand** the situation and the expected results that drive the need for change. Understanding includes the description of the situation and its information content that provides the: *who, what, where* and *when*. It involves the frame of reference of the actor, including assumptions and presuppositions. This can be referred to as surface knowledge, which was introduced in Chapter 2 and has a deeper treatment in Chapter 24/Part IV. As systems become more complicated or complex, their behavior and characteristics change, requiring different approaches to understanding (Wilson, 1998; Bennet & Bennet, 2004). Chickering et al. (2005) says that where deep learning is necessary, *we must create and re-create our own personal understanding*.

In addition to awareness and understanding, our actor must **believe** that the actions are real and will work as assumed. Believing something means that the actor accepts what they are aware of as true, and understands it really exists. Believing involves beliefs, fundamental neural patterns which are associated with many other patterns, and seem to dominate other patterns. They are central and strong patterns in the mind created by autobiographical experiences and closely related to emotions.

Thus, our beliefs significantly impact our attitudes, what we think about various subjects, and how we act. Believing that actions are real and will work is closely linked to our personal history of experiences.

Beliefs are frequently hidden from conscious thoughts and thereby can drive actions without the owner's realization. The expression *transformational learning* is used to describe a strong disorienting experience that results in an individual realizing that their beliefs and underlying assumptions are no longer valid or appropriate for a given aspect of reality. When this occurs, we typically have double-loop learning—a rapid shift in the frame of reference, the mindset or perspective of the individual relative to some experience. Double-loop learning is prevalent in Phase 2 of the Intellectual Social Change Journey.

Given awareness, understanding and believing, our actor must then *feel good* about taking the action. These feelings are what make the action important to the individual and worthy of their efforts. Zull (2002) considers emotions the foundation of learning, with the chemicals of emotion modifying the strength and contribution of each part of the learning cycle, directly impacting the signaling systems in each affected neuron. Similarly, Blackmore (2004) reminds us that reason cannot operate without emotions. Plotkin (1994) says that emotional content is almost always present in verbal and non-verbal communication. We would push that even further. All information coming into the body moves through the amygdala, that part of the brain that is,

> ... important both for the acquisition and for the on-line processing of emotional stimuli ... [with] Its processing encompassing both the elicitation of emotional responses in the body and changes in other cognitive processes, such as attention and memory (Adolphs, 2004, p. 1026).

As incoming information moves through the amygdala, an emotional "tag" is attached. If this information is perceived as life-threatening, then the amygdala takes immediate control, making a decision and acting on that decision before the individual is consciously aware of the threat! Haberlandt (1998) says that there is no such thing as a behavior or thought not impacted by emotions in some way. (This is discussed further in Chapter 19/Part III.) We agree. Even simple responses to information signals can be linked to multiple emotional neurotransmitters. As Mulvihill points out, because emotions are integrally linked with incoming information from all the senses, "it becomes clear that there is no thought, memory, or knowledge which is 'objective,' or 'detached' from the personal experience of knowing" (Mulvihill, 2003, p. 322). (Emotion as a human guidance system is discussed in Chapter 19/Part III.)

<<<<<<<<<>>>>>>>>

INSIGHT: **There is no such thing as a behavior or thought not impacted by emotions in some way.**

<<<<<<<<<>>>>>>>>

Unfortunately, even this emotional linking and sense of "knowing" may not be enough to initiate action. Our actor must also feel *ownership* of the action—a personal responsibility to act—and that he/she is *empowered* by the organization—and as a self—to take action, with the right, freedom, knowledge and confidence to take the action (self efficacy).

Knowledge empowers people. For purposes of this book, empowerment is considered the investing of power, or to supply an ability, to enable (American Heritage Dictionary, 2006). Thus, being empowered includes having *knowledge* of how, when and where to take the desired action as well as the courage to act. From learning theory, we know that individuals who *believe* they can learn, *can* learn (Lipton, 2005). Extrapolating this concept to empowerment, a person who believes they are empowered and can accomplish some task or worthwhile goal will have a much higher probability of success than an individual who does not believe they are empowered to do so (Bennet and Bennet, 2007b). The value of empowerment lies simultaneously in the freedom and the responsibility given to individuals to accomplish something, and in the internal recognition of the personal capacity and capability to do so.

In organizations, empowerment may be a formal doctrine and policy or informal expectations, trust and attitudes of managers and workers. With empowerment comes context knowledge, experience, and recognition of the scope within which empowerment applies. Where knowledge workers are concerned, empowerment is extremely important because it gives them the self-respect, trust, and opportunity to make maximum use of their knowledge and competencies (Bennet and Bennet, 2007b).

Although it is not included as part of our mnemonic representation of this model—which is AUBFOE—the final element is *impact*, what will happen if an action is taken and what will happen if it is not taken. Tied direct to belief in terms of outcome, impact includes the ability to perceive the effective outcome necessary to give the actor the confidence and motivation needed for success. If there is little or no impact, why should the actor take action?

While these elements are not necessarily sequential, together they represent a *significant force for energizing action* and initiating change. Under some circumstances they can occur nearly simultaneously. For example, if you as an adult are walking past a swimming pool where a small child falls into the water and no one else is around, you would almost instantly experience all of these elements and jump in to save the child, even if you don't know how to swim.

Applying the Model

Recall the stages of the individual change model presented above: awareness, understanding, belief, feelings, ownership and empowerment of self (knowledge of what to do and the courage to do it). These six stages can be used as impact factors to assess the level of change.

From the individual learning perspective, the impact factors can be looked at as moving through objective, relational, subjective and experiential phases, with each phase related to the specific approaches of instructing, teaching, coaching and mentoring, respectively. From the viewpoint of the individual, or learner, they first hear it (learning outside-in), then bring it into themselves, acting and creating (learning inside-out). An example of the first is listening to lectures; an example of the latter is involvement in simulations. Examples of these phases related to learning approaches are in Figure 6-2.

This model can also be used to assess effectiveness of a change strategy. When assessing impact factors from the viewpoint of a new initiative or process,[6-1] common activities that a change management program might include are:

1. **Build Infrastructure** to serve as foundation to the program. Infrastructure is the core foundation of the system of implementation. It may include the IT systems that accommodate the program, a space to collaborate on the program, the acquiring of tools to support the program, or even the building of capabilities of staffs to charter the program.

2. **Get management buy-in** and sponsor the program. Management acts as the role model and as the change ambassador.

3. **Training**. Staff must be trained to ride the wave of change. No matter whether the system is easy or complex, training is always a crucial part.

4. **Communication**. Continuously delivering the message to make sure the program is heard, the message is clear, and to create understanding.

5. **Promote & Reward**. This creates recognition and brings value to individuals.

6. **Embed practice into process**. This part is very crucial to make it stick.

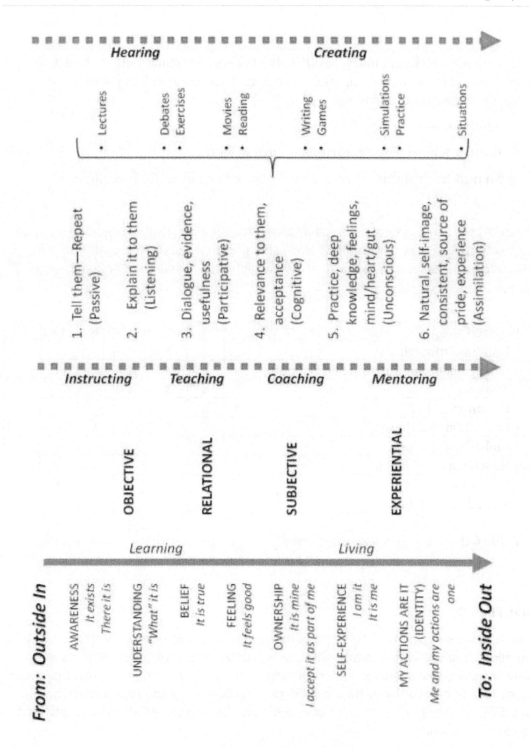

Figure 6-2. *The individual change model from the individual learning perspective*

7. **Provide and benchmark result/value return**. Benchmarking with easy to understand target with comparison of others in the same industry will boost awareness and understanding.

--- *Optional* ----

8. **Build a Knowledge Performance Index** (KPI)

9. **Shared team status**. This creates a "you are one of us" unity culture.

When these activities are assessed as a unit, they impact all six areas; however, no single activity can make this impact. See Table 6-2. In this example, activities 1-7 have covered all aspects of the factors. Hence, activities 8 and 9 are optional.

#	Activity	A	U	B	F	O	E
1	Building Infrastructure		X				
2	Management Sponsorship and Support	X	X	X			
3	Training	X	X	X			
4	Communication	X	X				
5	Promotion and Reward	X	X		X		
6	Embedded into process					X	X
7	Benchmark and Result	X	X		X		
8	KPI enforcement	X				X	X
9	Shared team status					X	X

Table 6-2. *Frame of reference for change program activities to assess whether personal action learning will take place at every level of the model.*

Final Thoughts

In any change strategy, the challenge of management and leadership becomes that of communicating and collaborating with the organization's knowledge workers to create an environment, and an understanding on the part of their workforce, that these change factors are worthy of their consideration, acceptance and personal attention and actions. When this happens, change will come from a knowledgeable, motivated and supportive workforce.

Unfortunately, leadership and management often use the outdated approach of telling workers what they are expected to do and how they are expected to change.

This is the approach historically used during Phase 1 of the Intelligent Social Change Journey, where the focus of work was on physical activity, but simply cannot work in the co-evolving of Phase 1I, where the focus of work is on mental activity. An approach that *can* work, and work well, is to let knowledge workers take the lead in selecting, creating and determining the changes needed throughout the organization. This empowerment and trust will then unleash the energy, knowledge and creativity of the workforce and, above all, they will have ownership. Through this approach, without realizing it, they will probably create their own personal acceptance of each of the seven change factors in the personal action learning change model. Paraphrasing Lao Tzu's description of the true leader,

> *Of a good leader, when his work is done, his aim fulfilled, They will say:*   *We did it ourselves.*

As indeed, they did.

Questions for Reflection:

Reflect on a change situation you have not fully adopted. At what level are you stuck?

How could you use the individual change model as an evaluation tool on your current project?

A Preview of Part IV: Co-Creating the Future
[Excerpt from Chapter 23]

Reality is essentially subjectively unknowable, existing as an image, perception, perspective or belief generated by an individual, a group or a society. Knowledge acquired from the external world comes through our senses, usually the result of physical, psychological and social interactions of our minds and bodies with an external world, or a perceived external world. Consciousness, because of its central role in our ontology, also plays a crucial part in shaping and filtering our epistemology. The physical characteristics of our brains, together with the emergence of language and higher-order consciousness, act as both filters and interpreters of the external world. However, no matter how much we know or think we know, the best we as evolutionary products of that world *can* know is a qualified reality, a reality limited by both our individual embodiment and our space-time location. Further limited by our genetic heritage, our developmental morphology, chance events and our external environment, the best we can hope for is a qualified understanding of ourselves and of our reality. "As mind pursues reality to its ultimate analysis, matter vanishes to the material senses but may still remain real to the mind." (*Urantia*, 1954, p. 1228)

Nevertheless, consciousness, supported by our unconscious mind/brain and bootstrapped through social collaboration, is the only resource available to observe, create and comprehend our existence. It is also the experiential lens through which we must look to interact with other beings and with the physical world. This lens is reminiscent of Plato's allegory of shadows in the cave.

According to Plato, all living beings in the sensible world are but imperfect copies of eternal forms residing in the world of Ideas...the world accessible to our senses is akin to the world of shadows experienced by the men in the cave. It is merely an imperfect manifestation of a perfect world—the world of Ideas, illuminated by the Sun of intelligibility. (Thuan, 2001, p. 300-301)

Another interpretation of a perfect world would be one in which everything in the Universe is exactly as it should be. What else could it be if we eliminate personal morality and accept the sentence as meaning that nature and the Universe work as they do, independent of but consistent with rocks and beetles and humans. Perhaps as Plato opined, it is only man that separates himself from nature and thereby creates the fuzziness and imperfections he then perceives. Does a true world of eternal and immutable ideas exist where mathematical relations and perfect geometrical structures reign supreme?

# # #

Appendix A: The Overarching ISCJ Model

The Intelligent Social Change Journey (ISCJ)

NOTE: Each model builds on the understanding gained from experiencing the previous phase

Phase 1: LEARNING FROM THE PAST
CHARACTERISTICS: Linear and Sequential, Repeatable, Engaging past learning, Starting from current state., Cause and effect relationships.

Phase 2: LEARNING IN THE PRESENT
CHARACTERISTICS: Recognition of patterns; Social interaction; Co-evolving with environment through continuous learning, quick response, robustness, flexibility, adaptability, alignment.

Phase 3: CO-CREATING OUR FUTURE
CHARACTERISTICS: Creative imagination; Recognition of global Oneness; Mental in service to the intuitive; Balancing senses; Bringing together past, present and future; Knowing; Beauty; Wisdom.

SOCIAL STATE (Depth of Connection)

SYMPATHY → EMPATHY → COMPASSION

MOVEMENT

EXPANDED CONSCIOUSNESS (Open to the Spiritual)

REDUCTION OF FORCES (Engage forces by choice)

INCREASED INTELLIGENT ACTIVITY (Growth of wisdom)

CONSCIOUSNESS is considered a state of awareness and a private, selective and continuously changing process, a sequential set of ideas, thoughts, images, feelings and perceptions and an understanding of the connections and relationships among them and our self.

INTELLIGENT ACTIVITY represents a perfect state of interaction where intent, purpose, direction, values and expected outcomes are clearly understood and communicated among all parties, reflecting wisdom and achieving a higher truth.

FORCES occur when one type of energy affects another type of energy in a way where they are moving in different directions. Bounded (inward focused) and/or limited knowledge creates forces.

KNOWLEDGE (The capacity (potential or actual) to take effective action)

- Expanded knowledge sharing, social learning, cooperation, collaboration
- Questioning of why?
- Pursuit of truth

- Recognition that with knowledge comes responsibility.
- Conscious pursuit of larger truth
- Knowledge selectively used as a measure of effectiveness

- Deeper development of conceptual thinking (higher mental thought)
- Connecting power of diversity and individuation to whole (Moving toward outward focus)
- Recognition of different world views; the exploration of information from different perspectives
- Expanded knowledge capacities.

- Valuing of creative ideas. Asking larger questions: How does this idea serve humanity? Are there any negative consequences?
- (Outward focus) Openness to other's ideas with humility. What if this idea is right? Are my beliefs or other mental models limiting my thought? Are hidden assumptions or feelings interfering with intelligent activity?

- Ability to recognize and apply patterns at all levels within a domain of knowledge to predict outcomes
- Growing understanding of complexity.
- Increased connectedness of choices; recognition of direction you are heading, expanded meaning-making
- Expanded ability to bisociate ideas; increased creativity

- Sense and knowing of Oneness
- Development of both lower (logic) and upper (conceptual) mental faculties, which work in concert with the emotional guidance system
- Application of patterns across knowledge domains for greater good
- Recognition of self as a co-creator of reality
- Ability to engage in intelligent activity.
- Developing the ability to tap into the intuitional plane at will

NATURE:
- Product of the past
- Context sensitive, situation dependent
- Partial, incomplete

REFLECTION:
- Review of interactions, feedback
- Determination of cause and effect (logic)
- (Inward focus) Questioning decisions and actions: What did I intend? What really happened? Why were there differences? What would I do the same? What would I do differently?

COGNITIVE SHIFTS:
- Recognition of importance of feedback
- Ability to recognize systems; impact of external forces
- Recognition and location of "me" in the larger picture (conscious awareness)
- Early pattern recognition and concept development

Taken from: Bennet, Bennet, et al. (2017). The Profundity and Bifurcation of Change. Parts I through V. Frost, WV: MQIPress.

Developed by Mountain Quest Institute. Contact alex@mountainquestinstitute.com for permissions

Appendix B: Five-Book Table of Contents

The Profundity and Bifurcation of Change
The Intelligent Social Change Journey

For Each:
Cover
Title Page
Quote from *The Kybalion*
Table of Contents
Tables and Figures
Appreciation

Preface

Introduction to the Intelligent Social Change Journey

Part I: LAYING THE GROUNDWORK

Part I Introduction

Chapter 1: Change is Natural
CHANGE AS A VERB...OUR CHANGING THOUGHTS...FINAL THOUGHT
Chapter 2: Knowledge to Action
KNOWLEDGE (INFORMING) AND KNOWLEDGE (PROCEEDING)...LEVELS OF KNOWLEDGE...FROM KNOWLEDGE TO ACTION...THE NATURE OF KNOWLEDGE...LEVELS OF COMPREHENSION...FINAL THOUGHTS
Chapter 3: Forces We Act Upon
AMPLITUDE, FREQUENCY AND DURATION...FROM THE VIEWPOINT OF THE INDIVIDUAL...CONTROL AS FORCE...REDUCING FORCES...THE SELF AND FORCES...FROM THE SPIRITUAL VIEWPOINT...STRATEGIC FORCES IN ORGANIZATIONS...THE CORRELATION OF FORCES...FINAL THOUGHTS
Chapter 4: The Ever-Expanding Self
THE SUBJECT/OBJECT RELATIONSHIP...THE PERSONALITY...CHARACTERISTICS OF PERSONALITY...DEVELOPMENT OF SELF...THE HEALTHY SELF…THE CONNECTED SELF...INDIVIDUATION...THE POWER OF HUMILITY…FINAL THOUGHTS
Chapter 5: The Window of Consciousness
PROPERTIES OF CONSCIOUSNESS...THE THRESHOLD OF CONSCIOUSNESS...LEVELS OF CONSCIOUSNESS...MEANING AND PURPOSE...CONSCIOUSNESS AS A QUANTUM FIELD...FLOW AS THE OPTIMAL EXPERIENCE...CONSCIOUSLY ACCESSING THE UNCONSCIOUS...FINAL THOUGHTS

APPENDICES:
Appendix A: The Overarching ISCJ Model
Appendix B: The Table of Contents for All Parts
Appendix C: *An Infinite Story*
Appendix D: Engaging Tacit Knowledge
Appendix E: Knowing
Appendix F: Values for Creativity

ENDNOTES

REFERENCES

About Mountain Quest
About the Authors

TOOLS

Part I: Introduction
3-1. Force Field Analysis
4-1. Self Belief Assessment
4-2. Humility
5-1. Engaging Tacit Knowledge (See Appendix D.)

Part II: Learning From the Past
7-1. Personal Plane-ing Process
7-2. The Five Whys
9-1. Engaging Outside Worldviews
9-2. Practicing Mental Imagining
10-1. Grounding through Nature
10-2. Relationship Network Management
11-1. Co-Creating Conversations that Matter

Part III: Learning in the Present
13-1. Trust Mapping
14-1. Building Mental Sustainability
16-1. Integrating Time into the Self Experience
16-2. Scenario Building
17-1. Thinking Patterns
17-2. Storying: Capture (see Appendix G)
17-3. Storying: Sculpt (see Appendix G)
17-4. Storying: Tell (see Appendix G)

Appendix C: *An Infinite Story*

There is such joy to be had soaring through the skies above this glorious Earth, diving into the oceans and seas, shifting to a sunny afternoon float atop a passing cloud, perhaps connecting with this energy and entangling with that pattern for awhile. Instant after instant after instant, a continuous awareness of Nows filled with a love of Being. We of One are many, expressing our light in an array of colors, sometimes seen and captured in pictures taken by those souls journeying in human form. Have you ever seen us? Have you ever wondered who we are?

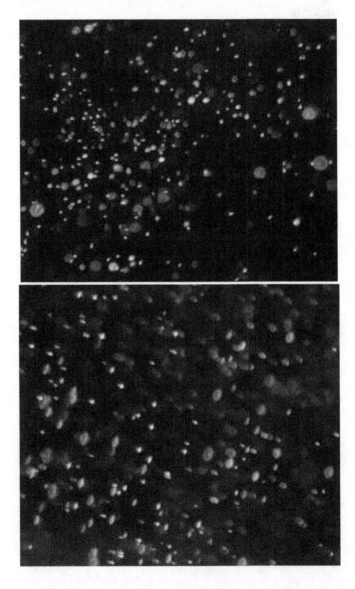

And then the Call goes out, a vibration of sound that comes from the heart of part of the One. What fun! In the instant we come together, a feeling of flowing breath riding the waves of life. And in that instant our light is stretched, moving out of the spherical form that is our natural setting and displaying the essence of a spectrum of color.

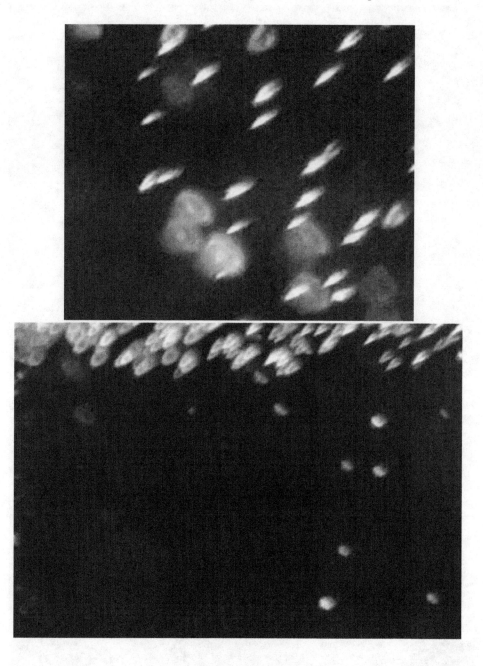

We expand as we connect with the mist in the air, moving as a collective, curving and shifting into form, sharing our energy, creating a pattern of Oneness.

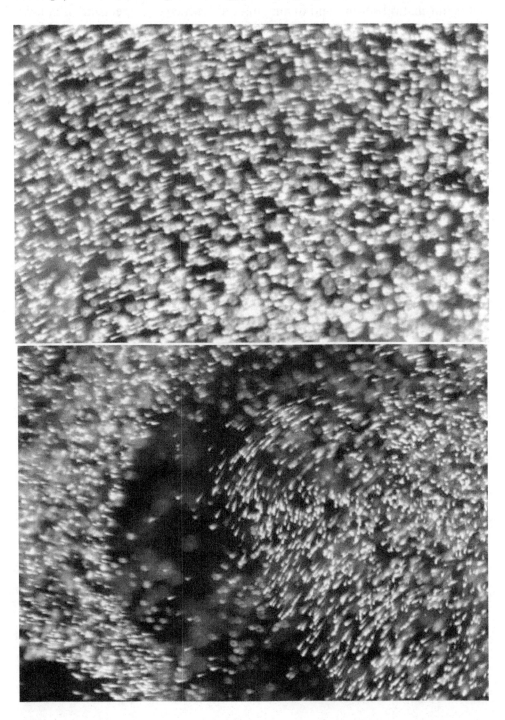

When we who respond to the Call are close in resonance, then oh the beautiful patterns we create! Some may perceive these as fractals. From one direction you will see an angle, and there is a split second when you can see our expansion. How gloriously bright the colors that present to the human eyes who choose to see us!

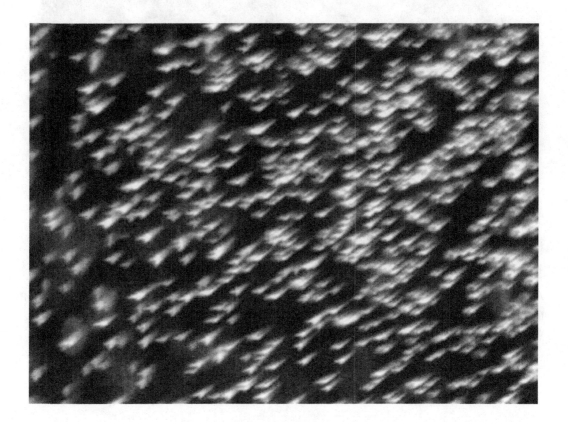

As we move closer and closer, we continue to expand, bringing in the water of the air to reassume comfortable spherical shapes producing faces within faces within form, with delight dissolving into the Oneness that we are.

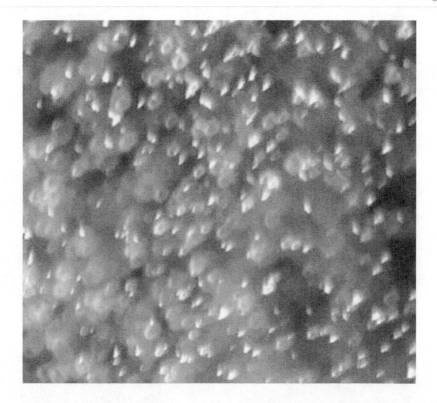

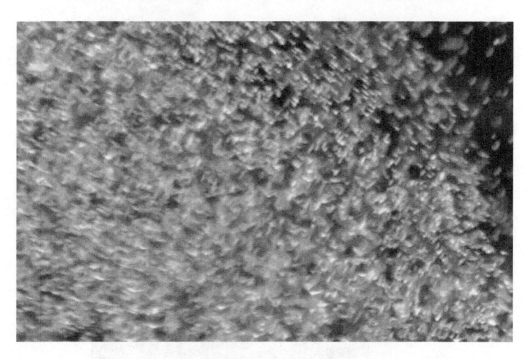

We *feel* the Joy of One as we create the *Myst* forms. We lighten into form, move into stillness, perhaps accenting the white of a full moon.

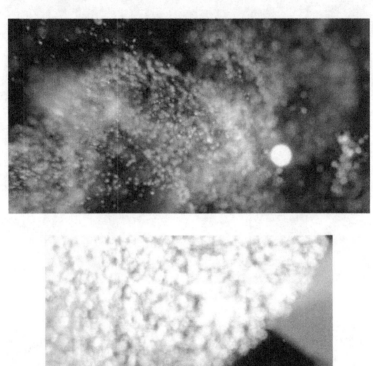

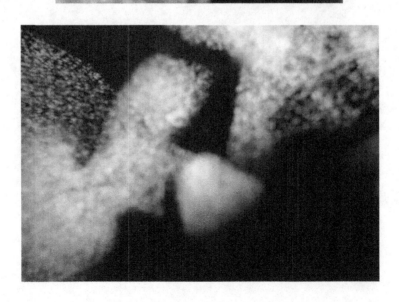

Oh, what beauty! Can you understand? We are individuated, yet one ... sharing our light, conveying a message, glowing in our delight! Can you see the faces? They represent our essence, the energy of us in a personalized fashion. And we love you.

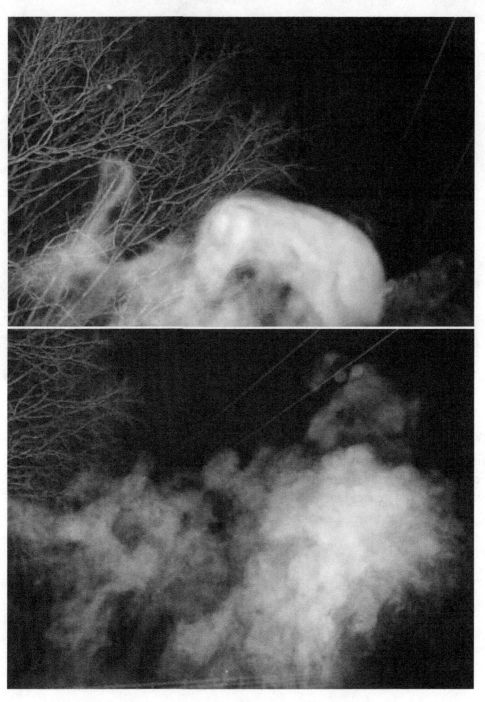

Now ...

we will share a secret. It is the same for all forms of life. There are inherent desires
and possibilities moving us towards cooperation and collaboration, the Connectedness
of love and joy and peace, Oneness.

Then, in an instant of ever-living Nows, the larger form releases. The circles of Orbs become skeletal, then dissipate, reducing into the spark of life that is so small, so large, so All.

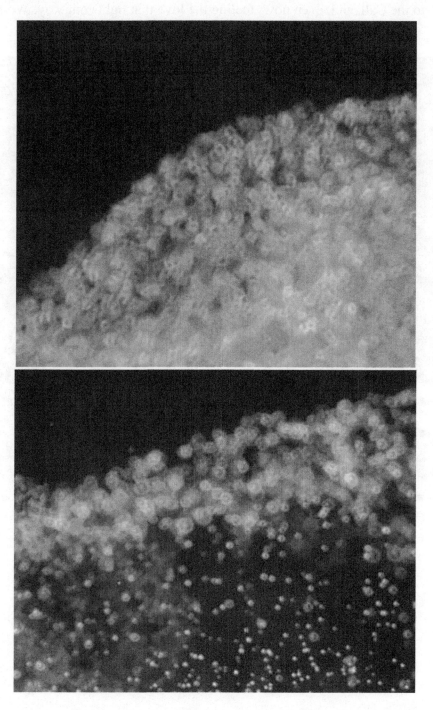

Do not be concerned. We do not really disappear. We are always here. When you are in joy, in the flash of a camera we will appear, and you will know us. You, too, are opening to the Call, and, even now, feeling the love that lights our way. We are One.

*[Excerpted from **Patterns in the Myst** (Bennet and Bennet, 2013)]*

Appendix D
Engaging Tacit Knowledge

[Detail for the Tool "Engaging Tacit Knowledge" introduced in chapter 5. Skip to the subtitle "Accessing Tacit Knowledge" below if you already understand the concepts of "knowledge", "tacit" and the four types of tacit knowledge: embodied, intuitive, affective and spiritual.]

SUBTOPICS: BACKGROUND ... THE TYPES OF TACIT KNOWLEDGE ... ACCESSING TACIT KNOWLEDGE ... SURFACING ... EMBEDDING ... SHARING ... INDUCING RESONANCE

FIGURE: D-1. CONTINUUM OF AWARENESS OF KNOWLEDGE SOURCE/CONTENT ... D-2. ACCESSING TACIT KNOWLEDGE

Background

Knowledge—the capacity (potential or actual) to take effective action—was introduced in Chapter 3. Our focus in this Part Is on that knowledge residing in the unconscious, that is, tacit knowledge (Item 1-E). Tacit knowledge is the descriptive term for those connections among thoughts that cannot be pulled up in words, a knowing of what decision to make or how to do something that cannot be clearly voiced in a manner such that another person could extract and re-create that knowledge (understanding, meaning, etc.). An individual may or may not know they have tacit knowledge in relationship to something or someone; but even when it is known, the individual is unable to put it into words or visuals that can convey that knowledge. We all know things, or know what to do, yet may be unable to articulate why we know them, why they are true, or even exactly what they are. To "convey" is to cause something to be known or understood or, in this usage, to transfer information from which the receiver is able to create knowledge.

As a point of contrast, explicit knowledge is information (patterns) and processes (patterns in time) that can be called up from memory and described accurately in words and/or visuals (representations) such that another person can comprehend the knowledge that is expressed through this exchange of information. This has historically been called declarative knowledge (Anderson, 1983). Implicit knowledge is a more complicated concept, and a term not unanimously agreed-upon in the literature. This is understandable since even simple dictionary definitions—which are generally unbiased and powerful indicators of collective preference and understanding—show a considerable overlap between the terms "implicit" and "tacit," making it difficult to differentiate the two. We propose that a useful interpretation of implicit knowledge is knowledge stored in memory of which the individual is not immediately aware which, while not readily accessible, may be pulled up when triggered (associated). Triggering can occur through questions, dialogue or reflective thought, or happen as a result of an external event. In other words, implicit knowledge is knowledge that the individual does not know they have, but is self-discoverable! However, once this knowledge is surfaced, the individual may or may not have the ability to adequately describe it such that another individual could create the same knowledge; and the "why and how" may remain tacit.

A number of published psychologists have used the term implicit interchangeably with our usage of tacit, that is, with implicit representing knowledge that once acquired can be shown to effect behavior but is not available for conscious retrieval (Reber, 1993; Kirsner et al, 1998). As described in the above discussion of implicit knowledge, what is forwarded here is that the concept of implicit knowledge serves as a middle ground between that which can be made explicit and that which cannot easily, if at all, be made explicit. By moving beyond the dualistic approach of explicit and tacit—that which can be declared versus that which can't be declared, and that which can be remembered versus that which can't be remembered—we posit implicit as representing the knowledge spectrum between explicit and tacit. While explicit refers to easily available, some knowledge requires a higher stimulus for association to occur but is not buried so deeply as to prevent access. This understanding opens the domain of implicit knowledge.

Tacit and explicit knowledge can be thought of as residing in "places," specifically, the unconscious and the conscious, respectively, although both are differentiated patterns spread throughout the neuronal system, that is, the volume of the brain and other parts of the central nervous system. On the other hand, implicit knowledge may reside in either the unconscious (prior to triggering, or tacit) or the conscious (when triggered, or explicit). Note there is no clean break between these three types of knowledge (tacit, implicit and explicit); rather, this is a continuum.

Calling them interactive components of cooperative processes, Reber agrees that there is no clear boundary between that which is explicit and that which is implicit (our tacit): "There is ... no reason for presuming that there exists a clean boundary between conscious and unconscious processes or a sharp division between implicit and explicit epistemic systems ..." (Reber, 1993, p. 23). Reber describes the urge to treat explicit and implicit (our tacit) as altogether different processes the "polarity fallacy" (Reber, 1993). Similarly, Matthews says that the unconscious and conscious processes are engaged in what he likes to call a "synergistic" relationship (Matthews, 1991). What this means is that the boundary between the conscious and the unconscious is somewhat porous and flexible.

Knowledge starts as tacit knowledge, that is, the initial movement of knowledge is from its origins within the Self (in the unconscious) to an outward expression (albeit driving effective action). What does that mean? Michael Polanyi, a professor of chemistry and the social sciences, wrote in The Tacit Dimension that, "We start from the fact that we can know more than we can tell" (Polanyi, 1967, p 108). He called this pre-logical phase of knowing tacit knowledge, that is, knowledge that cannot be articulated (Polanyi, 1958).

The Types of Tacit Knowledge

Tacit knowledge can be thought of in terms of four aspects: embodied, intuitive, affective and spiritual (Bennet & Bennet, 2008c). While all of these aspects are part of Self, each represents different sources of tacit knowledge whose applicability, reliability and efficacy may vary greatly depending on the individual, the situation and the knowledge needed to take effective action. They are represented in Figure D-1 along with explicit and implicit knowledge on the continuum of awareness.

Embodied tacit knowledge is also referred to as somatic knowledge. Both kinesthetic and sensory, it can be represented in neuronal patterns stored within the body. Kinesthetic is related to the movement of the body and, while important to every individual every day of our lives, it is a primary focus for athletes, artists, dancers, kids and assembly-line workers. A commonly used example of tacit knowledge is knowledge of riding a bicycle. Sensory, by definition, is related to the five human senses of form through which information enters the body (sight, smell, hearing, touch and taste). An example is the smell of burning rubber from your car brakes while driving or the smell of hay in a barn. These odors can convey knowledge of whether the car brakes may need replacing (get them checked immediately), or whether the hay is mildewing (dangerous to feed horses, but fine for cows). These responses would be overt, bringing to conscious awareness the need to take effective action and driving that action to occur.

	TACIT Kn			IMPLICIT Kn	EXPLICIT Kn
SPIRITUAL	INTUITIVE	AFFECTIVE	EMBODIED		
•Based on matters of the soul •Represents animating principles of human life •Focused on moral aspects, human nature, higher development of mental faculties •Transcendent power •Moves knowledge to wisdom •Higher guidance with unknown origin	•Sense of knowing coming from within •Linked to FOR •Knowing that may be without explanation (outside expertise or past experience) •24/7 personal servant of human being •Why (unknown)	•Feelings •Generally attached to other types or aspects of knowledge •Why (evasive or unknown)	•Expressed in bodily/material form •Stored within the body (riding bike) •Can be kinesthetic or sensory •Learned by mimicry and behavioral skill training •Why (evasive)	•Stored in memory but not in conscious awareness •Not readily accessible but capable of being recalled when triggered •Don't know you know, but self-discoverable •Ability may or may not be present to facilitate social communication. •Why (questionable)	•Information stored in brain that can be recalled at will •In conscious awareness •Can be shared through social communication •Can be captured in terms of information (given context) •Expressed emotions (visible changes in body state) •Why (understood)

UNCONSCIOUS AWARENESS   Level of Awareness of Origins /Content of Knowledge   IMPLICIT Kn   CONSCIOUS AWARENESS

Figure D-1. *Continuum of awareness of knowledge source/content.*

Intuitive tacit knowledge is the sense of knowing coming from inside an individual that may influence decisions and actions; yet the decision-maker or actor cannot explain how or why the action taken is the right one. The unconscious works around the clock with a processing capability many times greater than that at the conscious level. This is why as the world grows more complex, decision-makers will depend more and more on their intuitive tacit knowledge, a combination of life lessons. But in order to use it, decision-makers must first be able to tap into their unconscious.

Affective tacit knowledge is connected to emotions and feelings, with emotions representing the external expression of some feelings. Feelings expressed as emotions become explicit (Damasio, 1994). Feelings that are not expressed—perhaps not even recognized—are those that fall into the area of affective tacit knowledge. Feelings as a form of knowledge have different characteristics than language or ideas, but they may lead to effective action because they can influence actions by their existence and connections with consciousness. When feelings come into conscious awareness, they can play an informing role in decision-making, providing insights in a non-linguistic manner and thereby influencing decisions and actions. For example, a feeling (such as fear or an upset stomach) may occur every time a particular action is started which could prevent the decision-maker from taking that action.

Spiritual tacit knowledge can be described in terms of knowledge based on matters of the soul. The soul represents the animating principles of human life in terms of thought and action, specifically focused on its moral aspects, the emotional part of human nature, and higher development of the mental faculties (Bennet & Bennet, 2007c). While there is a "knowing" related to spiritual knowledge similar to intuition, this knowing does not include the experiential base of intuition, and it may or may not have emotional tags. The current state of the evolution of our understanding of spiritual knowledge is such that there are insufficient words to relate its transcendent power, or to define the role it plays in relationship to other tacit knowledge. Nonetheless, this area represents a form of higher guidance with unknown origin. Spiritual knowledge may be the guiding purpose, vision and values behind the creation and application of tacit knowledge. It may also be the road to moving information to knowledge and knowledge to wisdom (Bennet & Bennet, 2008d). In the context of this book, spiritual tacit knowledge represents the source of higher learning, helping decision-makers create and implement knowledge that has greater meaning and value for the common good.

Whether embodied, affective, intuitive or spiritual, *tacit knowledge represents the bank account of the Self*. The larger our deposits, the greater the interest, and the more we are prepared for co-evolving in a changing, uncertain and complex environment.

Accessing Tacit Knowledge

There are many ways to bring our tacit resources into our consciousness. For example, we propose a four-fold action model with nominal curves for building what we call extraordinary consciousness, that is, expanding our consciousness through accessing tacit resources. The four approaches to accessing include surfacing, embedding, sharing and inducing resonance. (See Figure D-2 below.)

Surfacing Tacit Knowledge.

As individuals observe, experience, study and learn throughout life they generate a huge amount of information and knowledge that becomes stored in their unconscious mind. Surfacing tacit knowledge is focused on accessing the benefit of that which is tacit by moving knowledge from the unconscious to conscious awareness. Three ways that tacit knowledge can be surfaced are through external triggering, self-collaboration and nurturing.

The process of triggering is primarily externally driven with internal participation. For example, conversation, dialogue, questions, or an external situation with specific incoming information may trigger the surfacing of tacit knowledge needed to respond. Triggering is often the phenomenon that occurs in "sink or swim" situations, where an immediate decision must be made that will have significant consequences.

Although collaboration is generally thought about as interactions among individuals and/or groups, a type of collaboration that is less understood is the process of *individuals consciously collaborating with themselves*. What this means is the conscious mind learning to communicate with, listen to, and trust its own unconscious based on a relationship built over time between the self and the personality. With the self in charge, the selection process and semantic complexing of all the experiences, learning, thoughts and feelings throughout life is consistent with the focus and purpose of the self. One way to collaborate with your self is through creating an internal dialogue.

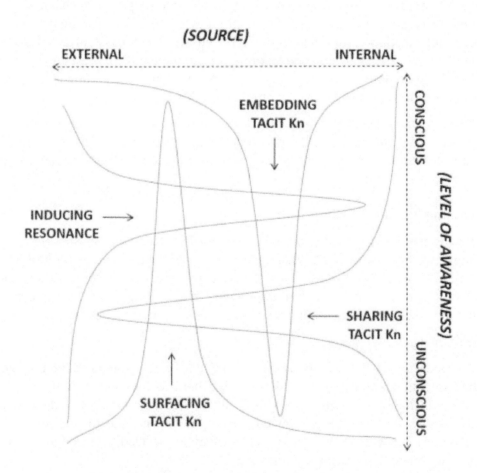

Figure D-2. *Accessing Tacit Knowledge.*

For example, accepting the authenticity of, and listening deeply to, a continuous stream of conscious thought while following the tenets of dialogue. Those tenets would include: withholding quick judgment, not demanding quick answers, and exploring underlying assumptions (Ellinor & Gerard, 1998, p. 26), *then* looking for collaborative meaning between what you consciously think and what you feel. A second approach is to ask yourself a lot of questions related to the task at hand. Even if you don't think you know the answers, reflect carefully on the questions, and be patient. Sleeping on a question will often yield an answer the following morning. Your unconscious mind processes information 24/7; it is not a figment of your imagination, or your enemy. To paraphrase the Nobel Laureate Neuroscientist Dr. Eric Kandel, your unconscious is a part of you. It works 24 hours a day processing incoming information on your behalf. So, when it tells you something via intuition, lucid dreaming, etc., you should listen carefully (but it may not always be right) (Kandel, 2006).

Although requiring time, openness and commitment, there are a number of approaches readily available for those who choose to nurture their sensitivity to tacit knowledge. These include (among others) meditation, inner tasking, lucid dreaming, and hemispheric synchronization. Meditation practices have the ability to quiet the conscious mind, thus allowing greater access to the unconscious (Rock, 2004). Inner tasking is a wide-spread and often used approach to engaging your unconscious. Tell yourself, as you fall asleep at night, to work on a problem or question. The next morning when you wake up, but before you get up, lie in bed and listen to your own, quiet, passive thoughts. Frequently, but not always, the answer will appear, although it must be written down quickly before it is lost from the conscious mind. Like meditation, the efficacy of this approach takes time and practice to develop (Bennet and Bennet, 2008e).

Lucid dreaming is a particularly powerful way to access tacit knowledge. The psychotherapist Kenneth Kelzer wrote of one of his lucid dreams:

> In this dream I experienced a lucidity that was so vastly different and beyond the range of anything I had previously encountered. At this point I prefer to apply the concept of the spectrum of consciousness to the lucid dream and assert that within the lucid state a person may have access to a spectrum or range of psychic energy that is so vast, so broad and so unique as to defy classification. (Kelzer, 1987)

Another way to achieve sensitivity to the unconscious is *through the use of sound*. For example, listening to a special song in your life can draw out deep feelings and memories buried in your unconscious. Sound and its relationship to humans has been studied by philosophers throughout recorded history; extensive treatments appear in the work of Plato, Kant and Nietzsche. Through the last century scientists have delved into studies focused on acoustics (the science of sound), psychoacoustics (the study of how our minds perceive sound) and musical psychoacoustics (the discipline that involves every aspect of musical perception and performance). As do all patterns in the mind, sound has the ability to change and shape the physiological structure of the brain.

For example, hemispheric synchronization (bringing both hemispheres of the brain into coherence) can be accomplished through the use of sound coupled with a binaural beat. (See Bullard and Bennet, 2013 or Bennet et al., 2015b for in-depth treatment of hemispheric synchronization.) Inter-hemispheric communication is the setting for brain-wave coherence which facilitates whole-brain cognition, assuming an elevated status in subjective experience (Ritchey, 2003). What can occur during hemispheric synchronization is a physiologically reduced state of arousal, quieting the body *while maintaining conscious awareness* (Mavromatis, 1991; Atwater, 2004; Fischer, 1971; West, 1980; Delmonte, 1984; Goleman, 1988; Jevning et al., 1992), thus providing a doorway into the unconscious. It is difficult to imagine the amount of learning and insights that might reside therein—and the expanded mental capabilities such access may provide—much less the depth and breadth of experience and emotion that has been hidden there, perhaps making such access a mixed blessing

Embedding Tacit Knowledge.

Every experience and conversation are *embedding* potential knowledge (information) in the unconscious as it is associated with previously stored information to create new patterns. Thinking about embedding as a process for improving our tacit knowledge can lead to new approaches to learning. Embedding is both externally and internally driven, with knowledge moving from the conscious to the unconscious through exposure or immersion, by accident or by choice. Examples include travel, regularly attending church on Sunday, or listening to opera and imitating what you've heard in the shower every day. Practice moves beyond exposure to include repeated participation in some skill or process, thus strengthening the patterns in the mind. For example, after many years of imitation (practice) look at what Paul Potts, an opera singer and winner of the *Britain's Got Talent* competition in 2007, accomplished!

Creating tacit knowledge occurs naturally through diverse experiences in the course of life as individuals become more proficient at some activity (such as public speaking) or cognitive competency (such as problem solving). When the scope of experience widens, the number of relevant neuronal patterns increases. As an individual becomes more proficient in a specific focus area through effortful practice, the pattern gradually becomes embedded in the unconscious, ergo it becomes tacit knowledge. When this happens, the reasons and context within which the knowledge was created often lose their connections with consciousness.

Embodied tacit knowledge requires new pattern embedding for change to occur. This might take the form of repetition in physical training or in mental thinking. For example, embodied tacit knowledge might be embedded through mimicry, practice, competence development or visual imagery coupled with practice. An example of this would be when an athlete training to become a pole vaulter reviews a video of his perfect pole vault to increase his athletic capability. This is a result of the fact that when the pole vaulter performs his perfect vault, the patterns going through his brain while he is doing it are the same patterns that go through his brain when he is watching himself do it. When he is watching the video, he is repeating the desired brain patterns and this repetition strengthens these patterns in unconscious memory. When "doing" the pole vault, he cannot think about his actions, nor try to control them. Doing so would degrade his performance because his conscious thoughts would interfere with his tacit ability.

In the late 1990's, neuroscience research identified what are referred to as mirror neurons. As Dobb's explains,

> These neurons are scattered throughout key parts of the brain—the premotor cortex and centers for language, empathy and pain—and fire not only as we perform a certain action, but also when we watch someone else perform that action. (Dobbs, 2007, p. 22)

Watching a video is a cognitive form of mimicry that transfers actions, behaviors and most likely other cultural norms. Thus, when we *see* something being enacted, our mind creates the same patterns that we would use to enact that "something" ourselves. As these patterns fade into long-term memory, they would represent tacit knowledge—both Knowledge (Informing) and Knowledge (Proceeding). While mirror neurons are a subject of current research, it would appear that they represent a mechanism for the transfer of tacit knowledge between individuals or throughout a culture. For more information on mirror neurons, see Gazzaniga, 2004.

Intuitive tacit knowledge can be nurtured and developed through exposure, learning, and practice. Knowledge (Informing) might be embedded through experience, contemplation, developing a case history for learning purposes, developing a sensitivity to your own intuition, and effortful practice. Effortful study moves beyond practice to include identifying challenges just beyond an individual's competence and focusing on meeting those challenges one at a time (Ericsson, 2006). The way people become experts involves the chunking of ideas and concepts and creating understanding through the development of significant patterns useful for solving problems and anticipating future behavior within their area of focus. In the study of chess players introduced earlier, it was concluded that "effortful practice" was the difference between people who played chess for many years while maintaining an average skill and those who became master players in shorter periods of time. The master players, or experts, examined the chessboard patterns over and over again, studying them, looking at nuances, trying small changes to perturb the outcome (sense and response), generally "playing with" and studying these *patterns* (Ross, 2006). In other words, they use *long-term working memory, pattern recognition and chunking* rather than logic as a means of understanding and decision-making. This indicates that by exerting mental effort and emotion while exploring complex situations, knowledge—often problem-solving expertise and what some call wisdom—becomes embedded in the unconscious mind. For additional information on the development of expertise see Ericsson (2006). An important insight from this discussion is the recognition that when facing complex problems which do not allow reasoning or cause and effect analysis because of their complexity, the solution will most likely lie in studying patterns and chunking those patterns to enable a tacit capacity to anticipate and develop solutions. For more on the reference to wisdom see Goldberg (2005).

Affective tacit knowledge requires nurturing and the development of emotional intelligence. Affective tacit knowledge might be embedded through digging deeply into a situation—building self-awareness and developing a sensitivity to your own emotions—and having intense emotional experiences. How much of an experience is kept as tacit knowledge depends upon the mode of incoming information and the emotional tag we (unconsciously) put on it. The stronger the emotion attached to the experience, the longer it will be remembered and the easier it will be to recall. Subtle patterns that occur during any experience may slip quietly into our unconscious and become affective tacit knowledge. For a good explanation of emotional intelligence see Goleman (1998).

Spiritual tacit knowledge can be facilitated by encouraging holistic representation of the individual and respect for a higher purpose. Spiritual tacit knowledge might be embedded through dialogue, learning from practice and reflection, and developing a sensitivity to your own spirit, living with it over time and exploring your feelings regarding the larger aspects of values, purpose and meaning. Any individual who, or organization which, demonstrates—and acts upon—their deep concerns for humanity and the planet is embedding spiritual tacit knowledge.

Sharing Tacit Knowledge

In our discussion above on surfacing tacit knowledge, it became clear that surfaced knowledge is new knowledge, a different shading of that which was in the unconscious. If knowledge can be described in words and visuals, then this would be by definition explicit; understanding can only be symbolized and to some extent conveyed through words. Yet the subject of this paragraph is sharing tacit knowledge. The key is that **it is not necessary to make knowledge explicit in order to share it**.

Sharing tacit knowledge occurs both consciously and unconsciously, although the knowledge shared remains tacit in nature. *There is no substitute for experience.* The power of this process has been recognized in organizations for years, and tapped into through the use of mentoring and shadowing programs to facilitate imitation and mimicry. More recently, it has become the focus of group learning, where communities and teams engage in dialogue focused on specific issues and experiences mentally and, over time, develop a common frame of reference, language and understanding that can create solutions to complex problems. The words that are exchanged serve as a tool of creative expression rather than limiting the scope of exchange.

The solution set agreed upon may retain "tacitness" in terms of understanding the complexity of the issues (where it is impossible to identify all the contributing factors much less a cause and effect relationship among them). Hence these solutions in terms of understanding would not be explainable in words and visuals to individuals outside the team or community. When this occurs, the team (having arrived at the "tacit" decision) will often create a rational, but limited, explanation for purposes of communication of why the decision makes sense.

Inducing Resonance.

Through exposure to diverse, and specifically opposing, concepts that are well-grounded, it is possible to create a resonance within the receiver's mind that amplifies the meaning of the incoming information, increasing its emotional content and receptivity. Inducing resonance is a result of external stimuli resonating with internal information to bring into conscious awareness. While it is words that trigger this resonance, it is the current of truth flowing under that linguistically centered thought that brings about connections. When this resonance occurs, the incoming information is consistent with the frame of reference and belief systems within the receiving individual. This resonance amplifies feelings connected to the incoming information, bringing about the emergence of deeper perceptions and validating the re-creation of externally-triggered knowledge in the receiver.

Further, this process results in the amplification and transformation of internal affective, embodied, intuitive or spiritual knowledge from tacit to implicit (or explicit). Since deep knowledge is now accessible at the conscious level, this process also creates a sense of ownership within the listener. The speakers are not telling the listener what to believe; rather, when the tacit knowledge of the receiver resonates with what the speaker is saying (and how it is said), a natural reinforcement and expansion of understanding occurs within the listener. This accelerates the creation of deeper tacit knowledge and a stronger affection associated with this area of focus.

An example of inducing resonance can be seen in the movie, *The Debaters*. We would even go so far as to say that the purpose of a debate is to transfer tacit knowledge. Well-researched and well-grounded external information is communicated (explicit knowledge) tied to emotional tags (explicitly expressed). The beauty of this process is that this occurs on *both sides* of a question such that the active listener who has an interest in the area of the debate is pulled into one side or another. An eloquent speaker will try to speak from the audience's frame of reference to tap into their intuition. Such a speaker will come across as confident, likeable and positive to transfer embodied tacit knowledge, and may well refer to higher order purpose, etc. to connect with the listener's spiritual tacit knowledge. An example can be seen in litigation, particularly in the closing arguments, where for opposing sides of an issue emotional tags are tied to a specific frame of reference regarding what has been presented.

[Excerpted from Bennet et al. (2015)]

Appendix E
The Art of Knowing

[We explore knowing from a more pragmatic viewpoint inclusive of brief exercises to expand our external sensing capabilities. To this end, a Knowing Framework developed for the U.S. Department of the Navy is utilized. For purposes of this discussion, Knowing is poetically defined as **seeing beyond images, hearing beyond words, sensing beyond appearances, and feeling beyond emotions.** *In this treatment, it is considered a sense that emerges from our collective tacit knowledge.]*

SUBTOPICS: Critical Areas of Knowing ... Principles of Knowing ... The Cognitive Capabilities ... The Cognitive Processes ... The Self as an Agent of Change

FIGURE: The Eternal Loop of Knowledge and Knowing

Every decision, and the actions that decision drives, is a learning experience that builds on its predecessors by broadening the sources of knowledge creation and the capacity to create knowledge in different ways. For example, as an individual engages in more and more conversations across the Internet in search of meaning, thought connections occur that cause an expansion of shallow knowledge. As we are aware, *knowledge begets knowledge*. In a global interactive environment, the more that is understood, the more that can be created and understood. This is how our personal learning system works. As we tap into our internal resources, *knowledge enables knowing, and knowing inspires the creation of knowledge.*

The concept of "knowing" is not easy to define, since the word and concept are used in so many different ways. We consider Knowing as a *sense* that is supported by our tacit knowledge. In this appendix, we provide a Knowing Framework (published as a chapter in Bennet & Bennet, 2013) that focuses on methods to increase individual sensory capabilities. This Framework specifically refers to our five external senses and to the increase of the ability to consciously integrate these sensory inputs *with our tacit knowledge*, that knowledge created by past learning experiences that is *entangled with* the flow of spiritual tacit knowledge continuously available to each of us. In other words, knowing—**driven by the unconscious as an integrated unit**—is the *sense* gained from experience that resides in the *subconscious* part of the mind, *and* the energetic connection our mind enjoys with the *superconscious*.

The subconscious and superconscious are both part of our unconscious resources, with the subconscious directly supporting the embodied mind/brain and the superconscious focused on tacit resources involving larger moral aspects, the emotional part of human nature and the higher development of our mental faculties. When engaged by an intelligent mind which has moved beyond logic into conscious processing based on trust and recognition of the connectedness and interdependence of humanity, these resources are immeasurable.

In Figure E-1 below, the superconscious is described with the terms spiritual learning, higher guidance, values and morality, and love. It is also characterized as "pre-personality" to emphasize that there are no personal translators such as beliefs and mental models attached to this form of knowing. In Chapter 26/Part IV, the flow of information from the superconscious is very much focused on the moment at hand and does not bring with it any awareness patterns that could cloud the decision-makers full field of perception.

In contrast, the memories stored in the subconscious are very much a part of the personality of the decision-maker, and may be heavily influenced by an individual's perceptions and feelings at the time they were formed. Embodied tacit knowledge would be based on the physical preferences of personality expression while affective tacit knowledge would be based on the feelings connected with the personality of the decision-maker. For example, if there was a traumatic event that occurred in childhood that produced a feeling of "helplessness," later in life there might be neuronal patterns that are triggered that reproduce this feeling when the adult encounters a similar situation. While these feelings may have been appropriate for the child, they would rarely be of service to a seasoned, intelligent decision-maker.

Descriptive terms for the subconscious include life learning, memory, associative patterning, and material intellect. The subconscious in an autonomic system serving a life-support function (see the discussion of personality in Chapter 4). We all must realize that **the human *subconscious* is in service to the conscious mind**. It is not intended to dominate decision-making. The subconscious expands as it integrates and connects (complexes) all that we put into it through our five external-connected senses. *It is at the conscious mind level that we develop our intellect and make choices that serve as the framework for our subconscious processing.*

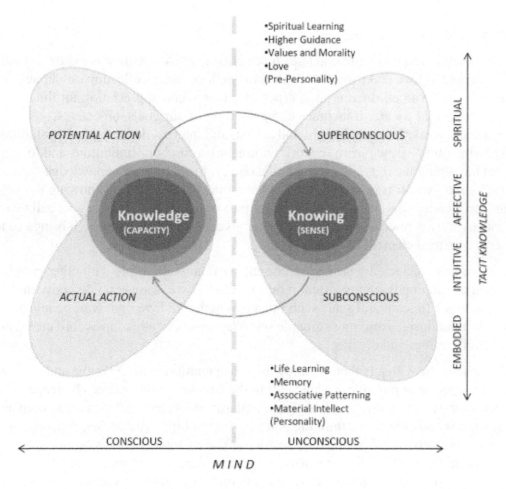

Figure E-1. *The Eternal Loop of Knowledge and Knowing*

Figure E-1 is a nominal graphic showing the continuous feedback loops between knowledge and knowing. Thinking about (potential) and experiencing (actual) effective action (knowledge) supports development of embodied, intuitive and affective tacit knowledges. When we recognize and use our sense of knowing—regardless of its origin—we are tapping into our tacit knowledge to inform our decisions and actions. These decisions and actions, and the feedback from taking those actions, in turn expand our knowledge base, much of which over time will become future tacit resources. Since our internal sense of knowing draws collectively from all areas of our tacit knowledge, the more we open to this inner sense, respond accordingly, and observe and reflect on feedback, the more our inner resources move beyond limited perceptions which may be connected to embedded childhood memories.

Critical Areas of Knowing

The Knowing Framework encompasses three critical areas. The first is "knowing our self," learning to love and trust ourselves. This includes deep reflection on our self in terms of beliefs, values, dreams and purpose for being, and appreciation for the unique beings that we are. It includes understanding of our goals, objectives, strengths and weaknesses in thought and action, and internal defenses and limitations. By knowing ourselves we learn to work within and around our limitations and to support our strengths, thus ensuring that the data, information, and knowledge informing our system is properly identified and interpreted. Further, knowing our self means recognizing that we are social beings, part of the large ecosystem we call Gaia and inextricably connected to other social beings around the world, which brings us to the second critical element: knowing others.

We live in a connected world, spending most of our waking life with other people, and often continuing that interaction in our dreams! There is amazing diversity in the world, so much to learn and share with others. Whether in love or at war, people are always in relationships and must grapple with the sense of "other" in accordance with their beliefs, values and dreams.

The third critical area is that of "knowing" the situation in as objective and realistic a manner as possible, understanding the situation, problem, or challenge in context. In the military this is called situational awareness and includes areas such as culture, goals and objectives, thinking patterns, internal inconsistencies, capabilities, strategies and tactics, and political motivations. The current dynamics of our environment, the multiple forces involved, the complexity of relationships, the many aspects of events that are governed by human emotion, and the unprecedented amount of available data and information make situational awareness a challenging but essential phenomenon in many aspects of our daily lives.

As we move away from predictable patterns susceptible to logic, decision-makers must become increasingly reliant on our "gut" instinct, an internal sense of knowing combined with high situational awareness. Knowing then becomes key to decision-making. The mental skills honed in knowing help decision-makers identify, interpret, make decisions, and take appropriate action in response to current situational assessments.

This construct of knowing can be elevated to the organizational level by using and combining the insights and experiences of individuals through dialogue and collaboration within teams, groups, and communities, both face-to-face and virtual. Such efforts significantly improve the quality of understanding and responsiveness of actions of the organization. They also greatly expand the scope of complex situations that can be handled through knowing because of the greater resources brought to bear—all of this significantly supported by technological interoperability.

Organizational knowing is an aspect of *organizational intelligence*, the capacity of an organization as a whole to gather information, generate knowledge, innovate, and to take effective action. This capacity is the foundation for effective response in a fast-changing and complex world. Increasing our sensory and mental processes contributes to the "positioning" understood by the great strategist Sun Tzu in the year 500 B.C. when he wrote his famous dictum for victory: *Position yourself so there is no battle* (Clavell, 1983). Today in our world of organizations and complex challenges we could say "Position ourselves so there is no confusion."

By exploring our sense of knowing we expand our understanding of ourselves, improve our awareness of the external world, learn how to tap into internal resources, and increase our skills to affect internal and external change. The Knowing Framework provides ideas for developing deep knowledge within the self and sharing that knowledge with others to create new perceptions and levels of understanding. Since each situation and each individual is unique, this Framework does not provide specific answers. Rather, it suggests questions and paths to follow to find those answers.

Principles of Knowing

In response to a changing environment, the Knowing Framework presented below in its expanded form was first developed at the turn of the century for the U.S. Department of the Navy. There are a number of recognized basic truths that drove its development. These truths became the principles upon which the Knowing Framework is based.

(1) Making decisions in an increasingly complex environment requires new ways of thinking.

(2) All the information in the world is useless if the decision-maker who needs it cannot process it and connect it to their own internal values, knowledge, and wisdom.

(3) We don't know all that we know.

(4) Each of us has knowledge far beyond that which is in our conscious mind. Put another way, we know more than we know we know. (Much of our experience and knowledge resides in the unconscious mind.)

(5) By exercising our mental and sensory capabilities we can increase those capabilities.

(6) Support capabilities of organizational knowing include organizational learning, knowledge centricity, common values and language, coherent vision, whole-brain learning, openness of communications, effective collaboration, and the free flow of ideas.

The concept of knowing focuses on the cognitive capabilities of observing and perceiving a situation; the cognitive processing that must occur to understand the external world and make maximum use of our internal cognitive capabilities; and the mechanism for creating deep knowledge and acting on that knowledge via the self as an agent of change. Each of these core areas will be discussed below in more detail.

The Cognitive Capabilities

The cognitive capabilities include observing, collecting and interpreting data and information, and building knowledge relative to the situation. The six areas we will address are: listening, noticing, scanning, sensing, patterning, and integrating. These areas represent means by which we perceive the external world and begin to make sense of it.

Listening

The first area, listening, sets the stage for the other five cognitive capabilities. Listening involves more than hearing; it is a sensing greater than sound. It is a neurological cognitive process involving stimuli received by the auditory system. The linguist Roland Barthes distinguished the difference between hearing and listening when he says: "Hearing is a physiological phenomenon; listening is a psychological act." What this means is that there is a choice involved in listening in terms of the listener choosing to interpret sound waves to potentially create understanding and meaning (Barthes, 1985).There are three levels of listening: alerting, deciphering and understanding. Alerting is picking up on environmental sound cues. Deciphering is relating the sound cues to meaning. Understanding is focused on the impact of the sound on another person. Active listening is intentionally focusing on who is speaking in order to take full advantage of verbal and non-verbal cues.

In developing active listening, imagine how you can use all your senses to focus on what is being said. One way to do this is to role-play, imagining you are in their shoes and feeling the words. Active listening means fully participating, acknowledging the thoughts you are hearing with your body, encouraging the train of thought, actively asking questions when the timing is appropriate. The childhood game of pass the word is an example of a fun way to improve listening skills. A group sits in a circle and whispers a message one to the next until it comes back to the originator. A variation on this theme is Chinese Whispers where a group makes a line and starts a different message from each end, crossing somewhere in the middle and making it to the opposite end before sharing the messages back with the originators. Another good group exercise is a "your turn" exercise, where one individual begins speaking, and another person picks up the topic, and so forth. Not knowing whether you are next in line to speak develops some good listening skills.

The bottom line is that what we don't hear cannot trigger our knowing. Awareness of our environment is not enough. We must listen to the flow of sound and search out meaning, understanding and implications.

Noticing

The second area, noticing, represents the ability to observe around us and recognize, i.e., identify those things that are relevant to our immediate or future needs. We are all familiar with the phenomenon of buying a new car and for the next six months recognizing the large number of similar cars that are on the streets. This is an example of a cognitive process of which we are frequently unaware. We notice those things that are recently in our memory or of emotional or intellectual importance to us. We miss many aspects of our environment if we are not focusing directly on them. Thus, the art of noticing can be considered the art of "knowing" which areas of the environment are important and relevant to us at the moment, and focusing in on those elements and the relationships among those elements. It is also embedding a recall capability of those things not necessarily of immediate importance but representing closely related context factors. *This noticing is a first step in building deep knowledge, developing a thorough understanding and a systems context awareness of those areas of anticipated interest.* This is the start of becoming an expert in a given field of endeavor, or situation.

A classic example of mental exercises aimed at developing latent noticing skills is repetitive observation and recall. For example, think about a room that you are often in, perhaps a colleague's office or a friend's living room. Try to write down everything you can remember about this room. You will discover that despite the fact you've been in this room often, you can't remember exactly where furniture is located, or what's in the corners or on the walls. When you've completed this exercise, visit the room and write down everything you see, everything you've missed. What pictures are on the walls? Do you like them? What personal things in the room tell you something about your colleague or friend? How does the layout of furniture help define the room? (These kinds of questions build relationships with feelings and other thinking patterns.) Write a detailed map and remember it. A few days later repeat this exercise from the beginning. If you make any mistakes, go back to the room again, and as many times as it takes to get it right. Don't let yourself off the hook. You're telling yourself that when details are important you know how to bring them into your memory. As your ability to recall improves, repeat this exercise focusing on a street, a building, or a city you visit often.

Scanning

The third area, scanning, represents the ability to review and survey a large amount of data and information and selectively identify those areas that may be relevant. Because of the exponential increase in data and information, this ability becomes more and more important as time progresses. In a very real sense, scanning represents the ability to reduce the complexity of a situation or environment by objectively filtering out the irrelevant aspects, or environmental noise. By developing your own system of environmental "speed reading," scanning can provide early indicators of change.

Scanning exercises push the mind to pick up details and, more importantly, patterns of data and information, *in a short timeframe*. This is an important skill that law enforcement officers and investigators nurture. For example, when you visit an office or room that you've never been in before, take a quick look around and record your first strong impressions. What feelings are you getting? Count stuff. Look at patterns, look at contrasts, look at colors. Try to pick up everything in one or two glances around the room. Make a mental snapshot of the room and spend a few minutes impressing it in your memory. As you leave, remember the mental picture you've made of the room, the way you feel. Impress upon yourself the importance of remembering this. This picture can last for days, or years, despite the shortness of your visit. Your memory can literally retain an integrated *gestalt* of the room. Realize that what you can recall is only a small part of what went into your mind.

Sensing

The fourth area, sensing, represents the ability to take inputs from the external world through our five external senses and ensure the translation of those inputs into our mind to represent as accurate a transduction process (the transfer of energy from one form to another) as possible. The human ability to collect information through our external sensors is limited because of our physiological limitations. For example, we only see a very small part of the electromagnetic spectrum in terms of light, yet with technology we can tremendously expand the sensing capability. As humans we often take our senses for granted, yet they are highly-sensitized complex detection systems that cause immediate response without conscious thought! An example most everyone has experienced or observed is a mother's sensitivity to any discomfort of her young child. The relevance to "knowing" is, recognizing the importance of our sensory inputs, to learn how to fine tune these inputs to the highest possible level, then use discernment and discretion to interpret them.

Exercise examples cited above to increase noticing, scanning, and patterning skills will also enhance the sense of sight, which is far more than just looking at things. It includes locating yourself in position to things. For example, when you're away from city lights look up on a starry night and explore your way around the heavens. Try to identify the main constellations. By knowing their relative position, you know where you are, what month it is, and can even approximate the time of day. The stars provide context for positioning yourself on the earth.

Here are a few exercise examples for other senses. Hearing relates to comprehension. Sit on a park bench, close your eyes and relax, quieting your mind. Start by listening to what is going on around you---conversations of passersby, cars on a nearby causeway, the birds chattering, the wind rustling leaves, water trickling down a nearby drain. Now stretch beyond these nearby sounds. Imagine you have the hearing of a panther, only multidirectional, because you can move your ears every direction and search for sounds. Focus on a faint sound in the distance, then ask your auditory systems to bring it closer. Drag that sound toward you mentally. It gets louder. If you cup one hand behind one ear and cup the other hand in front of the opposite ear, you can actually improve your hearing, focusing on noises from the back with one ear and noises from the front with the other. How does that change what you are hearing?

Next time you are in a conversation with someone, focus your eyes and concentrate on the tip of their nose or the point of their chin. Listen carefully to every word they say, to the pause between their words, to their breathing and sighs, the rise and fall of their voice. Search for the inflections and subtle feelings being communicated behind what is actually being said. When people are talking, much of the meaning behind the information they impart is in their feelings. The words they say are only a representation, a descriptive code that communicates thought, interacting electrical pulses and flows influenced by an emotion or subtle feeling. By listening in this way, with your visual focus not distracting your auditory focus, you can build greater understanding of the subtleties behind the words.

There are many games that accentuate the sense of touch. An old favorite is blind man's bluff; more current is the use of blindfolding and walking through the woods used in outdoor management programs. Try this at home by spending three or four hours blindfolded, going about your regular home activities. At first, you'll stumble and bump, maybe even become frustrated. But as you continue, your ability to manage your movements and meet your needs using your sense of touch will quickly improve. You will be able to move about your home alone with relatively little effort, and you'll know where things are, especially things that are alive, such as plants and pets. You will develop the ability to *feel* their energy. Such exercises as these force your unconscious mind to create, re-create, and surface the imagined physical world. It activates the mind to bring out into the open its sensitivity to the physical context in which we live.

Patterning

The fifth area, patterning, represents the ability to review, study, and interpret large amounts of data/events/information and identify causal or correlative connections that are relatively stable over time or space and may represent patterns driven by underlying phenomena. These hidden drivers can become crucial to understanding the situation or the enemy behavior. This would also include an understanding of rhythm and randomness, flows and trends. Recall the importance of structure, relationships, and culture in creating emergent phenomena (patterns) and in influencing complex systems.

A well-known example of the use of patterning is that of professional card players and successful gamblers, who have trained themselves to repeatedly recall complicated patterns found in randomly drawn cards. To learn this skill, and improve your patterning skills, take a deck of cards and quickly flip through the deck three or four at a time. During this process, make a mental picture of the cards that are in your hand, pause, then turn over three or four more. After doing this several times, recall the mental picture of the first set of cards. What were they? Then try to recall the second set, then the third.

The secret is not to try and remember the actual cards, but to close your eyes and recall the mental picture of the cards. Patterns will emerge. After practicing for awhile, you will discover your ability to recall the patterns---as well as your ability to recall larger numbers of patterns---will steadily increase. As you increase the number of groups of cards you can recall, and increase the number of cards within each group, you are increasing your ability to recall complex patterns.

Study many patterns found in nature, art, science, and other areas of human endeavor. These patterns will provide you with a "mental reference library" that your mind can use to detect patterns in new situations. Chess experts win games on pattern recognition and pattern creation, not on individual pieces

Integrating

The last area in the cognitive capabilities is integration. This represents the top-level capacity to take large amounts of data and information and pull them together to create meaning; this is frequently called sense-making. This capability, to pull together the major aspects of a complex situation and create patterns, relationships, models, and meaning that represent reality is what enables us to make decisions. This capability also applies to the ability to integrate internal organization capabilities and systems.

While we have used the word "integrating" to describe this capability, recall that the human mind is an associative patterner that is continuously complexing (mixing) incoming information from the external environment with all that is stored in memory. Thus, while the decision-maker has an awareness of integrating, the unconscious is doing much of the work and providing nudges in terms of feelings and speculative thought. Our unconscious is forever our partner, working 24/7 for us.

These five ways of observing represent the front line of cognitive capabilities needed to assist all of us in creative and accurate situational awareness and building a valid understanding of situations. To support these cognitive capabilities, we then need processes that transform these observations and this first-level knowledge into a deeper level of comprehension and understanding.

The Cognitive Processes

Internal cognitive processes that support the capabilities discussed above include visualizing, intuiting, valuing, choosing, and setting intent. These five internal cognitive processes greatly improve our power to understand the external world and to make maximum use of our internal thinking capabilities, transforming our observations into understanding.

Visualizing

The first of these processes, visualizing, represents the methodology of focusing attention on a given area and through imagination and logic creating an internal vision and scenario for success. In developing a successful vision, one must frequently take several different perspectives of the situation, play with a number of assumptions underlying these perspectives, and through a playful trial-and-error, come up with potential visions. This process is more creative than logical, more intuitive than rational, and wherever possible should be challenged, filtered, and constructed in collaboration with other competent individuals. Often this is done between two trusting colleagues or perhaps with a small team. While there is never absolute assurance that visualizing accurately represents reality, there are probabilities or degrees of success that can be recognized and developed

Intuiting

The second supporting area is that of intuiting. By this we mean the art of making maximum use of our own intuition developed through experience, trial-and-error, and deliberate internal questioning and application. There are standard processes available for training oneself to surface intuition. Recognize that intuition is typically understood as being the ability to access our unconscious mind and thereby make effective use of its very large storeroom of observations, experiences, and information. In our framework, intuition is one of the four ways tacit knowledge expresses.

Empathy represents another aspect of intuition. Empathy is interpreted as the ability to take oneself out of oneself and put oneself into another person's world. In other words, as the old Native American saying goes, "Until you walk a mile in his moccasins, you will never understand the person." The ability to empathize permits us to translate our personal perspective into that of another, thereby understanding their interpretation of the situation and intuiting their actions. A tool that can be used to trigger ideas and dig deeper into one's intuitive capability, bringing out additional insights, is "mind mapping." Mind mapping is a tool to visually display and recognize relationships from discrete and diverse pieces of information and data (Wycoff, 1991).

Valuing

Valuing represents the capacity to observe situations and recognize the values that underly their various aspects and concomitantly be fully aware of your own values and beliefs. A major part of valuing is the ability to align your vision, mission, and goals to focus attention on the immediate situation at hand. A second aspect represents the ability to identify the relevant but unknown aspects of a situation or competitor's behavior. Of course, the problem of unknown unknowns always exists in a turbulent environment and, while logically they are impossible to identify because by definition they are unknown, there are techniques available that help one reduce the area of known unknowns and hence reduce the probability of them adversely affecting the organization.

A third aspect of valuing is that of meaning, that is, understanding the important aspects of the situation and being able to prioritize them to anticipate potential consequences. Meaning is contingent upon the goals and aspirations of the individual. It also relies on the history of both the individual's experience and the context of the situation. Determining the meaning of a situation allows us to understand its impact on our own objectives and those of our organization. Knowing the meaning of something lets us prioritize our actions and estimate the resources we may need to deal with it.

Choosing

The fourth supporting area is that of choosing. Choosing involves making judgments, that is, conclusions and interpretations developed through the use of rules-of-thumb, facts, knowledge, experiences, emotions and intuition. While not necessarily widely recognized, judgments are used far more than logic or rational thinking in making decisions. This is because all but the simplest decisions occur in a context in which there is insufficient, noisy, or perhaps too much information to make rational conclusions. Judgment makes maximum use of heuristics, meta-knowing, and verication.

Heuristics represent the rules-of-thumb developed over time and through experience in a given field. They are shortcuts to thinking that are applicable to specific situations. Their value is speed of conclusions and their usefulness rests on consistency of the environment and repeatability of situations. Thus, they are both powerful and dangerous. Dangerous because the situation or environment, when changing, may quickly invalidate former reliable heuristics and historically create the phenomenon of always solving the last problem; yet powerful because they represent efficient and rapid ways of making decisions where the situation is known and the heuristics apply.

Meta-knowing is knowing about knowing, that is, understanding how we know things and how we go about knowing things. With this knowledge, one can more effectively go about learning and knowing in new situations as they evolve over time. Such power and flexibility greatly improve the quality of our choices. Meta-knowing is closely tied to our natural internal processes of learning and behaving as well as knowing how to make the most effective use of available external data, information, and knowledge and intuit that which is not available. An interesting aspect of meta-knowing is the way that certain errors in judgment are common to many people. Just being aware of these mistakes can reduce their occurrence. For example, we tend to give much more weight to specific, concrete information than to conceptual or abstract information. (See Kahneman et al., 1982, for details.)

Verication is the process by which we can improve the probability of making good choices by working with trusted others and using *their* experience and knowing to validate and improve the level of our judgmental effectiveness. Again, this could be done via a trusted colleague or through effective team creativity and decision-making.

Setting Intent

Intent is a powerful internal process that can be harnessed by every person. Intention is the source with which we are doing something, the act or instance of mentally setting some course of action or result, a determination to act in some specific way. It can take the form of a declaration (often in the form of action), an assertion, a prayer, a cry for help, a wish, visualization, a thought or an affirmation. Perhaps the most in-depth and focused experimentation on the effects of human intention on the properties of materials and what we call physical reality has been that pursued for the past 40 years by Dr. William Tiller of Stanford University. Tiller has proven through repeated experimentation that it is possible to significantly change the properties (ph) of water by holding a clear intention to do so. His mind-shifting and potentially world-changing results began with using intent to change the acid/alkaline balance in purified water. The ramifications of this experiment have the potential to impact every aspect of human life.

What Tiller has discovered is that there are two unique levels of physical reality. The "normal level" of substance is the electric/atom/molecule level, what most of us think of and perceive as the only physical reality. However, a second level of substance exists that is the magnetic information level. While these two levels always interpenetrate each other, under "normal" conditions they do not interact; they are "uncoupled." Intention changes this condition, causing these two levels to interact, or move into a "coupled" state. Where humans are concerned, Tiller says that what an individual intends for himself with a strong sustained desire is what that individual will eventually become (Tiller, 2007).

While informed by Spiritual, the Embodied, Intuitive and Affective tacit knowledges are *local expressions of knowledge*, that is, directly related to our expression in physical reality in a specific situation and context. Connecting Tiller's model of intention with our model of tacit knowledge, it begins to become clear that effective intent relates to an alignment of the conscious mind with the tacit components of the mind and body, that is Embodied, Intuitive, and Affective tacit knowledge. We have to *know* it, *feel* it, and *believe* it to achieve the coupling of the electric/atom/molecule level and magnetic information level of physical reality.

As we use our power of intent to co-create our future, it is necessary to focus from outcome to intention, not worrying about what gets done but staying focused on what you are doing and how you "feel" about what you are doing. Are we in alignment with the direction our decisions are taking us? If not, back to the drawing board— that's looking closer at you, the decision-maker, and ensuring that your vision is clear and your intent is aligned with that vision.

In summary, the five internal cognitive processes—visualizing, intuiting, valuing, choosing and setting intent—work with the six cognitive capabilities— listening, noticing, scanning, patterning, sensing, and integrating—to process data and information and create knowledge within the context of the environment and the situation. However, this knowledge must always be suspect because of our own self-limitations, internal inconsistencies, historical biases, and emotional distortions, all of which are discussed in the third area of knowing: the Self as an Agent of Change.

The Self as an Agent of Change

The third area of the knowing framework—the self as an agent of change—is the mechanism for creating deep knowledge, a level of understanding consistent with the external world and our internal framework. As the unconscious continuously associates information, the self as an agent of change takes the emergent deep knowledge and uses it for the dual purpose of our personal learning and growth, and for making changes in the external world.

Recall that deep knowledge consists of beliefs, facts, truths, assumptions, and understanding of an area that is so thoroughly embedded in the mind that we are often not consciously aware of the knowledge. To create deep knowledge an individual has to "live" with it, continuously interacting, thinking, learning, and experiencing that part of the world until the knowledge truly becomes a natural part of the inner being. An example would be that a person who has a good knowledge of a foreign language can speak it fluently; a person with a deep knowledge would be able to think in the language without any internal translation and would not need their native language to understand that internal thinking.

In the discussion of self as an agent of change, there are ten elements that will be presented. Five of these elements are internal: know thyself, mental models, emotional intelligence, learning and forgetting, and mental defenses; and five of these elements are external: modeling behaviors, knowledge sharing, dialogue, storytelling, and the art of persuasion

Internal Elements

Alexander Pope, in his essay on man (1732-3/1994), noted that: "Know then thyself, presume not God to scan; the proper study of mankind is man." We often think we know ourselves, but we rarely do. To really understand our own biases, perceptions, capabilities, etc., each of us must look inside and, as objectively as possible, ask ourselves, who are we, what are our limitations, what are our strengths, and what jewels and baggage do we carry from our years of experience. Rarely do we *take ourselves out of ourselves and look at ourselves*. But without an objective understanding of our own values, beliefs, and biases, we are continually in danger of misunderstanding the interpretations we apply to the external world. Our motives, expectations, decisions, and beliefs are frequently driven by internal forces of which we are completely unaware. For example, our emotional state plays a strong role in determining how we make decisions and what we decide.

The first step in knowing ourselves is awareness of the fact that we cannot assume we are what our conscious mind thinks we are. Two examples that most of us have experienced come to mind. The first is that we frequently do not know what we think until we hear what we say. The second example is the recognition that every act of writing is an act of creativity. Our biases, prejudices, and even brilliant ideas frequently remain unknown to us until pointed out by others or through conversations. Consciousness is our window to the world, but it is clouded by an internal history, experiences, feelings, memories, and desires.

After awareness comes the need to constantly monitor ourselves for undesirable traits or biases in our thinking, feeling, and processing. Seeking observations from others and carefully analyzing our individual experiences are both useful in understanding ourselves. We all have limitations and strengths, and even agendas hidden from our conscious mind that we must be aware of and build upon or control.

Part of knowing ourselves is the understanding of what mental models we have formed in specific areas of the external world. Mental models are the models we use to represent our own picture of reality. They are built up over time and through experience and represent our beliefs, assumptions, and ways of interpreting the outside world. They are efficient in that they allow us to react quickly to changing conditions and make rapid decisions based upon our presupposed model. Concomitantly, they are dangerous if the model is inaccurate or misleading.

Because we exist in a rapidly changing environment, many of our models quickly become outdated. We then must recognize the importance of continuously reviewing our perceptions and assumptions of the external world and questioning our own mental models to ensure they are consistent with reality (Senge, 1990). Since this is done continuously in our subconscious, we must always question ourselves as to our real, versus stated, motives, goals and feelings. *Only then can we know who we are, only then can we change to who we want to be.*

The art of knowing not only includes understanding our own mental models, but the ability to recognize and deal with the mental models of others. Mental models frequently serve as drivers for our actions as well as our interpretations. When creating deep knowledge or taking action, the use of small groups, dialogue, etc. to normalize mental models with respected colleagues provides somewhat of a safeguard against the use of incomplete or erroneous mental models.

A subtle but powerful factor underlying mental models is the role of emotions in influencing our perception of reality. This has been extensively explored by Daniel Goleman (1995) in his seminal book *Emotional Intelligence*. Emotional intelligence is the ability to sense, understand, and effectively apply the power and acumen of emotions as a source of human energy, information, connection, and influence. It includes self-control, zeal and persistence, and the ability to motivate oneself. To understand emotional intelligence, we study how emotions affect behavior, influence decisions, motivate people to action, and impact their ability to interrelate. Emotions play a much larger role in our lives than previously understood, including a strong role in decision-making. For years it was widely held that rationality was the way of the executive. Now it is becoming clear that the rational and the emotional parts of the mind must be used together to get the best performance in organizations.

Much of emotional life is unconscious. Awareness of emotions occurs when the emotions enter the frontal cortex. As affective tacit knowledge, emotions in the subconscious play a powerful role in how we perceive and act, and hence in our decision-making. Feelings come from the limbic part of the brain and often come forth before the related experiences occur. *They represent a signal* that a given potential action may be wrong, or right, or that an external event may be dangerous. Emotions assign values to options or alternatives, sometimes without our knowing it. There is growing evidence that fundamental ethical stances in life stem from underlying emotional capacities. These stances create the basic belief system, the values, and often the underlying assumptions that we use to see the world—our mental model. From this short treatment of the concept, it is clear that emotional intelligence is interwoven across the ten elements of the self as an agent of change. (See Goleman, 1995 and 1998.)

Creating the deep knowledge of knowing through the effective use of emotional intelligence opens the door to two other equally important factors: learning and forgetting. Learning and letting go—in terms of "filing" away or putting away on the bookshelf—are critical elements of the self as an agent of change because they are the primary processes through which we change and grow. They are also the prerequisite for continuous learning, so essential for developing competencies representing all of the processes and capabilities discussed previously. Because the environment is highly dynamic and will continue to become more complex, continuous learning will be more and more essential and critical in keeping up with the world.

Since humans have limited processing capability and the mind is easily overloaded and tends to cling to its past experiences and knowledge, "letting go" becomes as important as learning. Letting go is the art of being able to let go of what was known and true in the past. Being able to recognize the limitations and inappropriateness of past assumptions, beliefs, and knowledge is essential before creating new mental models and for understanding ourselves as we grow. It is *one of the hardest acts of the human mind* because it threatens our self-image and may shake even our core belief systems.

The biggest barrier to learning and letting go arises from our own individual ability to develop invisible defenses against changing our beliefs. These self-imposed mental defenses have been eloquently described by Chris Argyris (1990). The essence of his conclusion is that the mind creates built-in defense mechanisms to support belief systems and experience. These defense mechanisms are invisible to the individual and may be quite difficult to expose in a real-world situation. They are a widespread example of not knowing what we know, thus representing invisible barriers to change. Several authors have estimated that information and knowledge double approximately every nine months. If this estimate is even close, the problems of saturation will continue to make our ability to acquire deep knowledge even more challenging. We must learn how to filter data and information through vision, values, experiences, goals, and purposes using an open mind, intuition and judgment as our tools. This discernment and discretion within the deepest level of our minds provides a proactive aspect of filtering, thereby setting up purposeful mental defenses that reduce complexity and provide conditional safeguards to an otherwise open system. This is a fundamental way in which the self can simplify a situation by eliminating extraneous and undesirable information and knowledge coming from the external world.

The above discussion has identified a number of factors that can help us achieve an appropriate balance between change and our resistance to change. This is an important attribute: not all change is for the best, yet rigidity begets antiquity. This balance is situational and comes only from experience, learning, and a deep sense of knowing when to change and when not to change the self.

This section has addressed the self as an agent of change through internal recognition of certain factors that can influence self-change. Another aspect of change is the ability of the self to influence or change the external world. This is the active part of knowing. Once the self has attained deep knowledge and understanding of the situation and external environment, this must be shared with others, accompanied by the right actions to achieve success. We live in a connected world.

External Elements

The challenge becomes that of translating knowledge into behavior, thus creating the ability to model that behavior and influence others toward taking requisite actions. Role-modeling has always been a prime responsibility of leadership in the government as well as the civilian world. Having deep knowledge of the situation the individual must then translate that into personal behavior that becomes a role model for others to follow and become motivated and knowledgeable about how to act. Effective role-modeling does not require the learner to have the same deep knowledge as the role model, yet the actions and behaviors that result may reflect the equivalent deep knowledge and over time creates deep knowledge in the learner—but only in specific situations. This is how you share the effectiveness from learning and thereby transfer implicit knowledge.

Wherever possible, of course, it is preferable to develop and share as much knowledge as possible so that others can act independently and develop their own internally and situation-driven behavior. This is the reason Knowledge Management and communities of practice and interest require management attention. Since most deep knowledge is tacit, knowledge sharing can become a real challenge.

A third technique for orchestrating external change is through the use of dialogue. Dialogue is a process described by David Bohm (1992) to create a situation in which a group participates as coequals in inquiring and learning about some specific topic. In essence, the group creates a common understanding and shared perception of a given situation or topic. Dialogue is frequently viewed as the collaborative sharing and development of understanding. It can include both inquiry and discussions, but all participants must suspend judgment and not seek specific outcomes and answers. The process stresses the examination of underlying assumptions and listening deeply to the self and others to develop a collective meaning. This collective meaning is perhaps the best way in which a common understanding of a situation may be developed as a group and understood by others.

Another way of creating change and sharing understanding is through the effective use of the time-honored process of storytelling. Storytelling is a valuable tool in helping to build a common understanding of our current situation in anticipating possible futures and preparing to act on those possible futures. Stories tap into a universal consciousness that is natural to all human communities. Repetition of common story forms carries a subliminal message, a subtext that can help convey a deep level of complex meaning. Since common values enable consistent action, Story in this sense provides a framework that aids decision-making under conditions of uncertainty.

Modeling behavior, knowledge sharing, dialogue, and storytelling are all forms of building understanding and knowledge. Persuasion, our fifth technique, serves to communicate and share understanding with others who have a specific conviction or belief and/or to get them to act upon it. To change the external environment, we need to be persuasive and to communicate the importance and need for others to take appropriate action. The question arises: When you have deep knowledge, what aspects of this can be used to effectively influence other's behavior? Since deep knowledge is tacit knowledge, we must learn how to transfer this to explicit knowledge. Nonaka and Tageuchi (1995) and Polyani (1958) have done seminal work in this area. Persuasion, as seen from the perspective of the self, gets us back to the importance of using all of our fundamental values, such as personal example, integrity, honesty, and openness to help transfer our knowing to others.

As can be seen in the discussion above, **all four forms of tacit knowledge inform knowing**. The Knowing Framework seeks to engage our senses and hone our internal processing mechanisms to take full advantage of our minds/brains/bodies. By bringing our focus on knowing, we have the opportunity to move through relational, experiential, and cultural barriers that somewhere along the course of our lives have been constructed, and sometimes self imposed. This, however, is not the case for many of the young decision-makers moving into the workplace.

[Excerpted from Bennet and Bennet (2013)].

Endnotes

3-1. The Mountain Quest Institute, a research and retreat center located in the Allegheny Mountains of West Virginia, is located in the 40-mile radius surrounding the National Radio Astronomy Observatory in Greenbank, West Virginia. By law, cell phone towers are not allowed in this area. Thus, to date, it has proven a desirable location for individuals with IEI-EMF.

3-2. The term "incluessence" was coined by Jo Dunning (August 12, 2015, email to Alex). Jo talks about "True Incluessence" as the state of our Being that is far beyond the small drop of possibility we have come to accept as true. In our usage, we infer a future state that is far beyond that which we know to dream.

5-1. There are many scientists that have electromagnetic theories which are congruent. These would include: Harold Saxton Burr (Electric Fields of Life); Hameroff and Penrose (Orchestrated Reduction or Orch-OR); E. Roy John (Electromagnetic Information field); Ervin László (Akashic or A-Field); Benjamin Libet (Conscious Mental Field); Jibu and Yasue (Quantum Brain Dynamics); Johnjoe McFadden (CEMI Field Theory—CEMI is Conscious Electromagnetic Information); Michael Persinger (Electromagnetic Consciousness); Susan Pockett (EMF Field Theory—EMF is Electromagnetic Field); Hermes Romjin (EMF Photon Theory—EMF is Electromagnetic Field); Rupert Sheldrake (Morphic Fields/Morphic resonance); and William Tiller (K*Space).

6-1. The example of the application of the AUBFOE Individual Change Model used as impact factors to assess the level of change was developed by Chulatep Senivansa Na Ayudhaya, a committed Ph.D. student nearing completion of the program at Bangkok University Institute for Knowledge and Innovation Management.

References

Adolfs, R. (2004). "Processing of Emotional and Social Information by the Human Amygdala" in Gazzaniga, M.S. (Ed.), *The Cognitive Neurosciences III*. Cambridge, MA: The Bradford Press.

American Heritage Dictionary of the English Language (4th ed.) (2006). Boston: Houghton Mifflin Company.

Andreasen, N. (2005). *The Creating Brain: The Neuroscience of Genius*. New York: The Dana Foundation.

Anderson, J.R. (1983). *The Architecture of Cognition*. Cambridge, MA: Harvard University Press.

Argyris, C. (1990). *Overcoming Organizational Defenses: Facilitating Organizational Learning*. Englewood Cliffs, NJ: Prentice Hall.

Argyris, C. and Schon, D. (1978). *Organizational Learning: A Theory of Action Perspective*. Reading, MA: Addison-Wesley.

Atwater, F.H. (2004). *The Hemi-Sync Process*. Faber, VA: The Monroe Institute.

Axelrod, R. and Cohen, M.D. (1999). *Harnessing Complexity: Organizational Implications of a Scientific Frontier*. New York: The Free Press.

Barthes, R. (1985). *In the Responsibility of Forms*. New York: Hill and Wang.

Bateson, G. (1972). *Steps to an Ecology of the Mind*. New York: Ballantine.

Battram, A. (1996). *Navigating Complexity: The Essential Guide to Complexity Theory in Business and Management*. Sterling, VA: The Industrial Society.

Begley, S., (2007). *Train Your Mind Change Your Brain: How a New Science Reveals Our Extraordinary Potential to Transform Ourselves*. New York: Ballantine Books.

Bennet, A. and Bennet, D. (2013). *Decision-Making in The New Reality*. Frost, WV: MQIPress.

Bennet, A. and Bennet, D. (2010a). "Multidimensionality: Building the Mind/Brain Infrastructure for the Next Generation Knowledge Worker" in *On the Horizon*, Vol. 18, No. 3, 240-254.

Bennet, A. and Bennet, D. (2010b). "Leaders, Decisions and the Neuro-Knowledge System" in Wallis, S., *Cybernetics and Systems Theory in Management: Tools, Views and Advancements*. Hershey, PA: IGI Global

Bennet, A. and Bennet, D. (2008a). "The Depth of Knowledge: Surface, Shallow, or Deep?" in *VINE: The Journal of Information and Knowledge Management Systems,* Vol. 38, No. 4, 405-420.

Bennet, A. and Bennet, D. (2008b). "The Decision-Making Process for Complex Situations in a Complex Environment" in Burstein, F. and Holsapple, C.W. (Eds.), *Handbook on Decision Support Systems 1*, 2-20. New York: Springer-Verlag.

Bennet, A. and Bennet, D. (2008c). "The Fallacy of Knowledge Reuse" in *Journal of Knowledge Management*, 12(5), 21-33.

Bennet, A. and Bennet, D. (2008d). "Moving from Knowledge to Wisdom, from Ordinary Consciousness to Extraordinary Consciousness" in *VINE: Journal of Information and Knowledge Systems*, Vol. 38, No. 1, 7-15.

Bennet, A. and Bennet, D. (2007a). "CONTEXT: The Shared Knowledge Enigma" in *VINE: Journal of Information and Knowledge Systems*, Vol. 37, No. 1, 27-40.

Bennet, A. and Bennet, D. (2007b). *Knowledge Mobilization in the Social Sciences and Humanities: Moving From Research To Action*. MQIPress, Frost, WV.

Bennet, A. and Bennet, D. (2007c). "The Knowledge and Knowing of Spiritual Learning" in *VINE: The Journal of Information and Knowledge Management Systems*, 37 (2), 150-168.

Bennet, A. & Bennet, D. (2004). *Organizational Survival in the New World: The Intelligent Complex Adaptive System*. Boston, MA: Elsevier.

Bennet, A., Bennet, D. and Avedisian, J. (2015a). *The Course of Knowledge: A 21st Century Theory*. Frost, WV: MQIPress.

Bennet, A., Bennet, D. and Lewis, J. (2015c). *Leading with the Future in Mind: Knowledge and Emergent Leadership*. Frost, WV: MQIPress.

Bennet, D. (2001), "Loosening the World Knot", unpublished paper available at www.mountainquestinstitute.com

Bennet, D., Bennet, A. and Turner, R. (2015b). *Expanding the Self: The Intelligent Complex Adaptive Learning System*. Frost, WV: MQI Press.

Bennet, D. and Bennet, A. (2008e). "Engaging Tacit Knowledge in Support of Organizational Learning" in *VINE: Journal of Information and Knowledge Systems,* 38(1), 72-94.

Berman, M. (1981). *The Reenchantment of the World*. Ithaca, NY: Cornell University Press.

Blackmore, S. (2004). *Consciousness: An introduction*. New York: Oxford University Press.

Bohm, D. (1992). *Thought as a System*. New York: Routledge.

Bohm, D. (1980). *Wholeness and the Implicate Order*. London: Routledge & Kegal.

Bownds, M. D. (1999). *The Biology of Mind: Origins and Structures of Mind, Brain, and Consciousness*. Bethesda, MD: Fitzgerald Science Press.

Buchanan, M. (2004, Spring). "Power Laws and the New Science of Complexity Management" in *Strategy + Business, 34*, 70-79.

Buks, E., Schuster, R. Heiblum, M., Mahalu, D and Umansky, V. (1998). "Dephasing in Electron Interference by a 'Which-Path' Detector" in *Nature* (Vol. 391) (February 26), 871-874.

Buss, D.M. (1999). "Human Nature and individual Differences: The Evolution of Human Personality" in Pervin, L.A. and John, O.P. (Eds.), *Handbook of Personality: Theory and Research* (2nd Ed.). New York/London: The Gilford Press.

Byrnes, J. P. (2001). *Minds, Brains, and Learning: Understanding the Psychological and Educational Relevance of Neuroscientific Research*. New York: The Guilford Press.

Carroll, S. (2016). *The Big Picture: On the Origins of Life, Meaning, and the Universe Itself*. New York: Dutton.

Caspi, A. and Roberts, B.W. (1999). "Personality Continuity and Change across the Life Course" in Pervin, L.A. and John, O.P. (Eds.), *Handbook of Personality: Theory and Research* (2nd Ed.). New York/London: The Gilford Press.

Chalmers, D. (1999). *The Scientific American Book of the Brain*. New York: The Lyons Press

Chickering, A.W., Dalton, J.C. and Stamm, L. (2005). *Encouraging Authenticity & Spirituality in Higher Education*. San Francisco: Jossey-Bass.

Clavell, J. (Ed.) (1983). *The Art of War: Sun Tzu*. New York: Dell Publishing.

Collinge, W. (1998). *Where Ancient Wisdom and Modern Science Meet ... Subtle Energy: Awakening to the Unseen forces in Our Lives*. New York: Warner Books.

Conner, D.R. (1998). *Leading at the Edge of Chaos: How to Create the Nimble Organization*. New York: John Wiley & Sons, Inc.

Cooper, R. (2005). "Austinian Truth, Attitudes and Type Theory" in *Research on Language and Computation* 5: 333-362.

Cozolino, L., and Sprokay, S. (2006). "Neuroscience and Adult Learning" in Johnson, S. and Taylor, T. (Eds.), *The Neuroscience of Adult Learning*. San Francisco: Jossey-Bass, 11-19.

Crandall, B. Klein, G. and Hoffman, R.R. (2006). *Working Minds: A Practitioner's Guide to Cognitive Task Analysis*. Cambridge, MA: The MIT Press.

Crowley, V. (1999). *Jung: A Journey of Transformation*. Wheaton, IL: Quest Books.

Csikszentmihalyi, M. (1993). *The Evolving Self: A Psychology for the Third Millennium*. New York: HarperCollins Publishing.

Csikszentmihalyi, M. and Csikszentmihalyi, I.S. (Eds.) (1988). *Optimal Experience: Psychological Studies of Flow in Consciousness*. New York: Cambridge University Press.

Damasio, A.R. (2010). *Self Comes to Mind: Constructing the Conscious Brain*. New York: Vintage Books.

Damasio, A. R. (1994). *Descartes' Error: Emotion, Reason, and the Human Brain*. New York: G.P. Putnam's Sons.

Darwin, C. (1998). *The Descent of Man*. Amherst, NY: Prometheus Books.

Delmonte, M.M. (1984). "Electrocortical Activity and Related Phenomena Associated with Meditation Practice: A Literature Review" in *International Journal of Neuroscience*, 24: 217-231.

Dilts, R. (2003). *From Coach to Awakener*. Capitola, CA: Meta Publications.

Dobbs, D. (2007). "Turning Off Depression" in F. E. Bloom (Ed.), *Best of the Brain from Scientific American: Mind, Matter, and Tomorrow's Brain*. New York: Dana Press, 169-178.

Dunning, J. (2014). Discussion of consciousness via the Internet on December 13.

Edelman, G. and Tononi, G. (2000). *A Universe of Consciousness: How Matter Becomes Imagination*. New York: Basic Books.

Eilan, N.(1995). "Consciousness and the Self" in Bermudez, J.L., Marcel, A. and Eilan, N., *The Body and the Self*. Cambridge, MA: MIT Press.

Eldredge, N. and Gould, S.J. (1972). "Punctuated Equilibria: An Alternative to Phyletic Gradualism" in Schopf, TJM Freeman (Ed.), *Models in Paleobiology*. San Francisco: Cooper & Co, 82-115.

Ellinor, L. and Gerard, G. (1998). *Dialogue: Rediscover the Transforming Power of Conversation*. New York: John Wiley & Sons, Inc.

Encarta World English Dictionary (1999). New York: St Martin's Press.

Ericsson, K.A., Charness, N., Feltovich, P.J. and Hoffman, R.R. (Eds.) (2006). *The Cambridge Handbook of Expertise and Expert Performance*. New York: Cambridge University Press.

Fine, G. (2003). Introduction in Plato on *Knowledge and Forms: Selected essays*. New York: Oxford University Press.

Fischer, R. (1971). "A Cartography of Ecstatic and Meditative States" in *Science,* 174 (4012), 897-904.

Forrester, J. (1994). Personal communication with D. Porter, D. Bennet and A. Bennet.

Gazzaniga, M.S. (2008). *Human: The Science Behind What Makes Us Unique*. New York: HarperCollins.

Gazzaniga, M.S. (Ed.) (2004). *The Cognitive Neurosciences III*. Cambridge, MA: The MIT Press.

Gell-Mann, M. (1994). *The Quark and the Jaguar: Adventures in the Simple and the Complex*. NY: W.H.Freeman and Company.

Gettier, E. L. (1963). "Is Justified True Belief Knowledge?" in *Oxford Journals*, Oxford University Press. Retrieved 04/04/14 from http://rintintin.colorado.edu/~vancecd/phil1000/Gettier.pdf

Gibson, J.J. (1979). *The Ecological Approach to Visual Perception*. Boston: Houghton Mifflin.

Gladwell, M. (2005). *Blink: The Power of Thinking without Thinking*. New York: Little, Brown.

Gladwell, M. (2000). *The Tipping Point: How Little Things Can Make a Big Difference*. Boston: Little, Brown.

Glasser, W. (1998). *Choice Theory: A New Psychology of Personal Freedom*. New York: HarperCollins.

Goldberg, E. (2005). *The Wisdom Paradox: How Your Mind Can Grow Stronger as Your Brain Grows Older*. New York: Gotham Books.

Goldstein, K. (1939). *The Organism*. New York: American Book Co.

Goleman, D. (1998). "What Makes a Leader?" in *Harvard Business Review*, 93-102.

Goleman, D. (1995). *Emotional Intelligence*. New York: Bantam Books.

Haberlandt, K. (1998). *Human Memory: Exploration and Application*. Boston, MA: Allyn & Bacon.

Hawkins, D.R. (2002). *Power VS Force: The Hidden Determinants of Human Behavior*. Carlsbad, CA: Hay House.

Hodgkin, R. (1991). "Michael Polanyi—Profit of Life, the Universe, and Everything" in *Times Higher Educational Supplement*, September 27, 15.

James, W. (1890/1980). *The Principles of Psychology* (Vol. I.). New York: Holt, Rinehar & Winston.

Jensen, E. (2006). *Enriching the Brain: How to Maximize Every Learners Potential*. San Francisco, CA: Jossey-Bass.

Jensen, E. (1998). *Teaching with the Brain in Mind*. Alexandria, VA: Association for Supervision and Curriculum Development.

Jevning, R., Wallace, R.K., and Beidenbach, M. (1992). "The Physiology of Meditation: A Review" in *Neuroscience and Behavioral Reviews*, 16, 415-424.

Johnson, S. (2001). *Emergence*. New York: Scribner.

Jung, K. and Adler, G. (1972). Two Essays on Analytical Psychology (Collected Works of C.J. Jung Vol 7). Princeton, NJ: Princeton University Press.

Kahneman, D., P. Slovic and Tversky, A. (1982). *Judgment Under Uncertainty: Heuristics and Biases*. New York: Cambridge University Press

Kaku, M. (1997). *Visions*. New York: Anchor Books, Doubleday.

Kandel, E. R. (2006). *In Search of Memory: The Emergence of a New Science of Mind*. New York: W.W. Norton & Company.

Kelzer, K. (1987). *The Sun and the Shadow: My Experiment with Lucid Dreaming*. Virginia Beach: ARE Press.

Kirsner, K., Speelman, C., Maybery, M., O'Brien-Malone, A., Anderson, M. and MacLeod, C. (Eds.). (1998). *Implicit and Explicit Mental Processes*. Mahwah, NJ: Lawrence Erlbaum Associates, Publishers.

Klivington, K. (1989). *The Science of the Mind*. Cambridge, MA: MIT Press.

Kolb, D. A. (1984). *Experiential Learning: Experience as the Source of Learning and Development*. New Jersey: Prentice-Hall.

Konner, M. (1990). "Human Nature and Culture: Biology and the Residue of Uniqueness" in *The Boundaries of Humanity*, Sheehand, J.J. and Sosna, M. (Eds.). Berkeley: University of California Press, 103-24.

Kropotkin, P. (1902). *Mutual Aid: A Factor of Evolution*. London: Heinemann. Retrieved on 01/26/15 from http://libcom.org/files/Peter%20Kropotkin-%20Mutual%20Aid;%20A%20Factor%20of%20Evolution.pdf

Kurzweil, R. (2005). *The Singularity is Near: When Humans Transcend Biology*. New York: Viking.

The Kybalion (1940/1912). *The Kybalion: A Study of Hermetic Philosophy of ancient Egypt and Greece*. Yogi Pub. Society.

LeShan, Lawrence (1976). *Alternative Realities*. New York: Ballantine.

Lewin, K. (1946). "Force Field Analysis" in *The 1973 Annual Handbook for Group Facilitators*, 111-13.

Lewin, K. and Lewin, G.W. (Ed.) (1997). *Resolving Social Conflicts*. Washington, D.C.: American Psychological Association.

Lipton, B. (2005). *The Biology of Belief: Unleashing the Power of Consciousness*. Carlsbad, CA: Hay House.

Loveridge, D.J. (1977). "Shifting Foundations: Values and Futures" in Linstone, H.A. and Simmonds, W.H.C., *Futures Research: New Directions*. Reading, MA: Addison-Wesley Publishing Company, Inc.

MacFlouer, Niles (2004-16). *Why Life Is...* Weekly radio shows: BBSRadio.com (#1-#480) and KXAM (#1-#143). Retrieved from http://www.agelesswisdom.com/archives_of_radio_shows.htm

MacFlouer, Niles (1999). *Life's Hidden Meaning*. Tempe, AZ: Ageless Wisdom Publishers.

Mahoney, D. and Restak, R. (1998). *The Longevity Strategy: How to Live to 100 Using the Brain-Body Connection*. New York: John Wiley & Sons, Inc.

Marshall, I. and Zohar, D. (1997). *Who's Afraid of Schrödinger's Cat?* New York: William Morrow and Company, Inc.

Maslow, A. (1971). *The Farther Reaches of Human Nature*. New York: Viking Press.

Maslow, A. (1968). *Towards a Psychology of Being*. New York: Van Nostrand.

Matthews, R.C. (1991)."The forgetting algorithm: How fragmentary knowledge of exemplars can yield abstract knowledge" in *Journal of Experimental Psychology: General*, 120, 117-119.

Mavromatis, A. (1991). *Hypnagogia*. Routledge, New York, NY.

May, Rollo (1975). *The Courage to Create*. New York: Bantam.

McHale, J. (1977). "Futures Problems or Problems in Futures Studies" in Linstone, H.A. and Simmonds, W.H.C. (Eds.), *Futures Research: New Directions*. Reading, MA: Addison-Wesley Publishing Company, Inc.

McTaggart, L. (2002). *The Field: The Quest for the Secret Force of the Universe*. New York: Harper Perennial.

McWhinney, W. (1997). *Paths of Change: Strategic Choices for Organizations and Society*. Thousand Oaks, CA: SAGE Publications, Inc.

Medina, J. (2008). *Brain Rules: 12 Principles for Surviving and Thriving at Work, Home, and School*. Seattle, WA: Pear Press.

Mental Floss (2016). "16 Accelerated Facts About 'Quantum Leap'". Retrieved 08/28/16 from http://mentalfloss.com/article/79397/16-accelerated-facts-about-Quantum-leap

Merriam Webster (2016). Retrieved 06/22/2016 from www.merriam-wester.com/dictionary/faith; Retrieved 07/04/16 from http://www.merriam-webster.com/dictionary/propaganda ; Retrieved 07/06/16 from http://www.merriam-webster.com/dictionary/equal ; Retrieved 07/06/16 http://www.merriam-webster.com/dictionary/personality ; Retrieved 07/07/16 http://www.merriam-webster.com/dictionary/instinct ; Retrieved 08/26/16 http://learnersdictionary.com/definition/desire ; Retrieved 08/27/16 http://www.webster-dictionary.org/definition/Agape ; Retrieved 08/28/16 http://www.merriam-webster.com/dictionary/Quantum%20leap ; Retrieved 09/30/16 http://www.merriam-webster.com/dictionary/virtue ; Retrieved 10/01/16 http://www.merriam-webster.com/dictionary/sympathy ; Retrieved 10/01/16 http://www.merriam-webster.com/dictionary/serendipity ; Retrieved 11/07/16 http://www.merriam-webster.com/dictionary/karma

Moon, J.A. (2004). *A Handbook of Reflective and Experiential Learning: Theory and Practice*. New York: RoutledgeFalmer.

Morowitz, H. J., and Singer, J. L. (Eds.) (1995). *The Mind, the Brain, and Complex Adaptive Systems*. Reading, MA: Addison-Wesley.

Mulvihill, M.D. (2003). "The Catholic Church in Crisis: Will Transformative Learning Lead to Social Change through the Uncovering of Emotion?" in Weissner, C.A., Meyers, S.R., Pfhal, N.L. and Neaman, P.J. (Eds.), *Proceedings of the 5th International Conference on Transformative Learning*, 320-325. New York: Teachers College, Columbia University.

Munck, B., Kegan, R, Luskow Lahe, L. and Meyerson, D. (2002). *Harvard Business Review on Culture andCchange*. Boston, MA: Harvard Business Review Press.

Murphy, M. (1992). *The Future of the Body*. Los Angeles: Tarcher.

Myers, I. B. and Myers, P. B. (1995). *Gifts Differing: Understanding Personality Type*. Mountain View, CA: Davies-Black Publishing.

Noelle-Neumann, E. (2008). *A First Look at Communication Theory* (7th Ed). New York: McGraw-Hill.

Nonaka, I. and Takeuchi, H. (1995). *The Knowledge-Creating Company: How Japanese Companies Create the Dynamics of Innovation*. New York: Oxford University Press.

O'Dell, C. & Hubert, C. (2011). *The New Edge in Knowledge: How Knowledge Management is Changing the Way We Do Business*. Hoboken, NJ: John Riley & Sons, Inc.

Oxford English Dictionary (5th Ed) (2002). Volumes 1 and 2. Oxford: Oxford University Press.

Pert, C. B. (1997). *Molecules of Emotion: A Science Behind Mind-Body Medicine.* New York: Touchstone.

Plotkin, H. (1994). *Darwin Machines and the Nature of Knowledge.* Cambridge, MA: Harvard University Press.

Polanyi, M. (1967). *The Tacit Dimension.* New York: Anchor Books.

Polanyi, M. (1958). *Personal Knowledge: Towards a Post-Critical Philosophy.* Chicago, IL: The University of Chicago.

Pope, A. (1732-3/1994). Essay on Man and Other Poems. Dover.

Prigogine, I. (1996). *The End of Certainty: Time, Chaos, and the New Laws of Nature.* New York: The Free Press.

Reber, A.S. (1993). *Implicit Learning and Tacit Knowledge: An Essay on the Cognitive Unconscious.* New York: Oxford University Press.

Reiter, R.J. (1994). "Melatonin Suppression by Static and Extremely Low Frequency Electromagnetic Fields: Relationship to the Reported Increased Incidence of Cancer" in *Reviews of Environmental Health* 10(3-4): 171-86.

Ritchey, D. (2003). *The H.I.S.S. of the A.S.P.: Understanding the Anomalously Sensitive Person.* Terra Alta, WV: Headline Books, Inc.

Roberts, T. (1978). "Beyond Self-Actualization" in *Re-Vision, 1*, pp 42-46.

Rock, A. (2004), *The Mind at Night: The New Science of How and Why We Dream*, Basic Books, New York, NY.

Rohr, R. and Ebert, A. (2000). *Discovering the Enneagram: An Ancient Tool for a New Spiritual Journey.* New York: Crossroad Publishing Company.

Rose, Steven (2005). *The Future of the Brain: The Promise and Perils of Tomorrow's Neuroscience.* New York: Oxford University Press.

Ross, C.A. (2006). "Brain Self-Repair in Psychotherapy: Implications for Education" in Johnson, S. and Taylor, K., *The Neuroscience of Adult Learning: New Directions for Adult and Continuing Education.* San Francisco, CA: Jossey-Bass.

Ryle, G. (1949). *The Concept of Mind.* London: Hutchinson.

Sagan, C. (1973). *The Cosmic Connection: An Extraterrestrial Perspective.* Garden City, NY: Anchor Press/Doubleday.

Salk, J. (1973). *The Survival of the Wisest.* New York: Harper & Row.

Schein, E.H. (2004). *Organization Culture and Leadership.* San Francisco, CA: John Wiley & Sons.

Schrödinger, E. (1983). *My View of the World.* Oxford, England: Ox Bow Publishers.

Searle, J. R. (2000). "Consciousness, Free Action, and the Brain" in *Journal of Consciousness Studies*, Vol. 7, No. 10.

Seashore, C.N., Shawver, M.N., Thompson, G. & Mattare, M. (2004). "Doing Good by Knowing Who You Are: The Instrumental Self as an Agent of Change" in *OD Practitioner,* Vol. 36, No. 3., 42-46.

Seligman, M. E.P. (2011). *Flourish: A Visionary New Understanding of Happiness and Well-being.* New York: Free Press.

Senge, Peter (1990). *The Fifth Discipline.* New York: Doubleday.

Smith, M.K. (2003). "Michael Polanyi and Tacit Knowledge" in *The Encyclopedia of Informal Education,* 2, www.infed.org/thinkers/Polanyi.htm

Sousa, D.A. (2006). *How the Brain Learns.* Thousand Oaks, CA: Corwin Press.

Stacey, R. (1996). *Complexity and Creativity in Organizations.* San Francisco: Berrett-Koehler Publishers.

Stebins, L.H. (2010). "Development of Reality System Theory" in *Journal of Business & Economics Research* Vol. 8, No. 4, 1-22.

Stonier, T. (1997). *Information and Meaning: An Evolutionary Perspective.* London: Springer-Verlag.

Swomley, J. (2000). "Violence: Competition or Cooperation" in *Christian Ethics Today* 26, Vol. 6, No. 1.

Templeton, Sir John (2002). *Wisdom from World Religions: Pathways Toward Heaven on Earth.* Philadelphia, PA: Templeton Foundation Press.

Tiller, W. (2007). *Psychoenergetic Science: A Second Copernican-Scale Revolution.* DVD from www.illerfoundaion.com

Time-Life Books (undated). *The Enigma of Personality: Journey Through the Mind and Body.* Alexandria, VA: Time-Life Books.

Uleman, J. (2005). "Becoming Aware of the New Unconscious" in Hassin,R.R., Uleman, J.S. and Bargh, J.A. (Eds.), *The New Unconscious.* New York: Oxford University Press.

The Urantia Book (1955). Chicago: URANTIA Foundation.

Wade, J. (1996). *Changes of Mind: A Holonomic Theory of the Evolution of Consciousness.* Albany: SUNY Press.

Wagner, Roy (1975). *The Invention of Culture.* Chicago: University of Chicago.

Walsch, N.D. (2009). *When Everything Changes Change Everything: In a Time of Turmoil, a Pathway to Peace.* Ashland, OR: EmNin Books.

Walsh, R. (1999). *Essential Spirituality: Exercises from the World's Religions to Cultivate Kindness, Love, Joy, Peace, Vision, Wisdom and Generosity.* New York: John Wiley & Sons.

West, M.A. (1980). "Meditation and the EEG" in *Psychological Medicine,* 10: 369-375.

Wilber, K. (2001). *The Eye of Spirit: An Integral Vision for a World Gone Slightly Mad.* Boston: Shambhala publications.

Wilber, K. (2000). *Integral Psychology: Consciousness, Spirit, Psychology, Therapy*. Boston: Shambhala Publications.

Wilber, K. (1996). *A Brief History of Everything*. Boston: Shambhala.

Wilber, K. (1983). *Up From Eden: A Transpersonal View of Human Evolution*. Boulder, CO: Shambhala.

Wilson, E. O. (1998). *Consilience: The Unity of Knowledge*. New York: Alfred A. Knopf.

Wing, R.L. (Trans) (1986). *The Tao of Power: Lao Tzu's Classic Guide to Leadership, Influence, and Excellence*. New York: Doubleday.

Wycoff, J. (1991). *Mindmapping: Your Personal Guide to Exploring Creativity and Problem-Solving*. New York: The Berkley Publishing Group.

Zimmer, C. (2007). "The Neurobiology of the Self" in Bloom, F.E. (Ed.), *Best of the Brain from Scientific American: Mind, Matter, and Tomorrow's Brain*. New York: Dana Press, 47-57.

Zohar, D. & Marshall, I. (1994). *The Quantum Society: Mind, Physics, and the New Social Vision*. New York: William Morrow and Co., Inc.

Zull, J. E. (2002). *The Art of Changing the Brain: Enriching the Practice of Teaching by Exploring the Biology of Learning*. Sterling, VA: Stylus.

Index

About the Mountain Quest Institute

MQI is a research, retreat and learning center dedicated to helping individuals achieve personal and professional growth and organizations create and sustain high performance in a rapidly changing, uncertain, and increasingly complex world. Drs. David and Alex Bennet are co-founders of MQI. They may be contacted at alex@mountainquestinstitute.com

Current research is focused on Human and Organizational Systems, Change, Complexity, Sustainability, Knowledge, Learning, Consciousness, and the nexus of Science and Spirituality. MQI has three questions: The Quest for Knowledge, The Quest for Consciousness, and The Quest for Meaning. **MQI is scientific, humanistic and spiritual and finds no contradiction in this combination**. See www.mountainquestinstitute.com

MQI is the birthplace of Organizational Survival in the New World: The Intelligent Complex Adaptive System (Elsevier, 2004), a new theory of the firm that turns the living system metaphor into a reality for organizations. Based on research in complexity and neuroscience—and incorporating networking theory and knowledge management—this book is filled with new ideas married to practical advice, all embedded within a thorough description of the new organization in terms of structure, culture, strategy, leadership, knowledge workers and integrative competencies.

Mountain Quest Institute, situated four hours from Washington, D.C. in the Monongahela Forest of the Allegheny Mountains, is part of the Mountain Quest complex which includes a Retreat Center, Inn, and the old Farm House, Outbuildings and mountain trails and farmland. See www.mountainquestinn.com The Retreat Center is designed to provide full learning experiences, including hosting training, workshops, retreats and business meetings for professional and executive groups of 25 people or less. The Center includes a 26,000 volume research library, a conference room, community center, computer room, 12 themed bedrooms, a workout and hot tub area, and a four-story tower with a glass ceiling for enjoying the magnificent view of the valley during the day and the stars at night. Situated on a 430 acres farm, there is a labyrinth, creeks, four miles of mountain trails, and horses, Longhorn cattle, Llamas and a myriad of wild neighbors. Other neighbors include the Snowshoe Ski Resort, the National Radio Astronomy Observatory and the CASS Railroad.

About the Organizational Zoo Ambassadors Network

The Organizational Zoo Ambassadors Network (OZAN) is an international group of professionals interested in using The Organizational Zoo concepts as part of their capability development programs. Zoo Ambassadors have been trained in the application of OZAN Tools and approaches. They freely share their experiences through an international network which interacts primarily through a wiki supplemented by occasional face to face events and some on-line learning modules. See http://www.organizationalzoo.com/ambassadors/

About Quantra Leadership Academy

Quantra Leadership Academy (aka QLA Consulting) is a **transformational leadership and personal development training company run by** Dr. Theresa Bullard. **QLA is dedicated to helping individuals and organizations innovate their way of thinking to achieve breakthrough results.** There is one question that lies at the foundation of QLA: *What is your potential?* When you tap into your potential, greatness happens, you experience breakthroughs, "Ah-ha" moments occur, and you get into "The Zone" of peak performance. It is our passion to help you access your full potential, sustain what you achieve, and be able to refuel whenever you want. When you get to the point where you can do this on demand that is when you become a self-transforming agent of change. QLA shows you how to get there and gives you tools to accelerate your progress. By blending science, consciousness studies, and mental alchemy, or the art and science of transforming your mindset, we help you **reach your potential** and become more successful in essential areas of your work and life. *To help you* **access more of your potential,** *we offer a progression of transformative tools and trainings that integrate quantum principles, cutting-edge methods, and ancient wisdom for using your mind more creatively and effectively.* For more info: www.QLAconsulting.com

About the Authors

Dr. Alex Bennet, a Professor at the Bangkok University Institute for Knowledge and Innovation Management, is internationally recognized as an expert in knowledge management and an agent for organizational change. Prior to founding the Mountain Quest Institute, she served as the Chief Knowledge Officer and Deputy Chief Information Officer for Enterprise Integration for the U.S. Department of the Navy, and was co-chair of the Federal Knowledge Management Working Group. Dr. Bennet is the recipient of the Distinguished and Superior Public Service Awards from the U.S. government for her work in the Federal Sector. She is a Delta Epsilon Sigma and Golden Key National Honor Society graduate with a Ph.D. in Human and Organizational Systems; degrees in Management for Organizational Effectiveness, Human Development, English and Marketing; and certificates in Total Quality Management, System Dynamics and Defense Acquisition Management. Alex believes in the multidimensionality of humanity as we move out of infancy into full consciousness.

Dr. David Bennet's experience spans many years of service in the Military, Civil Service and Private Industry, including fundamental research in underwater acoustics and nuclear physics, frequent design and facilitation of organizational interventions, and serving as technical director of two major DoD Acquisition programs. Prior to founding the Mountain Quest Institute, Dr. Bennet was CEO, then Chairman of the Board and Chief Knowledge Officer of a professional services firm located in Alexandria, Virginia. He is a Phi Beta Kappa, Sigma Pi Sigma, and Suma Cum Laude graduate of the University of Texas, and holds degrees in Mathematics, Physics, Nuclear Physics, Liberal Arts, Human and Organizational Development, and a Ph.D. in Human Development focused on Neuroscience and adult learning. He is currently researching the nexus of Science, the Humanities and Spirituality.

Dr. Arthur Shelley is a capability development and knowledge strategy consultant with over 30 years professional experience. He has held a variety of professional roles including managing international projects in Australia, Europe, Asia and USA and has facilitated professional development program with organisations as diverse as NASA, Cirque du Soleil, World Bank, government agencies and corporates. He has facilitated courses in Masters programs on Executive Consulting, Leadership, Knowledge Management, Applied Research Practice and Entrepreneurship in face to face, blended and on-line modes. Arthur is the author of three books: *KNOWledge SUCCESSion (2017) Being a Successful Knowledge Leader (2009)*; *The Organizational Zoo, A Survival Guide to Workplace Behavior (2007)*. In 2014 he was awarded with an Australian Office of Learning and Teaching citation for "Outstanding contributions to student learning outcomes". Arthur is a regular invited speaker and workshop facilitator at international conferences to discuss his writing or to share experiences as the former Global Knowledge Director for Cadbury Schweppes. He is founder of The Organizational Zoo Ambassadors Network (a professional peer mentoring group), creator of the RMIT University MBA mentoring program and co-facilitator of the Melbourne KM Leadership Forum. Arthur has a PhD in Project Management, a Master of Science in Microbiology/Biochemistry, a Graduate Certificate in Tertiary Learning and Teaching and a Bachelor of Science. Arthur may be reached at arthur.shelley@rmit.edu.au

Dr. Theresa Bullard combines a Ph.D. in Physics with a life-long path of embracing the new paradigm of Science and Consciousness. Her passion and ability to bridge these worlds are her strengths and distinguish her as an exceptional teacher, speaker, leader and change-agent. Theresa is the founder of QLA Consulting Inc., President of the Board of Directors of Mysterium Center, an International Instructor with the Modern Mystery School, and co-founder of the Universal Kabbalah Network. She has over 15 years of experience in science research, international speaking, and transformational training. Author of *The Game Changers: Social Alchemists in the 21st Century*, along with several guided meditation albums and audio tools for accessing Quantum conscious states, her mission is to help individuals and organizations thrive in a changing world. Theresa may be contacted at Theresa@quantumleapalchemy.com

Dr. John Lewis is a speaker, business consultant, and part-time professor on the topics of organizational learning, thought leadership, and knowledge & innovation management. John is a proven leader with business results, and was acknowledged by Gartner with an industry "Best Practice" paper for an innovative knowledge management implementation. He is a co-founder at The CoHero Institute, creating collaborative leadership in learning organizations. John holds a Doctoral degree in Educational Psychology from the University of Southern California, with a dissertation focus on mental models and decision making, and is the author of *The Explanation Age*, which Kirkus Reviews described as "An iconoclast's blueprint for a new era of innovation." John may be contacted at John@ExplanationAge.com

Other Books by These Authors

Possibilities that are YOU! by Alex Bennet

     This series of short books, which are published under *Conscious Look Books*, are conversational in nature, taking full advantage of your lived experience to share what can sometimes be difficult concepts to grab onto. But, **YOU ARE READY!** We live in a world that is tearing itself apart, where people are out of control, rebelling from years of real and perceived abuse and suppression of thought. Yet, this chaos offers us as a humanity the opportunity to make a giant leap forward. *By opening ourselves to ourselves, we are able to fully explore who we are and who we can become.* With that exploration comes a glimmer of hope as we begin to reclaim the power of each and every mind developed by the lived human experience!

     These books share 22 large concepts from *The Profundity and Bifurcation of Change*. Each book includes seven ideas offered for the student of life experience to help you become the co-creator you are. Available in soft cover from Amazon.

Titles:

All Things in Balance
The Art of Thought Adjusting
Associative Patterning and Attracting
Beyond Action
The Bifurcation
Connections as Patterns
Conscious Compassion
The Creative Leap
The Emerging Self
The Emoting Guidance System
Engaging Forces
The ERC's of Intuition
Grounding
The Humanness of Humility
Intention and Attention
Knowing
Living Virtues for Today
ME as Co-Creator
Seeking Wisdom
Staying on the Path
Transcendent Beauty
Truth in Context

     A 23rd little book titled **The Intelligent Social Change Journey** provides the theoretical foundation for the **Possibilities that are YOU! series.** Also available in soft cover from Amazon

Other Books by MQI Press (www.MQIPress.net)

MQIPress is a wholly-owned subsidiary of Mountain Quest Institute, LLC, located at 303 Mountain Quest Lane, Marlinton, West Virginia 24954, USA. (304) 799-7267

Other Bennet eBooks available from in PDF format from MQIPress (US 304-799-7267 or alex@mountainquestinstitute.com) and Kindle format from Amazon.

The Course of Knowledge: A 21st Century Theory
by Alex Bennet and David Bennet with Joyce Avedisian (2015)

Knowledge is at the core of what it is to be human, the substance which informs our thoughts and determines the course of our actions. Our growing focus on, and understanding of, knowledge and its consequent actions is changing our relationship with the world. Because **knowledge determines the quality of every single decision we make**, it is critical to learn about and understand what knowledge is. **From a 21st century viewpoint,** we explore a theory of knowledge that is both pragmatic and biological. Pragmatic in that it is based on taking effective action, and biological because it is created by humans via patterns of neuronal connections in the mind/brain.

In this book we explore *the course of knowledge*. Just as a winding stream in the bowls of the mountains curves and dips through ravines and high valleys, so, too, with knowledge. In a continuous journey towards intelligent activity, context-sensitive and situation-dependent knowledge, imperfect and incomplete, experientially engages a changing landscape in a continuous cycle of learning and expanding. *We are in a continuous cycle of knowledge creation such that every moment offers the opportunity for the emergence of new and exciting ideas, all waiting to be put in service to an interconnected world.* Learn more about this **exciting human capacity**! AVAILABLE FROM AMAZON in Kindle Format. AVAILABLE FROM MQIPress in PDF.

Expanding the Self: The Intelligent Complex Adaptive Learning System
by David Bennet, Alex Bennet and Robert Turner (2015)

We live in unprecedented times; indeed, turbulent times that can arguably be defined as ushering humanity into a new Golden Age, offering the opportunity to embrace new ways of learning and living in a globally and collaboratively entangled connectedness (Bennet & Bennet, 2007). In this shifting and dynamic environment, life demands accelerated cycles of learning experiences. Fortunately, we as a humanity have begun to look within ourselves to better understand the way our mind/brain operates, the amazing qualities of the body that power our thoughts and feelings, and the reciprocal loops as those thoughts and feelings change our physical structure. This emerging knowledge begs us to relook and rethink what we know about learning, providing a new starting point to expand toward the future.

This book is a treasure for those interested in how recent findings in neuroscience impact learning. The result of this work is an expanding experiential learning model called the Intelligent Complex Adaptive Learning System, adding the fifth mode of social engagement to Kolb's concrete experience, reflective observation, abstract conceptualization and active experimentation, with the five modes undergirded by the power of Self. A significant conclusion is that should they desire, adults have much more control over their learning than they may realize. AVAILABLE FROM AMAZON in Kindle Format. AVAILALBE FROM MQIPress in PDF.

Decision-Making in The New Reality: Complexity, Knowledge and Knowing
by Alex Bennet and David Bennet (2013)

We live in a world that offers many possible futures. The ever-expanding complexity of information and knowledge provide many choices for decision-makers, and we are all making decisions every single day! As the problems and messes of the world become more complex, our decision consequences are more and more difficult to anticipate, and our decision-making processes must change to keep up with this world complexification. This book takes a consilience approach to explore decision-making in The New Reality, fully engaging systems and complexity theory, knowledge research, and recent neuroscience findings. It also presents methodologies for decision-makers to tap into their unconscious, accessing tacit knowledge resources and increasingly relying on the sense of knowing that is available to each of us.

Almost every day new energies are erupting around the world: new thoughts, new feelings, new knowing, all contributing to new situations that require new decisions and actions from each and every one of us. Indeed, with the rise of the Net Generation and social media, a global consciousness may well be emerging. As individuals and organizations, we are realizing that there are larger resources available to us, and that, as complex adaptive systems linked to a flowing fount of knowing, we can bring these resources to bear to achieve our ever-expanding vision of the future. Are we up to the challenge? AVAILABLE FROM AMAZON in Kindle Format. AVAILABLE FROM MQIPress in PDF.

Leading with the Future in Mind: Knowledge and Emergent Leadership
by Alex Bennet and David Bennet with John Lewis (2015)

We exist in a new reality, a global world where the individuated power of the mind/brain offers possibilities beyond our imagination. It is within this framework that thought leading emerges, and when married to our collaborative nature, makes the impossible an everyday occurrence. *Leading with the Future in Mind*, building on profound insights unleashed by recent findings in neuroscience, provides a new view that converges leadership, knowledge and learning for individual and organizational advancement.

This book provides a research-based *tour de force* for the future of leadership. Moving from the leadership of the past, for the few at the top, using authority as the explanation, we now find leadership emerging from all levels of the organization, with knowledge as the explanation. The future will be owned by the organizations that can master the relationships between knowledge and leadership. Being familiar with the role of a knowledge worker is not the same as understanding the role of a knowledge leader. As the key ingredient, collaboration is much more than "getting along"; it embraces and engages. Wrapped in the mantle of collaboration and engaging our full resources—physical, mental, emotional and spiritual—we open the door to possibilities. We are dreaming the future together. AVAILABLE FROM AMAZON in Kindle Format. AVAILABLE FROM MQIPress in PDF.

Also available from the authors and on Amazon..

The Game Changers: Social Alchemists in the 21ˢᵗ Century
by Theresa Bullard, Ph.D. (2013), available in hard and soft formats from Amazon.
Just about everywhere we look right now change is afoot. What is all this change about? Why now? And how do we best adapt? Many have called this time a "quickening", where the speed with which we must think, respond, and take action is accelerating. Systems are breaking down, people are rising up, and there is uncertainty of what tomorrow will bring. This book is dedicated to times such as these, times of great transformation. It can be seen as a companion guide on how to navigate the tumultuous tides of change. It aims to put such current events into a possible context within the evolutionary and alchemical process that humanity is going through. In it, author, physicist, and change-agent, Theresa Bullard, Ph.D., discusses emerging new paradigms, world events, future trends, and ancient wisdom that help reveal a bigger picture of what is happening. She offers insights and solutions to empower you, the reader, to become a more conscious participant in these exciting times of change. With this knowledge you will be more equipped to harness the *opportunities* that such times present you with. AVAILABLE FROM AMAZON in Kindle Format ... Paperback

The Organizational Zoo: A Survival Guide to Work Place Behavior
by Arthur Shelley (2006), available in hard and soft formats from Amazon.
Organizational Zoo is a fresh approach to organizational culture development, a witty and thought-provoking book that makes ideal reading for students and management. When you think of your organization as containing ants, bees, chameleons, and other creatures on through the alphabet, your work world becomes more manageable. Discover the secret strengths and weaknesses of each distinct animal so that you can communicate more productively—or manipulate more cunningly. Your choice! AVAILABLE FROM AMAZON in Paperback

The Explanation Age
by John Lewis (2013) (3rd Ed.), available in hard and soft formats from Amazon.
The technological quest of the last several decades has been to create the information age, with ubiquitous and immediate access to information. With this goal arguably accomplished, even from our mobile phones, this thought-provoking book describes the next quest and provides a blueprint for how to get there. When all organizational knowledge is framed as answers to our fundamental questions, we find ubiquitous and visual access to knowledge related to who, where, how, etc., yet the explanations are still buried within the prose. The question of "why" is arguably the most important question, yet it is currently the least supported. This is why business process methodologies feel like "box-checking" instead of "sense-making." This is why lessons learned are not actually learned. And this is why the consequential options and choices are captured better within a chess game than within the important decisions faced by organizations and society. With implications for business, education, policy making, and artificial intelligence, Dr. Lewis provides a visualization of explanations which promotes organizational sense-making and collaboration. AVAILABLE FROM AMAZON in Paperback

KNOWledge SUCCESSion: Sustained Capability Growth Through Strategic Projects
 by Arthur Shelley (2016), available in hard and soft formats from Amazon.
KNOWledge SUCCESSion is intended for executives and developing professionals who face the challenges of delivering business benefits for today, whilst building the capabilities required for an increasingly changing future. The book is structured to build from foundational requirements towards connecting the highly interdependent aspects of success in an emerging complex world. A wide range of concepts are brought together in a logical framework to enable readers of different disciplines to understand how they either create barriers or can be harvested to generate synergistic opportunities. The framework builds a way to make sense of the connections and provides novel paths to take advantage of the potential synergies that arise through aligning the concepts into a portfolio of strategic projects. AVAILABLE FROM AMAZON. Kindle Format ... Paperback

Knowledge Mobilization in the Social Sciences and Humanities: Moving from Research to Action
 by Alex Bennet and David Bennet (2007), available in hard and soft formats from Amazon.
This book takes the reader from the University lab to the playgrounds of communities. It shows how to integrate, move and use knowledge, an action journey within an identified action space that is called knowledge mobilization. Whether knowledge is mobilized through an individual, organization, community or nation, it becomes a powerful asset creating a synergy and focus that brings forth the best of action and values. Individuals and teams who can envision, feel, create and apply this power are the true leaders of tomorrow. When we can mobilize knowledge for the greater good humanity will have left the information age and entered the age of knowledge, ultimately leading to compassion and—hopefully—wisdom. AVAILABLE FROM AMAZON. Kindle Format ... Paperback
AVAILABLE FROM MQIPress in PDF and Softback.

Being a Successful Knowledge Leader: What Knowledge Practitioners Need to Know to Make a Difference.
 by Arthur Shelley (2009). AVAILABLE FROM AMAZON. Paperback
Being a Successful Knowledge Leader explores the challenges of leading a program of knowledge-informed change initiatives to generate sustained performance improvement. The book explores how to embed knowledge flows into strategic development cycles to align organizational development with changing environmental conditions. The high rate of change interferes with the growth of organizational knowledge because what is relevant only generates a competitive advantage for a short time. Also, the people who possess this knowledge are more mobile than previously. Combined, these factors can have a detrimental impact on performance and need to be mitigated against to ensure capabilities are built rather than diluted overtime. The characteristics for success that a knowledge leader needs to possess are explored from a unique perspective to stimulate creative thinking around how to develop and maintain these in emergent times.

Organizational Survival in the New World: The Intelligent Complex Adaptive System
by Alex Bennet and David Bennet (Elsevier, 2004), available in hard and soft formats from Amazon.
In this book David and Alex Bennet propose a new model for organizations that enables them to react more quickly and fluidly to today's fast-changing, dynamic business environment: The Intelligent Complex Adaptive System (ICAS). ICAS is a new organic model of the firm based on recent research in complexity and neuroscience, and incorporating networking theory and knowledge management, and turns the living system metaphor into a reality for organizations. This book synthesizes new thinking about organizational structure from the fields listed above into ICAS, a new systems model for the successful organization of the future designed to help leaders and managers of knowledge organizations succeed in a non-linear, complex, fast-changing and turbulent environment. Technology enables connectivity, and the ICAS model takes advantage of that connectivity by fostering the development of dynamic, effective and trusting relationships in a new organizational structure. AVAILABLE FROM AMAZON in Kindle Format ... Hardback ... Paperback

Other MQIPress books available in PDF format at www.MQIPress.net (US 304-799-7267 or alex@mountainquestinstitute.com) and Kindle format from Amazon.

REMEMBRANCE: Pathways to Expanded Learning with Music and Metamusic®
by Barbara Bullard and Alex Bennet (2013)
Take a journey of discovery into the last great frontier—the human mind/brain, an instrument of amazing flexibility and plasticity. This eBook is written for brain users who are intent on mining more of the golden possibilities that lie inherent in each of our unique brains. Begin by discovering the role positive attitudes play in learning, and the power of self affirmations and visualizations. Then explore the use of brain wave entrainment mixed with designer music called Metamusic® to achieve enhanced learning states. Join students of all ages who are creating magical learning outcomes using music and Metamusic.® AVAILABLE FROM AMAZON in Kindle Format.

The Journey into the Myst (Vol. 1 of The Myst Series)
by Alex Bennet and David Bennet (2012)
What we are about to tell you would have been quite unbelievable to me before this journey began. It is not a story of the reality either of us has known for well over our 60 and 70 years of age, but rather, the reality of dreams and fairytales." This is the true story of a sequence of events that happened at Mountain Quest Institute, situated in a high valley of the Allegheny Mountains of West Virginia. The story begins with a miracle, expanding into the capture and cataloging of thousands of pictures of electromagnetic spheres widely known as "orbs." This joyous experience became an exploration into the unknown with the emergence of what the author's fondly call the Myst, the forming and shaping of non-random patterns such as human faces, angels and animals. As this phenomenon unfolds, you will discover how the Drs. Alex and David Bennet began to observe and interact with the Myst. This book

shares the beginning of an extraordinary *Journey into the Myst*. AVAILABLE FROM AMAZON in Kindle Format. AVAILABLE FROM MQIPress in PDF.

Patterns in the Myst (Vol. 2 of The Myst Series)
 by Alex Bennet and David Bennet (2013)

The Journey into the Myst was just the beginning for Drs. Alex and David Bennet. Volume II of the Myst Series brings Science into the Spiritual experience, bringing to bear what the Bennets have learned through their research and educational experiences in physics, neuroscience, human systems, knowledge management and human development. Embracing the paralogical, patterns in the Myst are observed, felt, interpreted, analyzed and compared in terms of their physical make-up, non-randomness, intelligent sources and potential implications. Along the way, the Bennets were provided amazing pictures reflecting the forming of the Myst. The Bennets shift to introspection in the third volume of the series to explore the continuing impact of the Myst experience on the human psyche. AVAILABLE FROM AMAZON in Kindle Format. AVAILABLE FROM MQIPress in PDF.

The Profundity and Bifurcation of Change Part I: *Laying the Groundwork* by Alex Bennet and David Bennet with Arthur Shelley, Theresa Bullard and John Lewis

This book lays the groundwork for the **Intelligent Social Change Journey** (ISCJ), a developmental journey of the body, mind and heart, moving from the heaviness of cause-and-effect linear extrapolations, to the fluidity of co-evolving with our environment, to the lightness of breathing our thought and feelings into reality. Grounded in development of our mental faculties, these are phase changes, each building on and expanding previous learning in our movement toward intelligent activity. As we lay the groundwork, we move through the concepts of change, knowledge, forces, self and consciousness. Then, recognizing that we are holistic beings, we provide a baseline model for individual change from within.

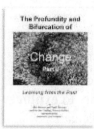

The Profundity and Bifurcation of Change Part II:

Learning from the Past by Alex Bennet and David Bennet with Arthur Shelley, Theresa Bullard and John Lewis

Phase 1 of the Intelligent Social Change Journey (ISCJ) is focused on the linear cause-and-effect relationships of logical thinking. Knowledge, situation dependent and context sensitive, is a product of the past. **Phase 1 assumes that for every effect there is an originating cause.** This is where we as a humanity, and as individuals, begin to develop our mental faculties. In this book we explore cause and effect, scan a kaleidoscope of change models, and review the modalities of change. Since change is easier and more fluid when we are grounded, we explore three interpretations of grounding. In preparation for expanding our consciousness, a readiness assessment and sample change agent's strategy are included. (Release 01/15/17)

The Profundity and Bifurcation of Change Part III:

Learning in the Present by Alex Bennet and David Bennet with Arthur Shelley, Theresa Bullard and John Lewis

As the world becomes increasingly complex, Phase 2 of the Intelligent Social Change Journey (ISCJ) is focused on **co-evolving with the environment**. This requires a deepening connection to others, moving into empathy. While the NOW is the focus, there is an increasing ability to put together patterns from the past and think conceptually, as well as extrapolate future behaviors. Thus, we look closely at the relationship of time and space, and pattern thinking. We look at the human body as a complex energetic system, exploring the role of emotions as a guidance system, and what happens when we have stuck energy. This book also introduces Knowledge Capacities, different ways of thinking that build capacity for sustainability.

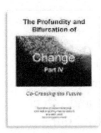

The Profundity and Bifurcation of Change Part IV: Co-Creating the Future by Alex Bennet and David Bennet with Arthur Shelley, Theresa Bullard and John Lewis

As we move into Phase 3 of the Intelligent Social Change Journey (ISCJ), **we fully embrace our role as co-creator**. We recognize the power of thought and the role of attention and intention in our ever-expanding search for a higher level of truth. Whether we choose to engage it or not, we explore mental discipline as a tool toward expanded consciousness. In preparing ourselves for the creative leap, there are ever-deepening connections with others. We now understand that the mental faculties are in service to the intuitional, preparing us to, and expanding our ability to, act in and on the world, living with conscious compassion and tapping into the intuitional at will.

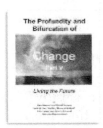

The Profundity and Bifurcation of Change Part V: Living the Future by Alex Bennet and David Bennet with Arthur Shelley, Theresa Bullard, John Lewis and Donna Panucci

We embrace the ancient art and science of Alchemy to **explore the larger shift underway for humanity** and how we can consciously and intentionally speed up evolution to enhance outcomes. In this conversation, we look at balancing and sensing, the harmony of beauty, and virtues for living the future. Conscious compassion, a virtue, is introduced as a state of being connected to morality and good character, inclusive of giving selfless service. We are now ready to refocus our attention on knowledge and consciousness, exploring the new roles these play in our advancement. And all of this—all of our expanding and growth as we move through the Intelligent Social Change journey—is giving a wide freedom of choice as we approach the bifurcation. What will we manifest?

Available in Softback from www.amazon.com

Available in Kindle format from www.amazon.com

Available in PDF format from www.MQIPress.net

Made in the USA
Middletown, DE
03 June 2023

31830713R00124